Outstanding [obscured] and learning 14-19

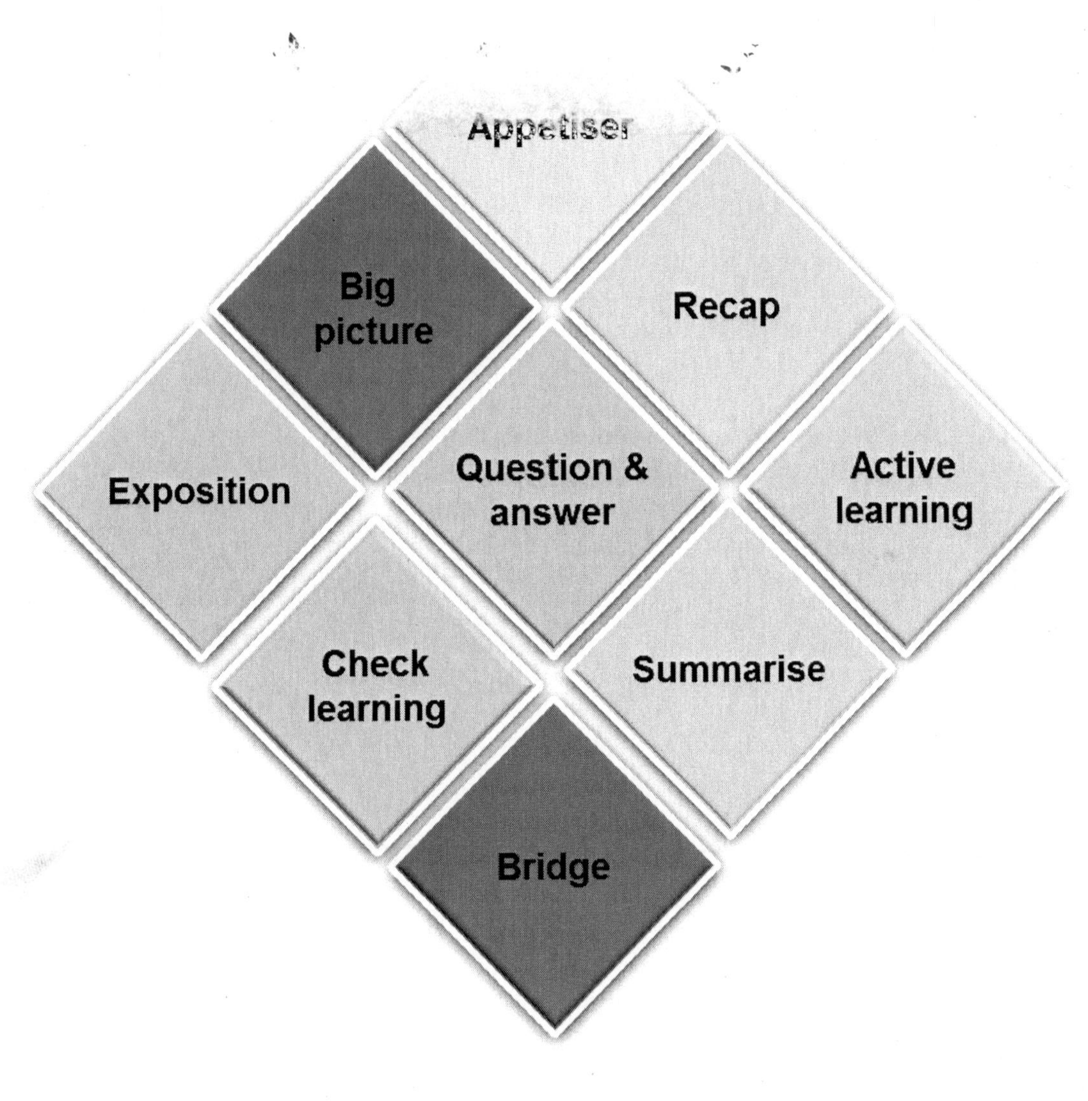

Bradley Lightbody

Publications

www.collegenet.co.uk

Outstanding teaching and learning 14-19

by

Bradley Lightbody M.Ed

A Collegenet publication, www.collegenet.co.uk
First published September 2009
Second Edition September 2012

First published September 2009
Second edition published September 2012
Collegenet Limited
53 Windmill Lane
Batley
West Yorkshire
WF17 0NT
United Kingdom

A catalogue entry for this book is available from the British Library.

ISBN 978-0-9563245-3-5

Printed and bound in the United Kingdom by
CPI Group (UK) Ltd, Croydon, CR0 4YY
www.cpibooks.co.uk

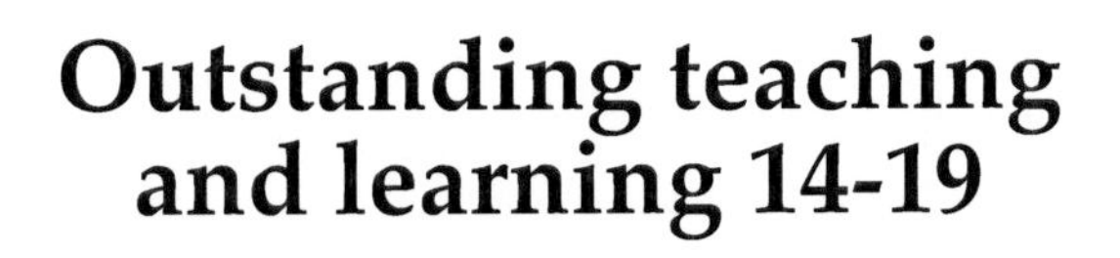

Outstanding teaching and learning 14-19

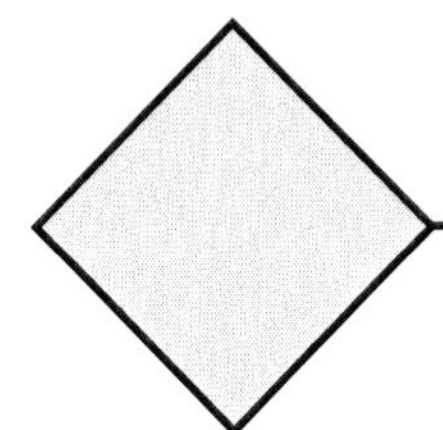

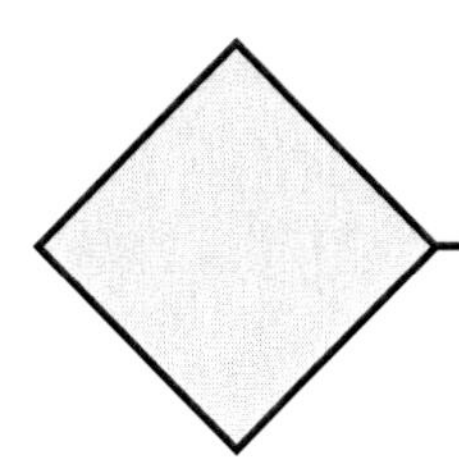

Acknowledgements

The publisher and author gratefully acknowledge the following for permission to reproduce copyright material:

Bilborough Sixth Form College, Northampton College, Professor John Hattie, Ofsted and official government departments and agencies reproduced under HMSO core licence C02W0007193. Quotations from, 'Essential Pieces of the Jigsaw: the Jigsaw of a Successful School' are used with the kind permission of Sir Professor Tim Brighouse and RM Plc of New Mill house, Milton Park, Abingdon, Oxon OX14 4SE (www.rm.com). Geoff Mitchell, Headteacher Tadcaster Grammar School, Teach First, Institute for Learning, Lifelong Learning UK, University of London, Hay Group, McKinsey Consultancy, Routledge, Random House, Orion, Hodder, Transworld, City and Guilds, Network Educational Press, Open University, News International, The Times Educational Supplement, The Guardian, Association for Supervision and Curriculum Development, Kim Smith, Gateshead college for the 'Wipeout' challenge task. The Commission for Equality and Human Rights, known as the Equality and Human Rights Commission ("the EHRC") has succeeded to the rights (including copyright and other intellectual property rights) and obligations of the former Disability Rights Commission ("the DRC"), the former Commission for Racial Equality ("the CRE") and the Equal Opportunities Commission ("the EOC") which ceased to exist on the 1st October 2007.

Every attempt has been made to contact all copyright holders and to gain responses but any omissions they will be corrected and addressed on notification.

My continuing debt to Carol for her support and understanding during many months of research and writing.

Preface

"Education is the kindling of a flame not the filling of a vessel".

(Socrates 470-399 B.C.)

Teaching is often a lonely business. You close your own classroom door and hope that by and large you are getting it right but there is always some nagging doubt. What do other teachers do? What are the most effective teaching and learning strategies? Those questions are very simple but clear answers are often elusive. Over the past 15 years I have observed well over 1,000 lessons and along with the students enjoyed many outstanding lessons. Often, I had to resist the urge to join in and in doing so I acknowledged the infectious passion and enthusiasm generated by the teacher for the subject. We were all being drawn into a vortex of interest, challenge and even excitement through a fast paced mix of whole class, individual, paired and group tasks and all richly resourced. This book draws on those experiences, recent academic research, professional criteria, student opinions and Ofsted findings. The approach is largely practical rather than theoretical but firmly grounded in academic research which has largely answered the first question, '*What do outstanding teachers do?*' The second question '*What are the most effective teaching and learning strategies?*' is largely answered by the Diamond Lesson Plan (Chapter Six) and hopefully the illustrations of each step in the subsequent chapters will trigger your own creativity. Ultimately outstanding teaching and learning is about passion i.e. your passion for your own subject and hopefully overtime a passion that many of your students will increasingly share. There are few rewards in teaching but knowing you have made a difference is the greatest reward of all.

Bradley Lightbody
September 2009.

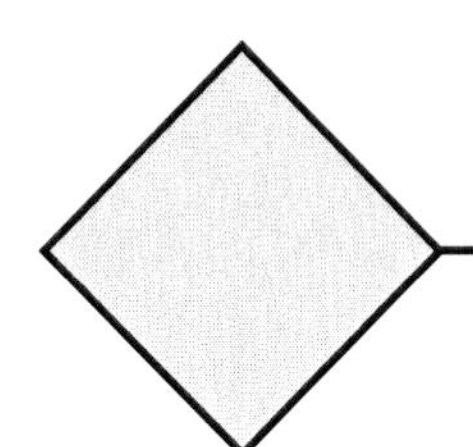

Preface to 2nd Edition

"Stay in college,
Get the knowledge
Stay there till you're through
If they can make penicillin from mouldy bread,
They can sure make something of you"

A poem by Muhammed Ali.

By age 14 too many young people have switched off learning and our most significant task as teachers is to re-awaken, re-invigorate and re-energise them with the benefits of engaging in learning. We can all act to transform lives by holding high expectations and by addressing the three fundamentals of outstanding practice, teaching, learning and assessment. Like Spinal Tap outstanding teachers go to 11. However, 'volume' does not have to mean alpha presentation skills but rather a well-planned brisk pace starting with an upbeat 'appetiser' to stir curiosity followed by a varied range of teaching and learning activities to capture and sustain interest. Learning, however, is the significant focus with care taken to focus on the learning outcomes of each activity and to model and guide how to learn. Finally at the heart of outstanding practice is assessment for learning and gaining feedback from each student on what they know and understand and crucially what they do not know. We must always remember that we do not teach classes but groups of individuals who all happen to be in the same room. What one student finds easy another will find difficult and our goal is to ensure all gain a sense of personal progress. Students who know they are making progress will gain higher motivation and will delve into independent learning and achievement will follow. This second edition has been extensively updated with academic, professional and Ofsted evidence of outstanding practice and all incorporated within the Diamond Lesson Plan. Please use it as starting point to develop your own outstanding practice.

Bradley Lightbody
1st September 2012.

Skills and attributes of outstanding teachers

"The one area of research that has been astonishingly consistent is children's views of good teaching. Whether you look at primary or secondary pupils, studies from the 30s right through to research we did last year, their opinions hardly vary. Children like teachers who can keep order, explain clearly, show enthusiasm for their subject, treat them as individuals, and who have a good sense of humour".[1]

The late Ted Wragg, Professor of Education at the University of Exeter speaking at the National Teaching Awards 31st October 2000.

Over the last century, as highlighted by the late Ted Wragg (1938-2005), a consensus on the skills and attributes of outstanding teachers has emerged and not just among children. Google[2] the question *'What makes an outstanding teacher?'* or any variation on this question e.g. a good teacher, a great teacher, or a brilliant teacher and you will be overwhelmed by a cascade of hits. Search You Tube in a similar way and you will also find thousands of videos uploaded by teachers, academics, organisations and students. All present very similar views and largely restate and/or expand upon Wagg's succinct summary. Since 2000 a number of key research reports have provided an in-depth analysis of the skills and attributes of outstanding teachers and the associated teaching and learning strategies.

Hay McBer Report 2000

The Hay McBer consultancy report (now just Hay group) was published in 2000 and entitled, *'Research into Teacher Effectiveness: A model of Teacher Effectiveness'*. Although the study was schools based the findings are equally applicable across the 14-19 sector. The report, concluded that, *"teachers really do make a difference"*.[3] This conclusion may seem obvious but it was made against a background of a debate on the impact of wider socio-economic influences on learning e.g. gender, ethnicity, poverty, disadvantaged communities and levels of parental support. The Hay McBer researchers concluded that the consistent factor driving successful learning across inner city districts as well as leafy suburbs was the skills and attributes of effective teachers. The wider socio-economic factors were not dismissed but set into context as barriers to learning that effective teachers and schools actively addressed and sought to mitigate primarily through holding high expectations, *"Expressing positive expectations of pupils – that they can and will learn and be successful – is one of the most powerful ways to influence pupils and raise achievement. It is one of the distinctive behaviours of high performing teachers who radiate confidence in their pupils and their potential, and never give up on them".*[4] The Hay McBer report identified three major skill sets of effective teachers as follows:

- Professional characteristics
- Teaching skills
- Classroom climate

In each case there was a significant emphasis upon the skills and attributes to motivate and to draw reluctant students into participation. The skills in relation to teaching were identified as follows:

Hay McBer skill characteristics of effective teachers

Characteristics	Descriptors
1. High Expectations	Challenge and inspire
2. Planning	Clear and detailed curriculum plans
3. Methods and strategies	Range of methods with a brisk pace
4. Lesson flow	Clarity and enthusiasm coupled with smooth transitions
5. Time on task	Engagement of all pupils
6. Pupil management and discipline	Clear rules universally understood and applied
7. Time and resource management	Achievable goals and varied resources
8. Assessment	Feedback and guidance on how to improve
9. Homework	Extension of learning via regular homework and opportunities for most able to extend learning.

'High expectations' is the first key characteristic identified by Hay McBer and this is clearly endorsed by Ofsted because the importance of holding high expectations is regularly repeated within Ofsted inspection criteria and the annual reports published by the Ofsted Chief Inspector. The Ofsted, *Handbook for the Inspection of Further Education and Skills 2012* states, *"learners benefit from high expectations...,*[5] and in a linked expansion *"whether high but realistic expectations are used to motivate learners"*.[6] This endorsement of holding high expectations is further reinforced by the criteria listed for the award of Ofsted Grade One, 'Outstanding', *'Staff have consistently high expectations of all learners and demonstrate this in a range of learning environments'*.[7] Nor is this focus on 'high expectations' just directed at the College sector. The equivalent criteria within the 2012 inspection criteria for the schools sector states, *'All teachers have consistently high expectations of all pupils'*.[8] Finally, the importance of maintaining high expectations is given further emphasis by the Ofsted 2012 criteria for Leadership and Management, *'demonstrate an ambitious vision, have high expectations for what all learners can achieve, and attain high standards of quality and performance'*.[9] The Hay McBer nine characteristics of effective practice are reflected across Ofsted and professional criteria and supported by wider educational research.

McKinsey Report 2007

The Hay McBer findings were substantially reinforced in September 2007 by the publication of the McKinsey Report which placed a spotlight on the skills of teachers as the dominant and primary factor underpinning achievement. The McKinsey Report was a major international comparative study of the effectiveness of the education systems in 25 of the world's leading economies. The common success factors of the top 10 performers (across internationally recognised benchmarks), were distilled and a devastatingly simple formula emerged.

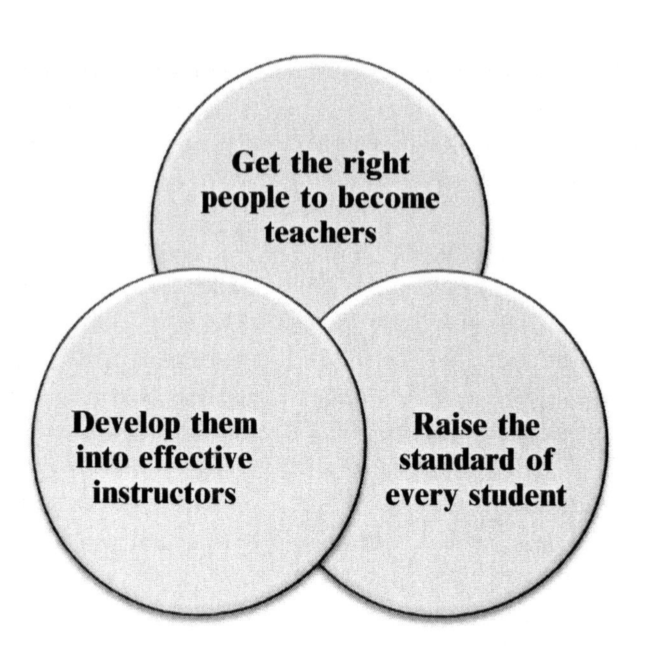

The above overlapping strategies were identified as the foundation steps for outstanding teaching and learning to flourish. McKinsey concluded that the most successful education systems advertise for and select highly skilled individuals as teachers, *"These mechanisms acknowledge that for a person to become an effective teacher they need to possess a certain set of characteristics that can be identified before they enter teaching: a high overall level of literacy and numeracy, strong interpersonal and communication skills, a willingness to learn and the motivation to teach. The selection procedures are therefore designed to test for these skills and attributes and to select those applicants that possess them"*.[10] Few teachers possessed all of those skills at the outset of their careers hence the McKinsey reference to *'develop them into effective instructors'*. This included seeking a commitment to continuous professional development to hone and perfect the high skill set required for effective teaching and to empower teaching teams to question, develop, refine and share effective teaching strategies and to adopt and apply common high standards. In one of the highest performing school systems (Hong Kong) the reported CPD commitment was 100 hours per year. The third major recommendation made by the McKinsey Report, was to ensure that the progress of all students was closely monitored against agreed learning targets and relevant achievement standards. Any slippage from the targets was expected to trigger early intervention to ensure that the student attained, as far as possible, the required standard. *"The very best systems intervene at the level of the individual student developing processes and structures within schools that are able to identify whenever a student is starting to fall behind and then intervening to improve that child's performance".* [11] Intervention was also recommended according to levels of perceived disadvantage according to community or home background to ensure that all students had an equal opportunity to succeed, *"The best systems have produced approaches to ensure that the school can compensate for the disadvantage resulting from the student's home environment". They start by setting clear and high expectations for what individual students should know, understand and be able to do"* [12] This focus on the individual and the reference to 'high expectations' is in clear accord with the earlier Hay McBer findings. McKinsey's significant conclusion was that despite decades of spending money on new buildings, new equipment, more teachers, new technology and funding smaller class sizes achievement in most countries showed little advancement. The issue was not one of 'hardware' but 'software' i.e. it is what happens in the classroom that makes the difference or in other words the skills of the teacher standing in front of the class. McKinsey reported, *'students placed with high performing teachers will progress three times as fast those placed with low performing teachers'.* [13] This conclusion has been substantially confirmed by extensive research undertaken by Eric Hanuskek, Senior Fellow of Stanford University. He revealed that the principal differences in student achievement were not between 'good' or 'bad' schools or factors like poverty, class size etc but between teachers, *"three years of good teachers in a row would overcome the average achievement deficit between low-income kids (those on free or reduced-price lunch) and others. In other words, high quality teachers can make up for the typical deficits that we see in the preparation of kids from disadvantaged backgrounds".*[14] Hanushek concluded that students are better off in 'bad' school with an effective teacher as opposed to being in a 'good' school with an ineffective teacher. On 2nd April, 2009, Professor Dylan Wiliam of the Institute of Education, one of the principal authors of *'Inside the Black Box',* published similar conclusions, *"Children in classes taught by the best teachers learn four times faster than those in classes taught by the poorest ones....It therefore matters much less which school a child attends than which classroom they are placed in..".*[15] In a further significant study, Professor Peter Tymms of Durham University tracked the progress of 73,000 primary school children from 1999 to 2005 and confirmed that poor teaching, above and beyond other factors, accounted for different rates of pupil progress. Consequently all schools and colleges should aim to address McKinsey's three core drivers of effective practice and devise and adopt appropriate strategies and policies.

Expert panel recommendations 2008

On 24th January 2008 an 'expert panel' was invited to contribute to a House of Commons seminar entitled, *'What makes a good teacher?'* Chaired by Barry Sheerman M.P. Professor Mary James of the Institute of Education presented ten key principles for effective teaching and learning based upon a ten year research programme conducted by the *Teaching and Learning Research Programme* (TLRP). The ten recommended learning interventions are quoted here, in full, as presented on the TLRP website (www.tlrp.org):[16]

1. Effective pedagogy equips learners for life in its broadest sense. Learning should aim to help individuals and groups to develop the intellectual, personal and social resources that will enable them to participate as active citizens, contribute to economic development and flourish as individuals in a diverse and changing society. This means adopting a broad conception of worthwhile learning outcomes and taking seriously issues of equity and social justice for all.

2. Effective pedagogy engages with valued forms of knowledge. Pedagogy should engage learners with the big ideas, key skills and processes, modes of discourse, ways of thinking and practising, attitudes and relationships, which are the most valued learning processes and outcomes in particular contexts. They need to understand what constitutes quality, standards and expertise in different settings

3. Effective pedagogy recognises the importance of prior experience and learning. Pedagogy should take account of what the learner knows already in order for them, and those who support their learning, to plan their next steps. This includes building on prior learning but also taking account of the personal and cultural experiences of different groups of learners.

4. Effective pedagogy requires learning to be scaffolded. Teachers, trainers and all those, including peers, who support the learning of others, should provide activities, cultures and structures of

intellectual, social and emotional support to help learners to move forward in their learning. When these supports are removed the learning needs to be secure.

5. Effective pedagogy needs assessment to be congruent with learning. Assessment should be designed and implemented with the goal of achieving maximum validity both in terms of learning outcomes and learning processes. It should help to advance learning as well as determine whether learning has occurred.

6. Effective pedagogy promotes the active engagement of the learner. A chief goal of learning should be the promotion of learners' independence and autonomy. This involves acquiring a repertoire of learning strategies and practices, developing positive learning dispositions, and having the will and confidence to become agents in their own learning.

7. Effective pedagogy fosters both individual and social processes and outcomes. Learners should be encouraged and helped to build relationships and communication with others for learning purposes, in order to assist the mutual construction of knowledge and enhance the achievements of individuals and groups. Consulting learners about their learning and giving them a voice is both an expectation and a right.

8. Effective pedagogy recognises the significance of informal learning. Informal learning, such as learning out of school or away from the workplace, should be recognised as at least as significant as formal learning and should therefore be valued and appropriately utilised in formal processes

9. Effective pedagogy depends on the learning of all those who support the learning of others. The need for lecturers, teachers, trainers and co-workers to learn continuously in order to develop their knowledge and skills, and adapt and develop their roles, especially through practice-based inquiry, should be recognised and supported.

10. Effective pedagogy demands consistent policy frameworks with support for learning as their primary focus. Organisational and system level policies need to recognise the fundamental importance of continual learning – for individual, team, organisational and system success – and be designed to create effective learning environments for all learners.

The TLRP top ten emphasises the 'communication' between teacher and student i.e. the process skills and support needed for students to access and assimilate new learning. As part of the seminar presentation, Professor Patricia Broadfoot, Vice-Chancellor of the University of Gloucestershire, listed the following characteristics of 'good' teaching:

- Creating an atmosphere of mutual respect and fairness in the classroom
- Providing opportunities for active learning
- Humour to encourage pupil engagement
- Making learning interesting
- Explaining things clearly.[17]

Broadfoot's list demonstrates a high degree of agreement with Ted Wragg's summary as quoted at the start of this chapter.

McKinsey 2010 – successful schools getting better

The considerable interest raised by the first McKinsey report (2007) prompted McKinsey to return to the topic and to deepen its research into the success factors underpinning the world's most successful education systems. The second McKinsey report published in November 2010 was entitled, *'How the world's most improved school systems keep getting better'*. The report detailed an extensive worldwide investigation into the improvement actions of the world's most successful education systems. The conclusion was the identification of four common developmental stages and six key 'interventions' to drive effective practice.

Developmental stages

The four stages identify a succession of key improvement actions to improve systems and teaching and learning from poor to excellent. The first stage is characterised by high levels of central control and direction to ensure the application of specified standards. Control is gradually relaxed as good practice is embedded until finally at the fourth stage autonomous curriculum teams largely govern and 'police' their own high standards of effective teaching and learning.

Stage	Characteristics
1 Poor to Fair	Assisting students to develop the standards of literacy and mathematical skills in particular to access the curriculum and enjoy success coupled with providing teachers with defined standards and models of good practice to drive consistency across all lessons i.e. a common tightly prescribed base pedagogy with firm central direction
2 Fair to Good	Establishing clear quality control though data monitoring to ensure that agreed good practice is consistently implemented, applying accountability and immediate interventions when performance targets are missed.
3 Good to Great	Raising the status of teachers as a profession with high standards, shared codes, incentives, rewards, motivational career paths and leadership.
4 Great to Excellent	A self-sustaining autonomous system that knows what good practice is and inducts all newcomers to the standards and encourages, innovation and experiments to further refine and build good practice.

McKinsey discovered many different pathways across the four stages and found no one set of steps that universally applied as the 'best' practice. All schools and colleges are invited to reflect on each stage and to set in motion relevant system and staff development improvement activities to advance from stage to stage until full autonomy is reached i.e. high achieving curriculum teams who are fully confident in their own systems, self-aware and able to maintain their own high standards with minimal external direction. However, McKinsey identified six common interventions, within and across all four stages as signposts and guides to effective reform:

1 Revising the curriculum and standards
2 Reviewing reward and remuneration structure
3 Building technical skills of teachers and principals
4 Assessing student learning
5 Utilising student data to guide delivery and
6 Establishing policy documents and education laws

The first intervention emphasises the need to closely specify what students should know, understand and be able to do and for teachers to identify the actions and strategies to achieve the specified learning goals and the relevant examination standards. Staff motivation should be addressed by appropriate recognition, including monetary reward for high performance against targets. In some cases McKinsey noted bonuses, equivalent to a month's salary were awarded for evidence of significant improvement. High entry standards to the teaching profession were specified with clear career paths that recognised and rewarded stages of competency from apprentice status to expert practitioner allied to the ability to coach and support others and to engage in regular peer support and Continuous Professional Development (CPD) to constantly review, question and raise standards. The progress of students was carefully monitored through standard assessment systems, barriers to learning were identified and prompt early support was provided for any students experiencing difficulty. Data on student progress was regularly gathered, discussed and analysed with clear accountability and as a prompt to further actions and support as necessary. Finally, policy documents provided clear guidance on the overall rationale, priorities and milestones and ensured all were fully aware of their responsibilities and roles. Those six interventions were identified as the core improvement actions of the world's most successful school systems although in varying forms across each of the four major developmental stages. McKinsey concluded that successful improvement is, *the disciplined craft of repeated practice and learning within the context of the system: the practice and internalization of the pedagogy.*[18] At the heart of this process is the teacher and the ability of the individual teacher to draw young people into effective participation, to identify their barriers to achievement, to coach improvement and most of all to build a belief in themselves that with effort a better future is attainable. In essence, teaching is a craft which we can learn, rehearse, review and perfect.

Dr. Robert J Marzano

Marzano is a prolific American researcher and writer who has undertaken extensive research into over 4,000 meta-analyses of the outcomes of educational research. His website marzanoresearch.com provides a gateway to his research and publications. Marzano's focus is primarily the classroom and his most well-known book, *Classroom Instruction That Works* (written in association with Debra Pickering and Jane Pollock) provides a practical and accessible guide to effective practice. Marzano, Pickering and Pollock identified nine key strategies for effective classroom practice.

Recommended learning strategies

No.	Learning strategies
1	Identifying similarities and differences *Breaking a concept down into clear steps often aided by 'big picture' charts and diagrams to show relationships*
2.	Summarising and note-taking *Recording key concepts and new learning in own words to encourage reflection, questions and deeper understanding*
3	Reinforcing effort and providing recognition *A 'can do' spirit – ability is not fixed and learning and progress is based on applying effort to succeed.*
4.	Homework and practice *Regular extended learning beyond the classroom*
5	Non-linguistic representations *Regular use of visuals, photographs, diagrams, models, objects to reinforce key concepts and learning*
6	Co-operative learning *Regular group working to explore key learning and build mutual learning support*
7	Setting objectives and feedback *Discuss learning targets and goals for a particular topic and encourage students to reflect on what they understand do not understand.*
8	Generating and testing hypotheses *Regularly posing key questions or hypotheses to trigger deeper thinking involving predictions and 'what if..'*
9.	Cues, questions and advance organisers *Signposting learning by sharing expected learning outcomes and identifying what students already know and how to extend their learning.*

Marzano, in common with the other research sources, emphasises that it is effective teachers that make the difference to learning and achievement much more so than home and community background. The effective teacher focuses upon developing learning and understanding by applying the above nine strategies.

Professor John Hattie

Perhaps the most significant research of all was the research undertaken by Professor John Hattie while Professor of Education at Auckland University. In 1999 Hattie presented a paper entitled, *Influences on Student Learning* as the subject of his inaugural lecture.

His paper summarised the conclusions of thousands of scientifically conducted teaching and learning research projects involving some 80 million students across the English speaking world. Hattie ranked each research project on an 'effect' scale for ease of comparison. The average 'effect' score for effective learning was calculated as 0.40. Any score above 0.40 identified a positive influence on learning and any score beyond 1.00 represented a highly significant advance in learning equivalent to a two grade leap at GCSE or improving the rate of learning by 50%. Hattie subsequently expanded his research and his most recent publication, *Visible Learning: A synthesis of over 800 meta-analyses relating to achievement, 2009*, details the outcomes of 800 world-wide meta-analyses related to student achievement compared to his initial study of 500 in 1999. Hattie has isolated 138 major influences on student learning and placed them into rank order in terms of significance. In March 2011 Hattie was appointed as the Director of the Education Research Institute, University of Melbourne and his most recent succinct good practice guidance to teachers, seeking to improve their practice, was to listen more and talk less.

Hattie's top ten

The following Top Ten list is Hattie's revised rank order based upon his additional and more extensive 2009 research. Consequently the rank order does differ from the rank order presented in his earlier research papers because of a greater volume of evidence of the effectiveness of individual strategies. The descriptions in the application column are not direct quotation but summarise the strategy. Hattie's top ten influences* on student learning are as follows.[19]

Rank	Effect	Influence	Application
1	1.44	Self-report grades	Learners self-awareness of their own progress against course and exam standards and seeking and acting on improvement guidance.
2	1.28	Piagetian programmes	Being alert to students' level of thinking skills in relation to Piaget's stages of learning and helping all to advance from concrete to abstract thinking.
3	0.90	Formative evaluation	Teacher reflection on effectiveness of lessons via self and peer assessment – effective observation feedback to answer 'how am I going'?

4	0.88	Micro teaching	Testing new strategies and reflecting on impact and offering short demonstration lesson, presentations of effective teaching.
5	0.88	Acceleration	Advancing the most able through the curriculum at a faster pace
6	0.80	Classroom behavioural	School and classroom interventions to curb any poor behaviour and promoting effective participation by students with learning difficulties..
7	0.75	Teacher clarity	Clear communication of learning goals learning guidance and checks on learning
8	0.74	Reciprocal teaching	Students encouraged to peer examine, review meaning of text and take the lead in discussions and take a turn at being the teacher.
9	0.73	Feedback	Discussing with students what they understand and what they do not understand.
10	0.72	Teacher-student relationship	Developing positive, motivational relationships involving listening, empathy, caring and mutual regard.

*Number Seven in Hattie's rank order is *'comprehensive interventions for learning disabled students'* but this is leapfrogged here to permit a focus on the top ten generic learning and teaching interventions.

Hattie has attached the 138 'influences on learning' to six major factors namely: student (19), home (7), school (27), curriculum (26), teacher (10) and teaching (49). As the figures in brackets indicate teaching is the most significant factor of all in terms of the numbers of studies and this is further magnified by the relatively high positions awarded to teaching studies within the overall rank order. Essentially it is what effective teachers do that makes the difference and here there is significant agreement between Marzano and Hattie on the most effective strategies. Many lower ranked strategies are also important and in practice teachers need to address a combination of overlapping strategies to generate the most effective teaching and learning. Hattie isolated three major attributes of the most effective teachers, "it is teachers *using particular teaching methods*, teachers *with high expectations for all students* and teachers who have *created positive student-teacher relationships* that are more likely to have above average effects on student achievement".[20] He concluded that students often face a lottery in terms of the skills of the teacher standing in their classroom, *"There appear as many teachers who have effects below this (below the positive 0.40 effect threshold), as there are above, and every year a student faces a huge gamble as to who is at the front of their class".*[21]

Successful schools and colleges ensure that this gamble does not exist through regular team talk, dissemination of good practice and observation schemes to drive the adoption and maintenance of commonly agreed standards often summarised within an agreed teaching and learning policy. The latter consideration is explored in Chapter Twelve.

The 'outstanding' pyramid

Picture a 3D pyramid with the four faces of the pyramid displaying the four key elements of outstanding teaching and learning as follows:

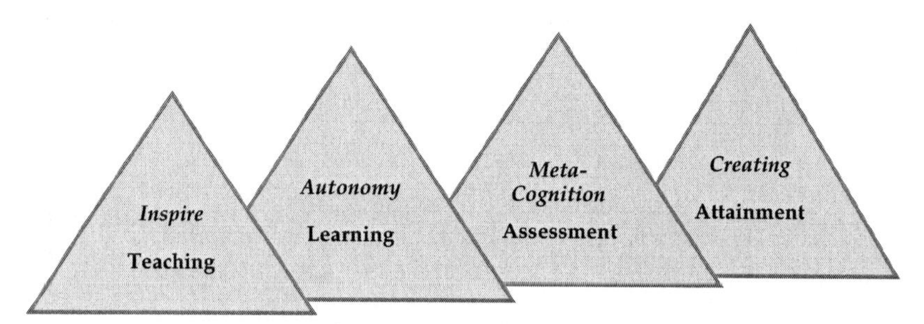

The most significant element or face of the pyramid is **teaching** because outstanding teaching and learning is driven by teachers who display a passion and enthusiasm for their subjects and who challenge and inspire their students to a greater effort. This greater effort significantly extends **learning** beyond the classroom, builds confidence and skills and leads students to gradually shift from being dependent on the teacher to becoming independent and ultimately autonomous learners. Progress is secured and advanced by an **assessment** process that delivers regular feedback within a coaching relationship. Low marks are questioned rather than ignored, self-assessment against marking criteria is encouraged and the students gain not only self-belief but meta-cognition in terms of their ability to seek and act on improvement guidance. The end result is high **attainment** as the students develop not only higher order thinking and reasoning skills but many will go further and apply their new skills and knowledge in creative ways and generate new and original applications, ideas or interpretations. Whereas in the time of Benjamin Bloom the highest level of attainment was 'evaluation' today it is regarded as 'creativity' in reflection of a much more individual, and entrepreneurial age. The above diagram is limited to displaying the apex of the pyramid and the 'outstanding' goals of:

- Inspiring
- Autonomy
- Meta-cognition
- Creating

However, in each case there is an underpinning taxonomy or hierarchy of skills and attributes. The teaching skills pyramid is presented below. The Skills hierarchy pyramid related to Learning is displayed in Chapter Eleven. The Assessment pyramid is part of Chapter Five and finally the Attainment pyramid is within Chapter Two.

Teaching skills pyramid

The pyramid below presents a hierarchy of the actions, skills and attributes of effective teachers. When the research into effective practice from all of the above major research sources, professional guidance and Ofsted reports is weighed and sifted four key themes emerge as illustrated in the teachers' skills pyramid.

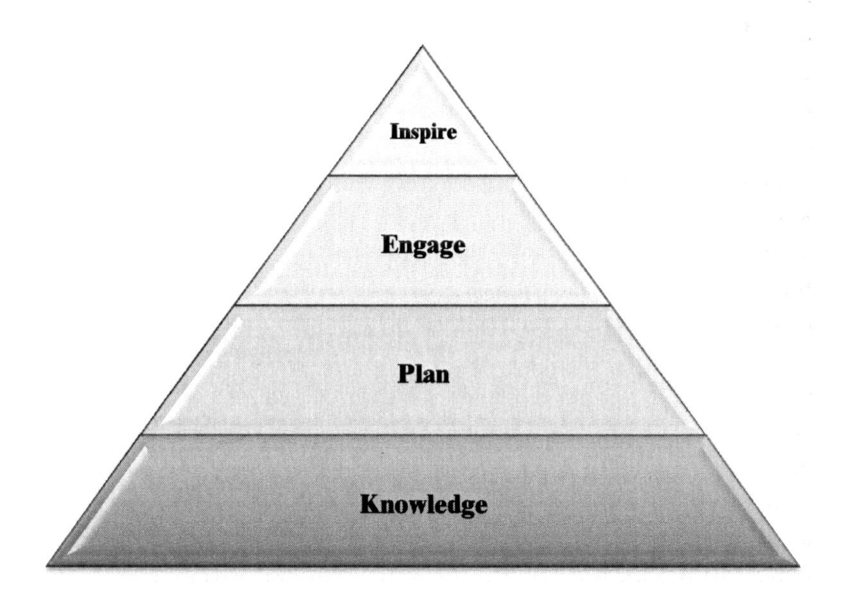

The four themes have a hierarchal relationship moving from a base of subject or skills knowledge, through planning and engagement skills to the prized ability to inspire students. Some teachers have the ability to enthuse and often inspire but lack the foundation skills of effective planning and organisation whereas others have clear knowledge and planning skills but struggle to enthuse or inspire. The outstanding teacher demonstrates effective practice at each stage of the pyramid.

Knowledge

Knowledge of a particular subject or skill is a teacher's bedrock. Clearly all teachers must possess good subject knowledge to be judged competent let alone outstanding. The importance of a sound knowledge base can be judged by the fact that it is still possible to commence a teaching career in Further Education (FE) purely on the basis of a specialist knowledge of a particular subject or skill whether it is Flower Arranging, Social Care, Motor Vehicle or History. Teacher training is required but can come second and catch-up, perhaps part-time over two years but a sound knowledge of subject is expected from the first day. A specialist knowledge is an expectation of any teacher but there is also an expectation that as time passes knowledge is kept up-to-date and especially within vocational areas. Most of us would be very unforgiving if a solicitor accountant or doctor was found to be relying upon outdated judgements, guidance or treatments. We expect expert knowledge from other professional groups and likewise students, parents and employers expect up-to-date knowledge from a teacher of a specialist subject or skill. Therefore it is no surprise that the Lifelong Learning standards for learning and teaching in FE state, " *Ensure that knowledge of own specialist area is current and appropriate to the teaching context*". [22] In September 2007 the status of FE teachers was significantly enhanced by the specification of professional standards by the *Institute for Learning* (IfL). The IFL introduced a 30 hour commitment to Continuous Professional Development (CPD), and has encouraged subject specific research, "*CPD…is any activity undertaken for the purposes of updating knowledge of the subject taught and developing teaching skills*".[23] The IfL notes that the 30 hour requirement is a minimum not a maximum because most teachers undertake many more hours. However the CPD minimum is enforced as a condition of a 'licence to practice', "*all members must demonstrate evidence of continuing professional development which links to subject specialism, teacher training, organisational and national requirements. Failure to comply with this is a disciplinary offence".*[24] This and related IfL regulations may seem stern but they place teaching in FE on a par with other professional groups by setting high standards for membership. The Tomlinson report of 2005 which reviewed the 14-19 curriculum commented, *"Where vocational areas are concerned this must also mean ensuring that teachers have up-to-date and accurate knowledge and recent experience of the area they teach."* [25] The expert panel who contributed to the House of Commons Seminar, *'What makes a good teacher?'* referred to knowledge in the following terms, *"Effective pedagogy depends on the learning of all those who support the learning of others. The need for lecturers, teachers, trainers and co-workers to learn continuously in order to develop their knowledge and skill, and adapt and develop their roles, especially through practice-based inquiry, should be recognised and supported."*[26] Professor Debra Myhill of Exeter University highlighted that whereas good subject knowledge and intellectual ability were important they were *"insufficient' to make a good teacher"*.[27] This is perhaps a view shared by many teachers who have often discovered that the visiting expert speaker struggled to explain their subject in terms that the average student could easily grasp. The Ofsted inspection framework for F.E. inspections 2009-12 was couched in the form of general principles and in relation to knowledge it confined itself to a basic expectation, *"Teaching staff have a sound knowledge of their subjects or are suitably skilled and experienced in their specialist area"*. [28] In comparison the parallel Ofsted inspection criteria for school inspections (Section 5 inspections) 2009-12 established a clear hierarchy of judgements, in relation to knowledge, as follows:

Satisfactory	*Teachers' subject knowledge is secure*
Good	*Teachers generally have strong subject knowledge which enthuses and challenges most pupils and contributes to their good progress.*
Outstanding	*Excellent subject knowledge is applied consistently to challenge and inspire pupils.*

The importance of knowledge was also emphasised by Ofsted in the 2005-8 inspection framework with a requirement to be up-to-date , " *show knowledge, technical competence and up-to-date expertise, at a level consistent with effective teaching, training and assessment of the course or programme".*[29] This was reinforced by Ofsted's 2008 criteria for vocational training which included the criterion, *"whether the activities reflect current commercial or industrial practice"*'[30] and the criteria for 'good or better' lessons included the criterion, *" accurate and up-to-date technical knowledge"*.[31] These explicit judgments on 'knowledge' have not been carried forward into the 2012+ inspection framework but it should not be assumed that they no longer apply. Rather expert and up-to-date knowledge is an embedded expectation as references to holding appropriate and specialist qualifications, building up-to-date knowledge and applying relevant safety guidelines appear across the 2012 inspection criteria for Further Education. The criteria for the award of Grade One 'outstanding' includes a reference to 'excellent' subject knowledge, *'Drawing on excellent subject knowledge and/or industry experience, teachers, trainers, assessors and coaches plan astutely and set challenging tasks based on systematic, accurate assessment of learners' prior skills, knowledge and understanding.*[32] A virtually identical criterion is included within the 2012 Grade One 'outstanding' criteria within the schools sector. The only difference is the removal of the references to industry experience, trainers and assessors. Ultimately, knowledge of subject is a base requirement and the significant skill is effective communication. This is reinforced by Hattie's rank order which places knowledge 125th out of 134 learning influences and with an 'effect score' of 0.09 far below the 0.40 threshold for significant learning influences. One explanation quoted by Hattie is, *"it is likely that subject matter knowledge influences teaching effectiveness up to some level of basic competence but less so thereafter"*.[33] Essentially it is rare for teachers not to know their subject – knowledge is a given. However, the notable edge applied by outstanding teachers is to display up-to-date or even expert knowledge. Indications of this may arise from references to current affairs, making connections to other subjects, new technology and new research, etc. Motivation increases when students can see the wider picture and appreciate the point and purpose of what they are studying. A simple reference to a relevant TV programme, museum collection, recommended book, new manufacturing process, newspaper article, new law, useful internet site, a blog, a new piece of equipment, an article in a library journal etc all help to bring the subject knowledge alive. In addition outstanding teachers can draw upon their up-to-date knowledge to offer multiple examples or explanations to help struggling students to overcome a learning block and to assimilate new learning. Many of the '*appetisers*' described in Chapter Seven and the '*bridge*' suggestions made in Chapter Ten are all designed to raise links to up-to-date knowledge and to promote independent learning.

Plan

Second to knowledge in the hierarchy of the skills pyramid is planning i.e. the ability to translate knowledge of a subject or skill into a clear step-by-step learning programme. In particular it is the ability to *plan for learning* and to monitor and adjust the pace and selection of teaching and learning strategies to support all students that makes the difference. Ofsted included within its 2009 criteria, *"how well staff plan sessions to take account of meeting the needs of different groups of learners fully"*. [34] In essence, can a teacher take students from no knowledge in September to mastery by June when the majority will pass and some will stretch further and gain a Distinction or a Grade A or A*? Or in a vocational programme pass/fail programme achieve the relevant commercial or technical standards? The theme of effective planning is extended within Ofsted's 2012 criteria for outstanding practice, "*...teachers, trainers, assessors and coaches plan astutely and set challenging tasks based on systematic, accurate assessment of learners' prior skills, knowledge and understanding. They use well-judged and often imaginative teaching strategies that, together with sharply focused and timely support and intervention, match individual needs accurately. Consequently, the development of learners' skills and understanding is exceptional*".[35] Here the planning is firmly focussed upon the individual in terms of an effective initial assessment process to capture individual learning needs and to set meaningful targets to stretch all to achieve their full potential. Note also the link made to '*imaginative teaching strategies*' and '*interventions*' planned to match the needs of students. To ensure that the majority of students can at least pass a course requires planning that goes far beyond simply listing the order of topics to be taught in a Scheme of Work and/or printing off a standard Scheme of Work from the National Curriculum or another official source. Is the pace and challenge right for the level of course and the different ability levels of the students enrolled? Are steps taken to closely monitor the progress of any 'at risk' students or identified 'at-risk' sub-groups and to narrow and/or close any known or emerging achievement gaps? Do the teaching methods, assessment methods and resources promote equality, diversity and good race relations? Are opportunities taken to build and reinforce effective functional and employability skills? Effective planning is also based upon a clear knowledge of the final exam or summative assessment or commercial skill standards against the entry standards of the students enrolled. Often not enough is known about the students in terms of their prior learning, their home circumstances, their abilities and their ambitions. Ofsted's 2012 criteria specifies, *'learners' additional support needs are quickly and accurately identified early in their programme through effective initial assessment, leading to appropriate planning and support throughout the duration of their programmes'.*[36] At the Further Education level the common complaint is that records rarely follow students from school to college or to training centres. In addition, within colleges, the initial assessment information, collated as a part of induction or enrolment processes, is often not shared with the wider teaching team. Essentially, effective teachers plan for the learning gap between the final exam standards and the entry standards of their students on an individual basis – they personalise learning. They focus on the teaching strategies and resources that will promote learning and set the challenge for each student just ahead of their current ability and adjust their planning in the light of the progress being made. They do this in conjunction with the students by planning for regular feedback within their lessons and at the transition points from one topic to another. They couch Schemes of Work and Lesson Plans and the expression of aims and objectives in the language of *how* to learn rather than *what* to learn. The focus on *how* rather than *what* is the hallmark of the effective teacher, although many might argue that this is an obvious point. The Board of Education Handbook for Teachers first published in 1904 states the teacher must be, " *a close and sympathetic student of the nature of his pupils. He must be able to range himself mentally alongside them and ready to modify his teaching to meet their needs...His starting point must be no rigid syllabus or subject , but the children as they really are: he must work always with the grain of their minds, try never to cut across it"*.[37] Compare the Board of Education statement with the following criterion taken from the Ofsted 2012 inspection framework for Further Education, *' staff work with learners to develop individual learning plans that are regularly informed by ongoing assessment ...learners are set challenging short and longer term goals that are reviewed and updated regularly'.* [38] The language is clearly different but the sentiment is the same. Personalisation, therefore, is not a new concept and we must always be alert to the fact that we do not teach classes but rather groups of individuals who all happen to be in the same room. Planning requirements will vary from school to school and college to college but ideally there should be a planning hierarchy from macro overview down to the micro i.e. individual target setting. At the macro level a *'Year Planner'* or other similar document is common i.e. a calendar or diary with a list of the key topics to be studied and in the recommended order. Next a Scheme of Work with a breakdown of the key topics but with the focus on ***how*** they will be taught, resourced and assessed rather than ***what*** will be taught. At the micro level individual lesson plans should provide a timed breakdown of the lesson and finally Individual Learning Plans (ILPs) should provide individual targets. All students should have an ILP which is reviewed regularly. The ILP is normally held and reviewed by Personal Tutors but in situations that involve individual working like an IT learning centre or an Art and Design studio each teacher should maintain ILPs. The effective teacher enters the classroom with a sharp awareness of what is to be learned and designs lessons to build the desired learning coupled with regular opportunities for the students to practice and improve functional and employability skills. A full overview of effective planning considerations is provided within Chapter Two.

Engage

An effective teacher, let alone an outstanding teacher, has to be able to command the room, maintain order and to motivate and engage the students in learning. The former demands good behaviour management skills and the latter good communication skills and lessons that involve a challenging sequence of tasks to capture and sustain the students' interest. Outstanding teachers also closely monitor students' learning and progress during the lesson and pause regularly to check and reinforce key learning by employing appropriate 'assessment for learning' strategies to check and advance progress. In essence they apply Hattie's top ten and are alert to Piagetian stages of development. Jean Piaget (1896-1980) identified four stages of maturation and cognitive development, Sensorimotor, Pre-Operational, Concrete Operational and Formal Operational.

Many students struggle with the transition from Concrete Operational to Formal Operational and need our intervention and support via multiple modes of explanation and exploration of new learning to assimilate and achieve. This cognitive hierarchy is also reflected in Bloom's Taxonomy and in practice it demands a sharp awareness of the skills and knowledge required not just to achieve a bare pass *(often reflects Concrete Operational or lower order of Bloom's Taxonomy)* but to gain a distinction or grade A *(often reflects Formal Operational or the higher order of Bloom's Taxonomy).* These considerations are explored in more depth in Chapter Two. Outstanding teachers address this learning gap and have strategies to bridge the gap to achieve at least pass standard for all students via real time monitoring and consolidation of learning. Some teachers fail to engage their students sufficiently because they overdo 'chalk and talk' and misjudge attention spans. After only 7-8 minutes the attention of most students will have begun to wander and therefore a good lesson plan will avoid too much time spent listening and place an emphasis on active involvement. To avoid over talking consider writing lesson plans that follow the simple formula of whole class presentation, individual task, paired task and in a longer lesson a group task as well. Entering the classroom with this plan of action will ensure the involvement of the students in the lesson and if the tasks are interesting and supported by a variety of resources full engagement will hopefully be achieved. The Hay McBer report emphasised this variety of learning activity as follows, *"effective teachers had well over 90% of the pupils on task through the lesson and flowed naturally to achieve a balance between whole class interaction, whole class lecture, individual work, group work and assessment".*[39] A similar point was made by the pioneering *Teach First* programme, *"The more flexible and innovative teachers are in their methods of delivery, the more engaged pupils will be. In short it is imaginative teaching more than imaginative curriculum content which makes the difference".*[40] A key factor in winning the engagement of students is to build the student-teacher relationship primarily by holding high expectations. Outstanding teachers convey to their students that learning cannot only enrich their lives but also offer them a satisfying career, a positive future and ultimately high levels of personal satisfaction. This was a key feature of the Hay McBer report and also commented upon by Hattie as follows, *"...teachers having expectations that all students can progress, that achievement for all is changeable (and not fixed), and that progress for all is understood and articulated".* [41] Ofsted 2012 criteria, as highlighted earlier, details the importance of high expectations but it does also temper this with realistic goals, *'whether high but realistic expectations are used to motivate learners'.*[42] Ultimately it is a question of personalising learning and focussing on learning pathways for each individual rather than tilting at the wider socio-economic issues beyond the control of the teacher and the individual. Consider the following extract from the motivational book, *Chicken Soup for the Soul:*[43]

> *"A tourist was walking along a deserted beach in Mexico at sunset when he noticed a local man in the distance bending down at the water's edge. As he drew nearer, he noticed that the man kept picking things up and throwing them far out into the water. Time and time again he kept hurling things out into the ocean.*
>
> *As he got closer he could see that the local man was picking up starfish that had been washed up onto the beach and, one at a time, he was throwing them back into the sea.*
>
> *As the tourist drew level he stopped and enquired, 'what are you doing'?*
>
> *The local man replied, 'I'm throwing these starfish back into the sea because if they are left here they will surely die once the sun comes up.*
>
> *'I understand,' replied the tourist,' but I can see thousands of starfish washed-up along the beach. You can't help all of them. There are simply too many. And don't you realise this is probably happening on hundreds of beaches all up and down this coast. Can't you see that you can't possibly make a difference'?*
>
> *The local man smiled, bent down and picked-up another starfish and threw it far out into the sea. He answered, 'I've made a difference to that one"!*

If you visit the 'Teacher of the Year' website (www.teachingawards.com) you will find many glowing tributes from students thanking individual teachers who made a difference. The following is a typical example from the 2012 awards, *"I found [my teacher] an inspiring and truly dedicated teacher, he paced the whole class through our GCSE maths, and helped me gain a grade A which I didnt think I was capable of. He pushed me right through from year 10 even when I was...well, quite a handful! I really hope he continues to teach as well as he did for us! And I would like to take this opportunity to thank him myself, and no doubt from our entire class! Thank you again."*[44] However, the challenges posed by socio-economic disadvantage are significant and not all students, can or will, participate in learning effectively. The outstanding teacher aims to win all but with the knowledge that some, because of overwhelming personal circumstances, will be unable to take advantage of the learning opportunities offered. The clear engagement of students in learning is expressed within the Ofsted 2012 inspection criteria as follow, *"learners benefit from high expectations, engagement, care, support and motivation from staff"*.[45] The additional emphasis placed here by the 2012 criteria compared to 2009-12 is *care and support*. In other words establishing a strong rapport but also ensuring an appropriate level of challenge consistent with the course level and for the different students within the lesson. Finally, an outstanding teacher watches body language very carefully. Are all of the students 'heads up' and on task or is there evidence of low attention, boredom or even disruptive behaviour? Exercising clear classroom control was sixth in Hattie's top ten. A lesson plan is a plan and the outstanding teacher will adjust the pace and flow of the lesson by truncating or extending learning activities according to the observed levels of progress. The key, as indicated, is to follow the actual learning rather than a pre-determined plan of expected learning.

Inspire

At the apex of the teachers' skill pyramid is the single word 'inspire'. However, Ofsted, academic and student opinion typically use three words to describe the edge presented by 'outstanding' teachers i.e. **inspiring, enthusiastic and passionate**. This is the dividing line between good and outstanding i.e. a motivational edge. Those three words pepper Ofsted 'outstanding' inspection reports, wider survey reports and Ofsted criteria. Consider the following quotation from the Ofsted inspection report for Kendal College published January 2011 which incorporated all three words, *"Outstanding lessons are characterised by passionate and enthusiastic teachers who use their extensive* *vocational expertise to inspire a culture of learning and challenge. In these lessons, teachers' expectations of their students are high, checks on learning and understanding are frequent, questions are probing and work is appropriately challenging".*[46] Kendal College achieved Ofsted's highest accolade of five Grade One 'outstanding' inspection grades. The Ofsted 2012 criteria for Further Education places an emphasis on inspire and challenge, *'how well teaching and learning methods – including training, coaching and mentoring – **inspire and challenge** all learners and enable them to extend their knowledge, skills and understanding'.*[47] Within the schools sector the Ofsted 2012 criteria also identifies a communication edge, *"the extent to which teachers enthuse, engage and motivate pupils to learn and foster their curiosity and enthusiasm for learning'.*[48] Highly motivational communication skills are the hallmark of outstanding teaching because they are associated with raising interest levels and triggering *independent research* which often translates into higher achievement. An example of this linkage is provided by the following student's comment placed on the Teacher of the Year website (www.teachingawards.com) in terms of how a new teacher successfully engaged him, *'She brought enthusiasm, knowledge, and fun into the classroom – allowing us all to have a laugh, but using dynamic teaching in order to make sure what was going in stayed in. I suddenly shot from a predicted E grade to a predicted B, and pulled off a B in GCSE English Lit and Language.*[49] Charisma is not what is meant by the key words *inspiring, enthusiastic* and *passionate* but rather fast-paced and challenging learning activities that motivate and even excite. In the Ofsted publication Twelve Excellent Schools 2008, a Headteacher remarked of his staff, *" their job is to 'light fires' and excite students about learning at school"*. [50] It is the pace and the challenge that produces an all-embracing sense of energy and purpose and encourages students to contribute personal research / experiences i.e. they become active participants in their own learning rather than passive recipients of information. A succinct description of the key features of outstanding teaching and learning appeared in the Ofsted publication, Why Colleges Succeed, published in November 2004: Here all three trigger words are present.

Teacher qualities

"Teachers are knowledgeable and enthusiastic, and the best are inspirational, skilfully imparting their passion to students. A feature of many of the

effective lessons is the enthusiasm teachers show for their subject. There is a pervasive culture of high expectations of both students and staff'.

Student qualities

'Learning is exceptional. Students are highly motivated, are intrinsically interested in learning new information and are enthusiastic about extending their understanding. They quickly develop good study habits, including independent research skills, and work hard to improve their knowledge. Much collaborative work in lessons is outstanding, with students co-operating most effectively on tasks set by the teacher".[51]

There is consistency of judgment in relation to effective teacher skills as indicated by the following identification of similar qualities in the Ofsted Chief Inspector's report 2011, *"Outstanding teaching and learning are characterised by highly skilled and enthusiastic teachers who use their extensive expertise to inspire a culture of learning and challenge".*[52] The Ofsted 2012 criteria for 'outstanding' within Further Education carries forward the importance of the attribute of enthusiasm as follows *"Staff generate high levels of enthusiasm for participation in, and commitment to, learning".*[53] A virtually identical criterion is included within the Ofsted 2012 'outstanding' criteria for the schools sector, *"Teachers and other adults generate high levels of enthusiasm for, participation in and commitment to learning.* [54] The outstanding teacher raises the high expectation that not only is every student capable of passing the course (all students selected and enrolled for a course should be capable of passing) but that a significant number can attain a high grade or apply the highest industry / commercial standard by following the learning directions given. If this is coupled with *raising horizons* in terms of what the future might hold for each individual the result is often higher personal motivation and a greater effort to succeed. Teachers should translate these high expectations into the relevant course level whether level 1, 2, 3 or 4 and set the pace accordingly and set 'challenging' targets appropriate for progression to the next level. Lifelong learning criteria which governs teacher training qualifications in F.E. includes the criterion, *"Implement appropriate and innovative ways to enthuse and motivate learners about own specialist area".*[55] The Tomlinson report of 2005 recommended that teachers should, *"inspire learners by delivering a varied, relevant and interesting curriculum in ways that motivate them ...and use their specialist expertise and passion for subject depth…"*[56] Hattie identified passion as the cement bonding effective learning and teaching as follows, *"we rarely talk about passion in education, as if doing so makes the work of teachers seem less serious, more emotional than cognitive, …. passion reflects the thrills as well as the frustrations of learning – it can be infectious, it can be taught, it can be modelled, and it can be learnt….it infuses many of the influences that make the difference to the outcomes…to wish to imbue others with a liking or even love of the discipline being taught.."* [57] Passion is not charisma because as Hattie indicates it can be 'learnt' and it does not have to be 'loud' but rather it reflects a deep personal interest and even love of subject. Students are quick to detect whether the subject means something to a teacher or not. Essentially, *enthusiasm, passion and inspiration* translate into, 'can you sell your subject and motivate'? The prize is to trigger independent learning and in some cases an intrinsic love of subject.

Skills pyramid criteria

The four key skill areas of the teachers' skills pyramid are reflected in both Lifelong Learning 2007[58] and Ofsted 2012 criteria[59] as follows.

Aspect	Lifelong Learning	Ofsted criteria 2012
Knowledge	Ensure that knowledge of own specialist area is current and appropriate to the teaching context	'Drawing on excellent subject knowledge and/or industry experience, teachers, trainers, assessors and coaches plan astutely and set challenging tasks
Plan	Plan teaching sessions which meet the aims and needs of individual learners and groups using a variety of resources, including new and emerging technologies.	how learning is planned to meet individual learners' needs and makes best use of staff knowledge and skills
Engage	Use a range of effective and appropriate teaching and learning techniques to engage and motivate learners and to encourage independence.	learners benefit from high expectations, engagement, care, support and motivation from staff… They use well-judged and often imaginative teaching strategies… the extent to which teaching, training and coaching encourages and develops independent learning

Inspire	Implement appropriate and innovative ways to enthuse and motivate learners about own specialist area.	Inspire and challenge all learners and enable them to extend their knowledge, skills and understanding...Staff generate high levels of enthusiasm for participation in, and commitment to, learning.

Note the high accord between the Lifelong Learning 2007 teacher training and Ofsted 2012 inspection standards. Ofsted has stated that within Further Education the Lifelong Learning professional standards will be included in lesson observation judgements.

Lifelong Learning professional standards

The Lifelong Learning professional standards were introduced in 2007 and govern all Further Education teaching qualifications. On 1st April 2011 responsibility for the standards and teacher training across Further Education was transferred to the Learning and Skills Improvement Service (LSIS). The standards for teachers in Further Education specify six domains of best practice:

A Professional values and practice
B Learning and teaching
C Specialist learning and teaching
D Planning for learning
E Assessment for learning
F Access and progression

Domain A provides an overarching set of values to govern all FE teaching and learning. The other five domains set standards for the identified key aspects of effective practice. Each standard has a preface letter S, K and P related to the expected *Scope, Knowledge, Practice*. The full standards for Domains B and C are as follows:

Domain B Learning and teaching	
They are committed to: BS 1 Maintaining an inclusive, equitable and motivating learning environment. BS 2 Applying and developing own professional skills to enable learners to achieve their goals. BS 3 Communicating effectively and appropriately with learners to enhance learning. BS 4 Collaboration with colleagues to support the needs of learners. BS 5 Using a range of learning resources to support learners.	
BK 1.1 Ways to maintain a learning environment in which learners feel safe and supported.	BP 1.1 Establish a purposeful learning environment where learners feel safe, secure, confident and valued.
BK 1.2 Ways to develop and manage behaviours which promote respect for and between others and create an equitable and inclusive learning environment.	BP 1.2 Establish and maintain procedures with learners which promote and maintain appropriate behaviour, communication and respect for others, while challenging discriminatory behaviour and attitudes.
BK 1.3 Ways of creating a motivating learning environment.	BP 1.3 Create a motivating environment which encourages learners to reflect on, evaluate and make decisions about their learning.
BK 2.1 Principles of learning and ways to provide learning activities to meet curriculum requirements and the needs of all learners.	BP 2.1 Provide learning activities which meet curriculum requirements and the needs of all learners.
BK 2.2 Ways to engage, motivate and encourage active participation of learners and learner independence.	BP 2.2 Use a range of effective and appropriate teaching and learning techniques to engage and motivate learners and encourage independence.
BK 2.3 The relevance of learning approaches, preferences and skills to learner progress.	BP 2.3 Implement learning activities which develop the skills and approaches of all learners and promote learner autonomy.
BK 2.4 Flexible delivery of learning, including open and distance learning and on-line learning.	BP 2.4 Apply flexible and varied delivery methods as appropriate to teaching and learning practice.
BK 2.5 Ways of using learners' own experiences as a foundation for learning.	BP 2.5 Encourage learners to use their own life experiences as a foundation for their development.
BK 2.6 Ways to evaluate own practice in terms of efficiency and effectiveness.	BP 2.6 Evaluate the efficiency and effectiveness of own teaching, including consideration of learner feedback and learning theories.
BK 2.7 Ways in which mentoring and/or coaching can support the development of professional skills and knowledge	BP 2.7 Use mentoring and/or coaching to support own and others' professional development, as appropriate.

BK 3.1 Effective and appropriate use of different forms of communication informed by relevant theories and principles.	BP 3.1 Communicate effectively and appropriately using different forms of language and media, including written, oral and non-verbal communication, and new and emerging technologies to enhance learning.
BK 3.2 A range of listening and questioning techniques to support learning.	BP 3.2 Use listening and questioning techniques appropriately and effectively in a range of learning contexts.
BK 3.3 Ways to structure and present information and ideas clearly and effectively to learners.	BP 3.3 Structure and present information clearly and effectively
BK 3.4 Barriers and aids to effective communication.	BP 3.4 Evaluate and improve own communication skills to maximise effective communication and overcome identifiable barriers to communication.
BK 3.5 Systems for communication within own organisation.	BP 3.5 Identify and use appropriate organisational systems for communicating with learners and colleagues.
BK 4. 1 Good practice in meeting the needs of learners in collaboration with colleagues.	BP 4.1 Collaborate with colleagues to encourage learner progress.
BK 5.1 The impact of resources on effective learning.	BP 5.1 Select and develop a range of effective resources, including appropriate use of new and emerging technologies
BK 5.2 Ways to ensure that resources used are inclusive, promote equality and support diversity.	BP 5.2 Select, develop and evaluate resources to ensure they are inclusive, promote equality and engage with diversity

Domain C Specialist learning and teaching

They are committed to:
CS 1 Understanding and keeping up to date with current knowledge in respect of own specialist area.
CS 2 Enthusing and motivating learners in own specialist area.
CS 3 Fulfilling the statutory responsibilities associated with own specialist area of teaching.
CS 4 Developing good practice in teaching own specialist area.

CK 1.1 Own specialist area including current developments.	CP 1.1 Ensure that knowledge of own specialist area is current and appropriate to the teaching context.
CK 1.2 Ways in which own specialism relates to the wider social, economic and environmental context.	CP 1.2 Provide opportunities for learners to understand how the specialist area relates to the wider social, economic and environmental context.
CK 2.1 Ways to convey enthusiasm for own specialist area to learners.	CP 2.1 Implement appropriate and innovative ways to enthuse and motivate learners about own specialist area.

CK 3.1 Teaching and learning theories and strategies relevant to own specialist area.	CP 3.1 Apply appropriate strategies and theories of teaching and learning to own specialist area.
CK 3.2 Ways to identify individual learning needs and potential barriers to learning in own specialist area.	CP 3.2 Work with learners to address particular individual learning needs and overcome identified barriers to learning.
CK 3.3 The different ways in which language, literacy and numeracy skills are integral to learners' achievement in own specialist area.	CP 3.3 Work with colleagues with relevant learner expertise to identify and address literacy, language and numeracy development in own specialist area.
CK 3.4 The language, literacy and numeracy skills required to support own specialist teaching.	CP 3.4 Ensure own personal skills in literacy, language and numeracy are appropriate for the effective support of learners.
CK 3.5 Ways to support learners in the use of new and emerging technologies in own specialist area.	CP 3.5 Make appropriate use of, and promote the benefits of new and emerging technologies.
CK 4.1 Ways to keep up to date with developments in teaching in own specialist area.	CP 4.1 Access sources for professional development in own specialist area.
CK 4.2 Potential transferable skills and employment opportunities relating to own specialist area.	CP 4.2 Work with learners to identify the transferable skills they are developing, and how these might relate to employment opportunities.

The equivalent standards for the schools sector were revised in 2011-12 by the Teaching Agency which is an executive arm of the Department of Education and replaced the General Teaching Council on 1st April 2012. The new national standards for teachers have eight sections as follows and came into force 1st September 2012;[60]

A teacher must:

1 Set high expectations which inspire, motivate and challenge pupils

- establish a safe and stimulating environment for pupils, rooted in mutual respect
- set goals that stretch and challenge pupils of all backgrounds, abilities and dispositions
- demonstrate consistently the positive attitudes, values and behaviour which are expected of pupils.

2 Promote good progress and outcomes by pupils

- be accountable for pupils' attainment, progress and outcomes
- be aware of pupils' capabilities and their prior knowledge, and plan teaching to build on these

- guide pupils to reflect on the progress they have made and their emerging needs
- demonstrate knowledge and understanding of how pupils learn and how this impacts on teaching
- encourage pupils to take a responsible and conscientious attitude to their own work and study.

3 Demonstrate good subject and curriculum knowledge

- have a secure knowledge of the relevant subject(s) and curriculum areas, foster and maintain pupils' interest in the subject, and address misunderstandings
- demonstrate a critical understanding of developments in the subject and curriculum areas, and promote the value of scholarship
- demonstrate an understanding of and take responsibility for promoting high standards of literacy, articulacy and the correct use of standard English, whatever the teacher's specialist subject
- if teaching early reading, demonstrate a clear understanding of systematic synthetic phonics7
- if teaching early mathematics, demonstrate a clear understanding of appropriate teaching strategies.

4 Plan and teach well structured lessons

- impart knowledge and develop understanding through effective use of lesson time
- promote a love of learning and children's intellectual curiosity
- set homework and plan other out-of-class activities to consolidate and extend the knowledge and understanding pupils have acquired
- reflect systematically on the effectiveness of lessons and approaches to teaching
- contribute to the design and provision of an engaging curriculum within the relevant subject area(s).

5 Adapt teaching to respond to the strengths and needs of all pupils

- know when and how to differentiate appropriately, using approaches which enable pupils to be taught effectively
- have a secure understanding of how a range of factors can inhibit pupils' ability to learn, and how best to overcome these

- demonstrate an awareness of the physical, social and intellectual development of children, and know how to adapt teaching to support pupils' education at different stages of development
- have a clear understanding of the needs of all pupils, including those with special educational needs; those of high ability; those with English as an additional language; those with disabilities; and be able to use and evaluate distinctive teaching approaches to engage and support them.

6 Make accurate and productive use of assessment

- know and understand how to assess the relevant subject and curriculum areas, including statutory assessment requirements
- make use of formative and summative assessment to secure pupils' progress
- use relevant data to monitor progress, set targets, and plan subsequent lessons
- give pupils regular feedback, both orally and through accurate marking, and encourage pupils to respond to the feedback.

7 Manage behaviour effectively to ensure a good and safe learning environment

- have clear rules and routines for behaviour in classrooms, and take responsibility for promoting good and courteous behaviour both in classrooms and around the school, in accordance with the school's behaviour policy
- have high expectations of behaviour, and establish a framework for discipline with a range of strategies, using praise, sanctions and rewards consistently and fairly
- manage classes effectively, using approaches which are appropriate to pupils' needs in order to involve and motivate them
- maintain good relationships with pupils, exercise appropriate authority, and act decisively when necessary.

8 Fulfil wider professional responsibilities

- make a positive contribution to the wider life and ethos of the school
- develop effective professional relationships with colleagues, knowing how and when to draw on advice and specialist support

- deploy support staff effectively
- take responsibility for improving teaching through appropriate professional development, responding to advice and feedback from colleagues
- communicate effectively with parents with regard to pupils' achievements and well-being.

Take a few moments to slowly read the above criteria for Further Education and/or Schools as appropriate and reflect on the underpinning skill sets and the different aspects of planning and expertise. The full set of Lifelong Learning standards may be downloaded from the Lifelong Learning legacy website incorporated within the LSIS website www.lsis.org.uk and the full Teacher Standards' publication is available from www.education.gov.uk.

Personal attributes and skills

The core of the Lifelong Learning and schools' criteria is high interpersonal and intrapersonal skills and this is in accord with academic research. For instance Hattie summarises the skill set of 'accomplished teachers' as, *" those who engage them, turn them on to the subject, who inspire them, and who communicate a passion for learning"*. [61] This is a significant skills demand and it is notable that many schools and colleges do advertise for high levels of interpersonal and intrapersonal skills. Consider this example of teacher selection criteria provided by the Headteacher of Tadcaster Grammar School in North Yorkshire, Mr Geoff Mitchell:[62]

- *"An inspiring and successful teacher at all levels and within all abilities*
- *Knowledgeable and passionate about their teaching subject*
- *Energetic, enthusiastic and motivated, committed to continuous improvement*
- *Rigorous in their approach to challenging underachievement and setting high standards*
- *Fully up-to-date with all the recent changes within the curriculum and the examination system*
- *Committed to a culture of success and celebration of achievement*
- *Keen to promote the wider aspects of their subject across the curriculum and within the community*

- *Able to work in a team*
- *An effective form tutor who commands respect from students".*

Mr Mitchell wrote this specification long before any of the professional and inspection standards discussed were published and note the inclusion of the attributes of enthusiasm, passion and inspiration. All colleges and schools need to specify the skills and attributes of effective teachers and to actively seek the relevant skill set at interview and of equal importance to 'grow' the skill set via Continuous Professional Development (CPD) within existing staff teams. A glance at the job adverts in the Times Educational Supplement (TES) every Friday demonstrates that most schools and colleges do focus on the applicant's ability to enthuse and communicate their subjects well. It is notable that Higher Education advertisements largely depart from this pattern and place their emphasis upon knowledge and research skills with often no specification of teaching skills at all. Universities are rapidly reappraising their appointment criteria because students, paying high fees, are becoming increasing vocal and intolerant of large lecture theatre presentations delivered by dull lecturers and accompanied by dense bullet-point dominated Powerpoint slides. Knowledge and research skills alone, as discussed earlier, do not make a good teacher. The overall consensus from the Primary sector forward is that schools and colleges are actively seeking to employ teachers with high levels of interpersonal and intrapersonal skills. In 2006, as Chief education adviser to London schools, Sir Professor Tim Brighouse specified the need to appoint staff with the right level of skills, *"Appointing the right staff is therefore crucial....what if I hear you say, "we are desperate and there really is nobody else"? This is the most dangerous position for any school: the temptation to appoint anyone living and walking is almost irresistible. Yet resist you must. Make it temporary, alter the curriculum. Bring in someone temporarily. Do anything but don't appoint".*[63] How far do teacher training or professional development courses focus on developing high interpersonal and intrapersonal skills as opposed to theoretical knowledge? In addition how often does your school or college offer training opportunities in effective presentational skills? Such courses are fairly standard in the world of business to hone and perfect communication and presentational skills but surprisingly rare in our schools and colleges. Visit a good bookshop and note the high number of books on presentational skills within the business section compared to few, if any, on the education shelves. The former Secretary of State for Children, Schools and Families, Ed Balls, in recalling his own days at school gave the following description of outstanding teachers, "*The thing that makes an outstanding teacher is first a passion that every child has talent and that with the right support that talent can come to the fore and the child can do well. Great teachers don't write any child off. You have to care about your subject, and learning and ideas, and you've got to be able to communicate and inspire. You need quite a lot of patience, too*".[64] From the ex-Secretary of State down we all perhaps have similar individual memories of effective teaching and learning and why we enjoyed going to some lessons more than others. It is notable that Ed Balls instinctively refers to the qualities of *passion* and *inspiration*. However, what skills and attributes should teachers (and in particular outstanding teachers) seek to develop and perfect?

Fento standards

Prior to the inception of Lifelong Learning the Further Education National Training Organisation (FENTO) set the national standards for Further Education 1999-2007. Fento specified the following set of personal attributes[65]

- "personal impact and presence
- enthusiasm
- self-confidence
- energy and persistence
- reliability
- intellectual rigour
- integrity
- appreciation of FE values and ethics
- commitment to education and to learners' progress and achievement
- readiness to adapt to changing circumstances and new ideas
- realism
- openness and responsiveness to others
- acceptance of differing learning needs, expectations and styles
- empathy, rapport and respect for learners and colleagues
- assertiveness".

The Fento attributes emphasised the ability to communicate effectively and to build positive relationships with students. The attribute *personal impact and presence* is one that all teachers should consider. How you dress, greet, welcome, stand, move and speak are all important to establishing clear classroom control and respect. Commenting on dress is often regarded as controversial but it simply means do you distinguish between leisure dress and professional dress? All other professional groups do. The attribute *'intellectual rigour'* also raises a high aspiration in terms of displaying depth and breadth of knowledge. All teachers are currently being encouraged to undertake a master's degree to deepen their research and subject expertise .

Teacher of the Year

Further evidence of the links between effective personal and communication skills and outstanding teaching and learning arise from the UK *Teachers of the Year* awards. The annual teaching awards are a well-established feature of the educational landscape in the UK and celebrate the skills of outstanding teachers. Let's reflect upon the skills and attributes of the seven regional winners of ***Teacher of the Year* 2012** within the Secondary Schools sector as described by colleagues, pupils and the judging panels:[66]

Cathy McGowan – Northern Ireland
"An outstanding teacher of English who has a gift for motivating, inspiring and encouraging students".

Sion Jones – Wales
"An outstanding teacher who is inspirational...enthusiastic and caring...He has empathy and humour...He also has a well-deserved reputation for providing stimulating lessons".

Sue King – North
"She is an inspirational teacher who uses her exceptional subject knowledge to deliver creative and innovative lessons that fully engage all pupils".

Stewart Shovlin – Midlands
"His lessons are both amazing and exciting students are simultaneously transfixed and transported".

Lindsay Elliot – East
"Her subject is Product Design, a creative subject and her own flair, passion and enthusiasm shine through her teaching to inspire and motivate".

Rapdha Jaipersal – South East including London
"Her enthusiasm for her subject is infectious and there is always an excited buzz in her class...She has high expectations of all her pupils and a passion to help them reach their potential".

Ian Taylor – South West
"Take five words to describe Ian Taylor and they are likely to be visionary, talented, innovative, perceptive and creative".

All of the above testimonials focus on effective communication skills with the oft repeated words, enthusiasm, passion and inspiration in evidence.

Students' and children's opinions

Perhaps the most important people to ask, 'what makes an outstanding teacher' are students and children? They are after all the 'customers' and observe teachers in action every day and are therefore in a position to make comparisons and to identify good practice. Some colleges are currently experimenting with adding students to their lesson observation teams and it is often common, in schools, for pupils to sit on interview panels or to offer the appointments panel feedback following a demonstration lesson by an applicant.

Thank a Teacher

The Teaching Awards website referred to above also features a 'thank a teacher' section and the following three examples of students' comments further reinforce that outstanding teachers motivate and inspire:

- *"You are one of the most inspiring people I have ever met and I feel privileged to have been taught by you. Thank you for all your effort, enthusiasm and support that you have shown me over the past few years."*

- *"His enthusiasm for the subject, combined with an engaging teaching style fired my own interest in it. I went on to study Management Science at Warwick University and now work for Goldman Sachs in London. Goes to show what an impact excellent teaching can have".*
- *"Her enthusiasm in class helped me get involved in the classroom, and her supportive attitude will always stick with me. From underachieving at a C grade, she showed me English could be not just interesting and useful but fun…I want to thank her so much because of the opportunities she has given me. [My teacher] is a truly inspirational teacher and anyone who has her as their English teacher are destined to succeed.*

You can read many more personal messages of thanks to teacher who made a difference at www.teachingawards.com.

UNESCO Survey

In 1996 UNESCO conducted a survey on the theme of, 'what makes a good teacher' and children from around the world participated. Here are some of their answers:[67]

" I think a good teacher should be…curious, passionate, interested about their pupils' interests, wishes and feelings".
(Mirjana Kazija, Rijeka, Croatia)

"enthusiastic and enjoys teaching and should be honest and imaginative".
(Sheeba Ramachandran Buraidha, Saudi Arabia)

"A good teacher is an effective communicator…".
(Marie Garcia, Osyter Bay, N.Y. USA)

"A good teacher must have up-to-date knowledge…".
(Sajjad Haider, Islamabad, Pakistan)

"Arrives in time to start a lesson and ends the lesson on time because of good organisation and planning".
(Berit Hencke, Keil, Germany)

"A good teacher is someone who is a learner herself".
(Astrid, Perth, Australia)

"A good teacher always thinks to improve the teaching techniques".
(Mohammed Hazawawi Yusuf, Perah, Malaysia)

It would be difficult to quibble with any of the above judgements and they chime well with more formal academic research.

A student opinion

In 2005 the winner of the UK Centre for Legal Education, 'Student of the Year' prize, Farina Jussab was asked what made a good teacher. Farina listed the following qualities of a good teacher:[68]

- *"the most important quality is the ability to inspire,*
- *relate the theory to current issues,*
- *actively involve students by asking questions,*
- *visual aids do wonders ...can trigger your memory in exams,*
- *clear outlines, simple diagrams,*
- *instil enthusiasm,*
- *good planning,*
- *help students to get used to writing within certain time limits,*
- *assess individual needs,*
- *encourage teamwork...an important skill within the workplace".*

Overall students, in general, find little difficulty in identifying the key characteristics of effective teaching and as Farina commented the characteristics of less effective teaching, *"It is not very motivating to listen to a tutor who has absolutely no enthusiasm for what they teach. The lack of enthusiasm becomes obvious through the tone and demeanour of teachers. This lack of passion transfers to the students and they too begin to feel that it is too much of a bother to listen or even to study."*[69] Farina, in common with other sources quoted, has instinctively highlighted that effective teachers display, *enthusiasm* and *passion*. The UK Centre for Legal Education subsequently commissioned research into the qualities and attributes of outstanding teachers and in a paper presented to the Society of Legal Scholars conference 2008 Tracey Varnava concluded that outstanding teachers *" display an active interest in and development of approaches to teaching that influence, motivate and inspire students to learn".*[70]

Post 16 learner opinions

In 2001 the Further Education National Training Organisation (FENTO) and the Association of Colleges (AOC) invited a sample of 700 FE students to comment on the most important skills of effective teachers. [71] The top five qualities cited by the students were:

- "sound subject knowledge
- understanding and gives good advice
- creative, interesting and imaginative
- warm and cheery
- clear instruction and presentation".

Overall, the students placed an emphasis upon effective communication and relationship skills. Perhaps we should all consider how far we greet and welcome students and are *warm and cheery.*

Bilborough College survey

In 2009 Bilborough Sixth Form College, Nottingham[72] hit upon a very simple but powerful way of surveying student opinions as part of its Learner Involvement strategy. All new students were invited to contribute to a 'comment wall' by posting notes on what motivated them and what de-motivated them to learn. Pink post-it notes were motivators and blue post-it notes were de-motivators. The comments that follow are verbatim students' comments in random order but with no direct link between the two columns. The students' comments in relation to effective lessons are presented in Chapter Five.

Motivators	De-motivators
Help from teachers	Boring teachers
Support from teachers	Unconfident teachers
When subjects (easy or hard) are taught enthusiastically and interestingly = engage students and motivate them to find out more about it, work on it.	When teachers talk for most of the lesson, from the start on which they stand at the whiteboard to the end of the lesson.

Good teaching motivates me	unsupportive teachers
the way he talks about what we can achieve it we work	When pile of work is given without teacher talking about it or explaining it.
Enthusiastic teachers	Grumpy teachers, monotone voices
Enthusiasm from the teacher	A boring rubbish teacher
When teachers are enthusiastic	Strict teachers who don't involve the class in a fun way
Teacher talking in front of class	When teachers talk in a monotone fashion and act as if they don't care – because then I don't care
Enthusiastic teachers	When the teacher talks for most of the lesson
Enthusiastic teacher, one that gets excited about what they're teaching	Just skim over books and material, don't go into concepts
When a teacher has enthusiasm about their subject rather than teaching for the money then enjoyment. Make discussion fun like General Studies	When teachers tell us their life story and give us unnecessary information that's not relevant to the topic
When the teachers are passionate about their subject and pass that enthusiasm onto you	Negative teachers who pester students, and who don't create aims for lessons
When teachers give us tasks that help us understand topic and give us the opportunity to discuss	Teachers spoon feeding information
Good organisation of structure, help the lesson go smoothly Teachers enthusiasm when teaching	Lack of enthusiasm in both teachers and pupils
Humour and originality	Teachers that can't control the classroom so that other students mess around
A teacher with energy and varied activities	If the teacher has a monotone voice and doesn't care about the lesson themselves
Enthusiastic teaching	Sitting down listening to the teacher ALL lesson

An enthusiastic teacher and atmosphere	Monotone teachers
Light hearted teaching and discussion	When teachers call me dumb
The teachers – tell jokes	Not being rewarded with encouragement from teachers/peers
Enthusiastic teachers – Having an all round knowledge of the subject even if its not all relevant to the course eg French and Spanish – extra info about the culture makes it more interesting.	I am demotivated by teachers who see the class as a whole and ignore individuals
Teacher that involves all the students.	Teacher just talks and you don't understand what they're on about
Encouraging words from teacher	teachers that like to talk
I am motivated by the teachers being enthusiastic, and stick to the point of the lesson.	When teachers start talking off subject (nothing to do with lesson)
In class I am motivated by enthusiastic teachers that believe in you.	When the teacher isn't enthusiastic
I am motivated by teachers who don't go on about something. If they are interesting, let you get on and help you then I find them motivational	No clear, achievable goal
An enthusiastic teacher who is passionate about their subject.	Teachers who can't be bothered! And making notes!
Teachers that are passionate about their subjects and not ashamed to let it show	No constructive feedback
Vibrant teachers – interacting and moving about.	When teachers are not bothered and don't set good example
An enthusiastic teacher who is passionate about the subject they teach.	Boring teaching ie copying from board

I'm motivated by teachers who are generally friendly and happy.	I am demotivated by teachers who are dull with no charisma
Enthusiastic teachers.	Having to listen to teachers moaning about other people's ability to hand in work.
Passion for subject	Using a monotone voice (the teacher) and having a lack of varying teaching skills
Tutor or teacher saying positive things	Pressure from teachers (I know when the deadlines are!)
Good teachers – enthusiastic and helpful	Boring teachers.
When the teacher is enthusiastic	Lack of enthusiasm
When the teachers are lively	When the teachers aren't very enthusiastic
Enthusiastic teacher	Teachers constantly talking to the class – I switch off!!

In terms of 'motivators' look how often the students repeat the words 'enthusiasm' and 'passion'. The students want a teacher who makes the topic interesting and displays their own love of subject. In terms of 'demotivators' the words 'monotone' and 'boring' are regularly used. In particular the students are critical of teachers who over-talk and provide insufficient challenge.

Hay McBer Children's survey

Finally this chapter started with the views of children so let's end this consideration of what makes an outstanding teacher by giving the final word to children. The Hay McBer report contains the following description of a good teacher by Year Seven and Eight pupils. [73]

"A good teacher:
is kind
is generous
listens to you
encourages you
has faith in you
keeps confidences
likes teaching
likes teaching their subject
takes time to explain things
helps you when you are stuck
tells you how you are doing
allows you to have your say
doesn't give up on you
cares for your opinion
makes you feel clever
treats people equally
stands up for you
makes allowance
tells the truth
is forgiving".

The overall theme of the children's criteria places an emphasis upon a positive relationship with the teacher and ultimately 'caring' qualities. However, note that children, as young as 12 years old, are quite perceptive and have concluded that some teachers do not like teaching or even their own subject! This is a fundamental question for any teacher – do you love your own subject or is teaching just a job? Hattie emphasised that the most effective teachers, *"cared about teaching the students their passion for their subject, gave students confidence in themselves as learners and as people, treated the student as a person, and instilled a love of learning of their subject(s)"*. [74] Interestingly the new Teachers' Standards released by the Department for Education 1st September 2012 include the prescription, *"promote a love of learning and children's intellectual curiosity"*.[75] and the revised inspection criteria published by Ofsted in June 2012 for Further Education includes the attributes of care and support, *' learners benefit from high expectations, engagement, care, support and motivation from staff"*.[76] Perhaps Ofsted has read the children's comments? Love of subject is perhaps the key attribute for outstanding teaching and learning because it drives a never ending search for new ways of making the subject interesting. Do you love your subject?

Planning for learning

"Primarily, inspection evaluates how individual learners benefit from their courses and learning programmes".[1]

(Ofsted Inspectors' Handbook for Further Education 2012)

Outstanding teaching and learning can arise spontaneously. Most teachers have had the experience of entering a lesson with only a rudimentary lesson plan but nevertheless generating enjoyable and productive learning. However, how often will limited planning produce an outstanding or even a satisfactory lesson? For every unplanned lesson that does generate enjoyable and productive learning there will be many more that fail to delight or engage. In particular planning must, as the above Ofsted quotation indicates, focus on the individual because we do not teach classes but groups of individuals who all happen to be in the same room. Effective planning therefore starts with the individual and ends with the individual in terms of their progress and progression. Both aspects are significant in terms of progress relative to each student's starting position and background and progression to a higher course, employment and/or university.

Planning consideration

Effective course and lesson planning involves:

- awareness of the socio-economic, ethnic and gender profile of the community served and particularly in terms of any 'at risk' groups;
- awareness of the major local and regional employment opportunities and associated entry standards and related employability skill requirements;
- awareness of wider national, European and World employment and/or Higher Education opportunities to raise ambition and aspirations;

- awareness of up-to-date research and technological advances within own vocational or academic programmes and updating Schemes of Work as appropriate;
- awareness and application of appropriate safety guidance and safe working within vocational areas;
- identification and promotion of opportunities for self-employment;
- awareness of the examination board's latest specification and in particular assessment and examination schedule;
- breaking the content of the examination board or other specification down into key topics;
- setting the sequence of topics and the number of lessons to be devoted to each one;
- considering the level of the course and the appropriate level of challenge;
- identifying key formative assessment points and the related skill / knowledge demands placed on the students;
- identifying key summative assessment or examination points and the related skill / knowledge demands placed on the students;
- considering the skills / knowledge requirements for pass, merit and distinction levels of achievement (or grades AB, C or D/E) and how to stretch all to achieve their best potential i.e. effective differentiation;
- addressing the learning and study skills required for the next level course or Higher Education;
- selecting a range of teaching strategies to interest, engage and build motivation and learning over time;
- introducing a varied range of learning resources, especially ILT, and including the timing of any visiting speakers or educational visits;
- integrating opportunities to practice and improve functional, employability and digital skills;
- introducing ramped learning i.e. minor learning goals in the first few weeks to ease all into the course (but with suitable challenge for all) and thereafter quickening the pace and increasing the demands made of all students;
- considering the entry skills of the students and any relevant generic and specific barriers to learning;
- considering social, ethnic, religious, linguistic and gender

backgrounds and ensuring appropriate responses and sensitivity;
- addressing individual support needs and ensuring appropriate resources / assistance for each stage of the course;
- directing the work / contribution of any support / technician staff;
- attaching extension tasks to promote independent learning and to stretch the most able within a Virtual Learning Environment (VLE);
- evaluating own lessons and adapting Schemes of Work and Lesson Plans in light of student feedback and any feedback from lesson observations.

The above list of considerations may appear daunting but the task is essentially to translate a specification into an enjoyable programme of study that takes all students from no knowledge to at least pass standard and preferably beyond.

Team planning

Whereas planning a new course is demanding it should also be a stimulating and a professionally satisfying task involving creativity and perhaps innovation. The term innovative practice is a feature of professional and Ofsted criteria as well as the Ofsted injunction to '*inspire and challenge*'.[2] There are no national standards within teacher training or Ofsted criteria (beyond broad guidance) for the format or content of Lesson Plans, Schemes of Work and Individual Learning Plans. All colleges and schools are free to adopt their own formats and content as they feel appropriate. However, Ofsted will judge how far planning documentation promotes or hinders good practice. Ofsted is interested in the outcomes of planning rather than the process itself or any fixed opinion on the style or form of planning documentation. However, consistency is regularly identified as an aspect of good practice in terms of consistency between staff within a particular teaching team or across a whole school or college as to how standards of teaching, learning and assessment are discussed, maintained and disseminated. Ideally managers should ensure that good standards for students are not a lottery i.e. at the whim of individual teachers but that team discussion refines and agrees procedures and systems and that these are consistently and uniformly enacted. This focus on consistency is an endorsement of the principle of Continuous Professional Development (CPD) whereby at staff meetings there is regular discussion around how to improve teaching and learning or how to improve assessment systems or actions for improvement following feedback from lesson observation programmes. Team best practice is preferable to individual best practice because as Ofsted data tells us only 11% of lessons nationally are judged outstanding. There are too few naturally occurring 'outstanding' teachers and so without team action to propagate outstanding practice the significant majority of students will not experience inspiring and challenging teaching. Inspectors will often study the minutes of staff meetings for evidence of staff development and collaborative practice and seek evidence that managers do focus on leading improvements to teaching and learning. The Ofsted 2012 criteria for Leadership and Management in Further Education includes the criterion, *"leaders and managers constantly review and develop the performance of teachers and trainers through dialogue, coaching, mentoring and support and training"* and *"Leaders seek out and share best practice contributing to a coherent programme of professional development"*.[3] Collaboration is also a significant feature of effective practice within the schools sector as evidenced by this quotation from Ofsted publication, Twelve Outstanding Secondary Schools, *" time is ring-fenced for staff to work in teams: engaging in productive discussion about pedagogy, planning, lessons that inspire students to become independent and effective learners and being reflective rather simply dealing with administration"*.[4] The simple question, 'How can I inspire and challenge my students?' is perhaps the best staff development. The individual answer is good but a team answer is better because it will improve teaching and learning for most students rather than a few.

Professional guidance

The major sources of general professional guidance and support to improve teaching and learning are as follows:

Schools

Department for Education www.education.gov.uk
The Teaching Agency www.education.gov.uk

The Standards and Testing Agency www.education.gov.uk
Teaching and Learning Academy www.tla.ac.uk

Further Education

Department for Business, Innovation and skills www.bis.gov.uk
Institute for Learning www.ifl.ac. uk
Learning and skills Improvement Service www.lsis.org.uk

The Office for Standards in Education, Children's Services and Skills (Ofsted) has a remit across both schools and Further Education. The above sources of professional guidance all emphasis the primacy of effective planning to sustain effective teaching and learning.

Teachers' Standards 2012

Within the schools sector the Teachers' Standards, introduced in September 2012 (see Chapter One), highlight many significant planning considerations above and beyond subject knowledge. The focus is the individual *"be aware of pupils' capabilities and their prior knowledge, and plan teaching to build on these"*[5] The Ofsted 2012 criteria for 'outstanding' within the schools sector reflects this standard, *"teachers plan astutely and set challenging tasks based on systematic, accurate assessment of pupils' prior skills, knowledge and understanding".*[6] Consequently there is a significant need to plan for differentiation, to stretch and challenge, to raise ambition and to address any barriers to learning in relation to students with learning difficulties or disabilities and for those whose first language is not English. Good behaviour management is also a significant aspect of the Schools inspection framework and the promotion of positive attitudes and values. All school staff, regardless of subject background, are also charged with raising standards of literacy and in particular reinforcing and improving the application of standard English. Finally, there is an expectation that homework and extended learning tasks will be regularly set to promote independent learning beyond the classroom. All of these aspects emphasise the importance of team planning to agree and apply consistent strategies and common standards and procedures to build and sustain effective teaching and learning.

Lifelong Learning UK standards

Within Further Education the Lifelong Learning professional standards set similar expectations to the Teachers' Standards. The full set may be accessed within the Lifelong Learning legacy website within the Learning and Skills Improvement Service (LSIS) website www.lsis.org.uk. There are six domains of professional standards in total and Domain D specifies the standards for course and lesson planning as follows:[7]

Figure 2. Lifelong Learning Professional standards **Domain D Planning for Learning**	
They are committed to: DS 1 Planning to promote equality, support diversity and to meet the aims and learning needs of learners. DS 2 Learner participation in the planning of learning. DS 3 Evaluation of own effectiveness in planning learning.	
DK 1.1 How to plan appropriate, effective, coherent and inclusive learning programmes that promote equality and engage with diversity.	DP 1.1 Plan coherent and inclusive learning programmes that meet learners' needs and curriculum requirements, promote equality and engage with diversity effectively.
DK 1.2 How to plan a teaching session	DP 1.2 Plan teaching sessions which meet the aims and needs of individual learners and groups, using a variety of resources, including new and emerging technologies.
DK 1.3 Strategies for flexibility in planning and delivery.	DP 1.3 Prepare flexible session plans to adjust to the individual needs of learners.
DK 2.1 The importance of including learners in the planning process.	DP 2.1 Plan for opportunities for learner feedback to inform planning and practice.
DK 2.2 Ways to negotiate appropriate individual goals with learners.	DP 2.2 Negotiate and record appropriate learning goals and strategies with learners.
DK 3.1 Ways to evaluate own role and performance in planning learning.	DP 3.1 Evaluate the success of planned learning activities.
DK 3.2 Ways to evaluate own role and performance as a member of a team in planning learning.	DP 3.2 Evaluate the effectiveness of own contributions to planning as a member of a team.

The above Planning for Learning standards also stress the importance of meeting the needs of each individual and this is emphasised within the Ofsted 2012 criteria for Further Education, *"staff initially assess learners' starting points and monitor their progress, set challenging tasks, and build on and extend learning for all learners".*[8] This stipulation relates not only to advance course and lesson planning but also to progress within each lesson in terms of adjusting the pace of lessons in response to actual rather than planned progress. The full Lifelong Learning standards for teaching and learning (as presented in Chapter One) also focus on promoting independence and autonomy, creating motivating learning environments, gaining regular feedback from students, employing ILT and building functional skills and employability skills. In addition the Lifelong Learning standards place a significant focus on embedding equality and diversity good practice. This is also a major planning consideration within Ofsted criteria for schools and colleges. Chapter Four 'Equality and Diversity' provides in-depth guidance on the relevant Ofsted standards and related good practice. Ofsted has also raised, in the 2012 inspection framework for Further Education, the importance of planning for the integration of employability skills across the curriculum and the application of new technology and particularly the development of Virtual Learning Environments (VLE) to support and promote independent learning, *"the promotion and development of independent learning skills, for example, through the use of a range of technologies, including a virtual learning environment".*[9] This reflects the changing nature of employment as Britain embraces the 21st Century, Knowledge Age.

Employability skills

Over the past thirty years Britain has experienced a revolution in employment with a sharp decline in unskilled or semi-skilled industrial employment and a rapid rise in high skilled employment within the Service Sector. The associated rise of a global market place and digital working environments have raised a demand for a more flexible and highly skilled workforce i.e. higher levels of functional, employability and independent learning skills and more workers with graduate level qualifications. In 2009, the then Department for Children, Schools and Families, introduced the 14-19 diploma programme by highlighting key future trends:

"Our world is changing...fast,

- *By 2020 there will be 5 million fewer low skilled jobs in Britain than there are today*

- *40% of all jobs in 2020 will require a graduate qualification*
- *The top 10 jobs that will be in demand in 2010 did not exist in 2004*
- *Today's learners will have 10-14 jobs...by age 38*
- *We are currently preparing students for jobs that don't yet exist".*[10]

Today 76% of the UK economy is Service Sector based employment and rising. The industrial and manufacturing sectors that dominated employment in the Twentieth Century have gone. The coal mines, shipyards, steel plants and textile mills that employed hundreds of thousands of workers in unskilled jobs are closed and in their place are jobs within the ever expanding retail, tourism, banking, insurance, catering, leisure and sports markets. The Service Sector thrives on a highly literate, numerate and IT proficient workforce and therefore course and lesson planning should identify opportunities to practice and build effective functional and employability skills. The Government White Paper February 2005 emphasised the need to embed the development of functional skills as follows, "*In addition to functional skills, young people need a range of learning and social skills. Success in further and higher education and in employment depends on the ability to adapt to new or changing circumstances. Independent learning skills are essential for study at university level. Businesses want skilled and enthusiastic employees who can help them respond to the rapidly changing demands of a competitive global economy. These skills are not separately taught, but brought out by expert teachers through the methods they use to teach the curriculum subjects.*[11] The latter statement raises an expectation for more individual, paired and group tasks within lessons to build personal and functional skills rather than passive 'chalk and talk' based lessons. In December 2006 Lord Leitch published his final UK skills report entitled *'Prosperity for all in the global economy-world class skills'*, and made similar observations, "*The UK economy has changed significantly over time. Today the service sector accounts for around three quarters of the UK economy.... service sector jobs require different types of skills to the more traditional low skill jobs, such as basic manufacturing, which they are replacing. In particular, they place greater emphasis on customer handling, team working and communication skills, which are essential in a service economy.* [12] In 2006 the Vision 2020 report, (Chaired by the then Chief Inspector of Ofsted, Christine Gilbert), drew many of these threads together and presented a list of the 'soft skills' required for success in the highly competitive world economy by 2020:

- *being able to communicate orally at a high level*
- *reliability, punctuality and perseverance*
- *knowing how to work with others in a team*
- *knowing how to evaluate information critically*
- *taking responsibility for, and being able to manage, one's own learning and developing the habits of effective learning*
- *knowing how to work independently without close supervision*
- *being confident and able to investigate problems and find solutions*
- *being resilient in the face of difficulties*
- *being creative, inventive, enterprising and entrepreneurial.*[13]

CBI Employability skills 2012[14]

The Confederation of British Industry (CBI) represents the views of many British employers nationally and since 2008 they have engaged in surveying their members' opinions on employability skills. The CBI has specified the importance of the following seven employability skills and invited schools and colleges to consider their integration into teaching and learning:

Self-management – readiness to accept responsibility, flexibility, time management, readiness to improve own performance
Teamworking – respecting others, co-operating, negotiating, persuading, contributing to discussions
Business and customer awareness – basic understanding of the key drivers for business success and the need to provide customer satisfaction
Problem solving – analysing facts and circumstances and applying creative thinking to develop appropriate solutions
Communication and literacy – application of literacy, ability to produce clear, structured written work and oral literacy, including listening and questioning.
Application of numeracy – manipulation of numbers, general mathematical awareness and its application in practical contexts
Application of information technology – basic IT skills, including familiarity with word processing, spreadsheets, file management and use of internet search engines.

Employer satisfaction with School/ College leavers' employability skills %

The most recent CBI report on employability skills was published in June 2012, and entitled, *'Learning to Grow: what employers need from education and skills'*. Their earlier 2011 report also included satisfaction levels with the skills of graduates by way of comparison. The employers surveyed expressed their levels of satisfaction (figures in percentages) across a range of employability skills as follows.

Skills aspect	Very Satisfied	Satisfied	Not Satisfied
Use of IT	12	75	13
Basic numeracy	4	65	30
Basic literacy / use of English	4	61	35
Teamwork	3	65	33
Positive attitude to work	5	59	37
Knowledge about job / career	3	53	44
Problem solving	1	53	46
International cultural awareness	0	42	57
Self-management	2	37	61
Business & Customer awareness	2	29	69
Foreign language skills	1	29	69

The 2012 report highlights a rise in employer satisfaction rates from 2011 with regard to literacy and numeracy but the 'not satisfied' rates of 35% and 30% respectively are still regarded as too high. The 'use of IT' gains the highest satisfaction ratings and no doubt reflects the digital skills of the rising i-generations but many still lack competences in work applied IT i.e. comfortable across Microsoft Office. Concern is also expressed about the low levels of cultural awareness and business and customer awareness within an expanding global marketplace. However, the highest dissatisfaction rates are reserved for the low level of foreign language skills and this perhaps reflects that most young people drop foreign languages at age 14. The top five 'in demand' foreign languages are:

- French,
- Mandarin,
- German,
- Spanish and
- Arabic.

The acquisition of effective employability skills is significant because 82% of employers surveyed by the CBI rank competence across employability skills above degree subject and degree classification. This is something both school-leavers and graduates should reflect upon when writing CVs and letters of application. Evidence of effective functional and employability skills may counteract low examination results. In terms of planning how far do your lessons offer learning activities to develop and build the skill set required for 21st century employment? The Ofsted 2012 criteria for Further Education specifies the importance of *"broader skills relevant to learners' progression and career aims, such as communication, teamwork, leadership, taking responsibility, reflective thinking, problem solving, independent enquiry and employability"*[15] In addition in relation to functional skills the relevant 2012 criterion is *" teaching and learning develop English, mathematics and functional skills and support the achievement of learning goals and career aims".* [16] Similarly within the 2012 Ofsted criteria for schools inspectors will judge, *"how well teaching enables pupils to develop skills in reading, writing, communication and mathematics"*.[17] The first true digital generation who know nothing of life before the internet, Generation Z, will enter Further Education in September 2016. They are the generation born since 2000 and they are already in our High Schools. They will enter the world of work in 2020+ and enter a world of global multicultural trade, 24 hour business operations, digital information processing, digital communication, mobile working via Tablet and Smartphone, and regular innovations in products and services. The global marketplace will demand high employability skills or more popularly '21st Century skills'. However care must be taken not to misapply the term 21st century skills to describe skills that were just as important and in demand in the 20th century. The 21st Century difference rests in skills in relation to *digital competencies* and *creativity*. Our world already turns on digital competencies for all aspects of 21st century living and working. Consequently scan through your Scheme of Work and consider how far there are opportunities to practice and develop competence across

Microsoft Office and/or Apple equivalents within the relevant 'creative' vocational fields. Creativity, however, is perhaps the defining skill for the 21st Century service and hi-tech led economy in terms of the ability to identify problems, find solutions, add value and design new products and services. Creativity as detailed below is regarded as the highest level of cognitive ability in a re-working of Bloom's Taxonomy. Ultimately the adage of the 1950s employers, 'give me the three Rs, reading, writing and arithmetic' still resonates but all staff should plan for the skill requirements of the future and not the past. A full overview of the 'Knowledge Age' and the implications for the future of teaching and learning may be gained from the textbook, ***'The i-Learning Revolution: A new pedagogy*** also by Bradley Lightbody. Purchase direct via Collegenet.co.uk or Amazon.co.uk

The planning hierarchy

Effective course and lesson planning should move from the macro to the micro. The chart below illustrates a hierarchy of key planning documents from Year Planner (macro) to Individual Learning Plan (micro). These four documents, in different forms, are fairly standard features in our schools and colleges. The Year Planner provides students with a 'big picture' overview of the whole course followed by increasing levels of detail specified within the Scheme of Work and the Lesson Plan. At the micro level an Individual Learning Plan (ILP) records initial and diagnostic assessment outcomes and should set challenging but achievable learning targets. The ILP or similar record is ordinarily held by a Personal Tutor or Mentor and reviewed with the student at key formative assessment points. However, in situations where individual working is the dominant mode of learning e.g. Art and Design studio, a vocational workshop, lessons for Students with Learning Difficulties or Disabilities (SLDD) then lesson specific ILPs should be used in place of a standard lesson plan.

The focus of the above planning hierarchy should be students and learning. Effective teachers identify what students should know and understand about each key topic with close reference to the relevant examination and/or commercial standards. They select relevant teaching strategies and resources and plan how to capture and sustain interest and attention. However, most teachers are sharply aware of

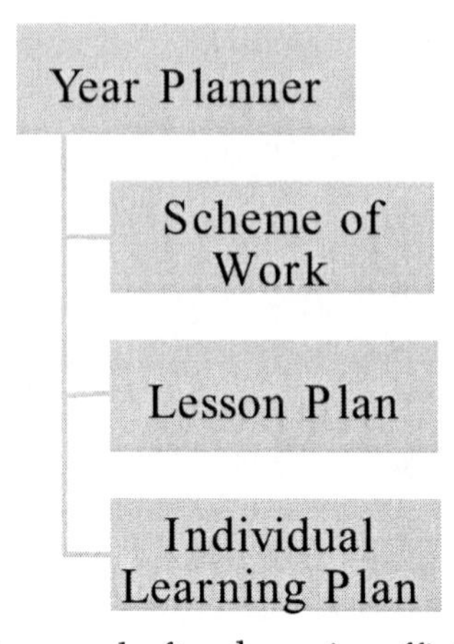

their limited class-time and often have insufficient time to develop topics in-depth to stretch and challenge the most able or to repeat information to support the least able. However, the rise of the internet and the ease of finding information online and the ability to place extended learning and support materials onto a Virtual Learning Environment (VLE) is part of the answer. Students can access a VLE anytime, anyplace and learning can continue outside of the classroom and promote and aid deeper learning. The benefits of this online learning extension are highlighted within Ofsted 2012 criteria for Further Education, *"the extent to which teaching , training and coaching encourages and develops independent learning"* and in an expanded statement *"how learning materials are used during and outside learning sessions including those available in a Virtual Learning Environment"*.[18] The ability to access learning materials online and to work independently raises the issue of the study and learning skills of our students and their levels of motivation and effort outside of the classroom. Our planning process should address strategies to build independent learning skills and to promote effort over ability. The McKinsey report detailed in Chapter One referred to the need, *'to raise the standard of every student'* or in other words to raise their capacity to learn. It is often overlooked that Ofsted has criteria for students and their role in learning but in 2008 Ofsted published the following criteria in relation to the responsibilities of students:

> *"Good teaching enables learners to make the most of their potential and advance their knowledge, understanding and skills well beyond those they had when they started their course. Inspectors will assess, through observation and discussion with learners, the extent to which*

learners (irrespective of their age, gender, race, ethnicity, learning difficulty or disability):

- *acquire knowledge and skills, develop ideas and increase their understanding*
- *become confident in what they are doing*
- *understand how well they are progressing and what they need to do to improve*
- *work productively and make effective use of their time*
- *are interested in their work and able to sustain their concentration*
- *think and learn for themselves*
- *make use of the resources available to them, for example in libraries and ICT centres and other learning technologies*
- *show determination to complete assignments on time and see problems through to resolution*
- *are prepared to seek help and act on advice they receive".*[19]

How far do you plan for and address the development of the above skill set to build and support independent learning? Gaining active participation in independent learning and associated peer learning beyond the classroom will not only cover more of the curriculum but also build and improve personal learning and thinking skills ready for the demands of future university and/or employment. The key steps to build and support learning skills are detailed in Chapter Eleven.

Year Planner

The term *'Year Planner'* is used here but the title of the document will vary from college to college and school to school. However, the common aim is to provide students with an immediate overview of the entire course so that the students can see 'at a glance' the key course content and major assessment points. Some colleges will issue a Year Planner as a separate document or include it within a general course guidance booklet. In addition some colleges, and schools, may issue academic year 'planner' diaries or student booklets containing key course information along with planning pages for evaluation and the recording of assignment and homework or extended learning tasks. At its most straightforward a Year Planner can be presented in an A4 circular format i.e. A3 paper folded to yield a title page, two inner pages and a back page. This can be a vehicle to address the Ofsted direction to *inspire and challenge.* Design the title page as a bright welcome page dominated by a relevant photograph or image and some motivational text coupled with an exhortation to work hard.

Year Planner title page

Enter school or college title here

Year Planner

Enter course title here

Welcome to your course programme for…? Please use this brief Year Planner to identify your term dates, key study targets and the major assessment points. Aim to study ahead and to make best use of the resources on the VLE to extend your learning. Aim high and aim to be the best you can be. The past is the past and the future is yet to be written.

Insert photo or image

Insert name of course leader

You can of course decide what to present but keep to good design parameters and avoid too much clutter. Our aim is to motivate and to stir curiosity and to raise interest levels about the benefits of the course programme and where it might lead. References to current affairs can be effective with perhaps the title page featuring a photograph of a new relevant product, piece of equipment, new research etc. Imagery of this type is quite powerful in delivering currency and a sense of significance and importance in terms of the coverage of the course programme.

Year Planner inner pages

Consider making the first inner page a calendar page and extend the examples below into a full A4 page.

Week	Date	Key Topic	Events
1	?? September	Insert key topics	Insert key dates for assessment, trips, progress evenings etc
2	?? September		
3	?? September		
5	?? September		
6.	?? September		
7.	?? October		
8.	?? October		
9.	**?? October**	**Half term**	**holiday**
10.	?? October		

Use the full width and depth of an A4 page to list the weeks from the first week of term in September through to the end of the school or college year in July. Clearly this assumes a one year course programme and should be adjusted for shorter programmes. The table should be completed by inserting the week number, week commencing dates followed by the related key topics and finally in the right hand column any key assessment or examination dates including any major course events e.g. progress evenings, careers fairs, educational visits. If placed online on a Virtual Learning Environment (VLE) many of the headings can be converted into clickable links to access more detailed information e.g. programme area or department overview, the examination board, progress evening arrangements, staff email links. It may be necessary to adjust the layout of the Year Planner to achieve a best fit with the screen layout of your VLE platform. The immediate benefit is a shared programme of study, key events to look forward to and raising awareness of the timing of key assessment points. Our overall aim is to encourage and facilitate student autonomy and independent working.

The second inner page might be devoted to 'how to learn' guidance with upbeat suggestions on how to organize folders and files, reminders of key equipment or textbook requirements and the addresses of key websites for further support including an introduction to the resources of the VLE and the Learning Centre. Wider college or school support services might also be highlighted.

Year Planner back page

The back page of the Year Planner might be devoted to careers information including the employability skills associated with the vocational area and generic independent learning skills. Too many students are often uncertain of the jobs linked to their programme and/or university course and a simple suggestion may provide a direction and perhaps also raising the possibility of future self-employment. Stimulate their interest from the first day and effort will follow. Finally, the completed Year Planner could be tweaked and adapted as a first newsletter to parents or guardians to alert them to the demands and opportunities of the course programme and suggestions for how they could support and assist their son or daughter to learn.

Schemes of Work

A Scheme of Work is a summary of the learning and teaching programme for the whole academic year. It should list not only the major curriculum topics but also how they are going to be taught, resourced and assessed. Listing topics is straightforward but the creative part and the real craft of teaching is not listing ***what*** you are going to teach but ***how*** you are going to teach it. This is the skill that separates teachers from subject experts i.e. the selection of teaching and learning strategies and resources to bring each topic alive and to aid and promote learning and understanding.

Title page

Start by designing a clear title page for the Scheme of Work that addresses students and raises the expectation that students will refer to the Scheme of Work to plan and work ahead. Specify the key course aims and objectives but also include reference to functional, and employability skills. Also include reference to the major summative assessment and examination points. If necessary carry this over onto a second page in order to provide a longer and more student friendly introduction. Note there is an assumption here that the Scheme of Work will be shared with students. It should be a working document for both teachers and students to aid and promote learning rather than a chore to be written, filed and forgotten.

Scheme of Work grid

The Scheme of Work grid illustrated below is fairly universal in our colleges and schools albeit with variations in the headings used. It should be completed with sufficient detail to be useful to students and to prompt independent study. In order not to overwhelm students, the Scheme of Work may be released term by term or module by module. This staged release may be a useful device to trigger a review of learning and to highlight the key learning targets for the new term or module.

Example of a Scheme of Work grid

Scheme of work					
Week	**Topic**	**Knowledge & skills content**	**Learning and teaching activities**	**Resources**	**Assessment methods**
1 3-9-??					
2. 10-9-??					
3. 17-9-??					

The Scheme of Work grid should be completed as follows:

- **Week** – insert the relevant week commencing date which should match the dates listed in the Year Planner.
- **Topic** – insert the relevant topic which should match the topic listed in the Year Planner. In situations of more than one lesson per week you may choose to alter this column heading to 'lesson' and insert lesson headings for each individual lesson. Otherwise advancing topic by topic is satisfactory.
- **Knowledge and skills content** – this is the ***'what'*** part i.e. what

you are going to teach. Provide a short summary statement of the topic content and highlight any functional skills, employability skills and/or any equality and diversity considerations.

- **Learning and teaching activities** – this is the **'how'** part i.e. how the students are going to learn and how you are going to teach the topic content. Keep this short and sharp. Completing this column will help to ensure variety of teaching methods over time and methods to build and develop functional and employability skills.
- **Resources** – list the key resources you will need to support the learning and teaching activities identified. This will also help to promote variety because if you are regularly citing textbook, handout and whiteboard then it might prompt consideration of using wider resources. Also examine and review all resources with a view towards maximizing any opportunities to address and embed equality and diversity good practice.
- **Assessment** – list the key formative and summative assessment points and highlight the key learning outcomes expected.

Addressing all of the above considerations may seem very daunting. However, it often takes three years to develop a comprehensive Scheme of Work for a new course. The first year is dominated by testing the pace and challenge in terms of the order and time allocated to each major topic and monitoring the effectiveness of different teaching and learning strategies and resources. Try to take your Scheme of Work into every lesson and annotate it with what worked well and what might be improved and your own spontaneous additions in terms of resources and learning activities. The second year builds on this experience by deepening and confirming the range of teaching and learning strategies and resources. Finally, the third and subsequent years will involve minor refinements and adjustments in the light of student feedback, lesson observation feedback, examiners', reports, EV guidance etc. Therefore for new courses the Scheme of Work is very much a 'working document' but for established courses this development process should be complete. Invest the detail in the core topics because some changes to programmes and examinations are inevitable. However, core topics will always survive and the relevant parts of the Scheme of Work can be 'cut and pasted' into any new framework.

Ofsted reports

In outstanding schools and colleges the Ofsted evidence is of considerable staff collaboration in the writing of effective Schemes of Work linked to online resources and study guidance. In November 2004 the OFSTED report, *'Why Colleges Succeed'* referred to Schemes of Work in the best performing colleges as follows, *"There is uniformity of practice in relation to the use of schemes of work and lesson plans: Schemes of Work are well structured, give details of resources and suggested learning activities and are implemented consistently across course teams."*[22] This raises a management responsibility which goes beyond agreeing and disseminating a Scheme of Work grid. Effective managers read and approve Schemes of Work and offer relevant mentor support for new teachers and encourage peer development and the display of Schemes of Work online and/or on notice boards as working tools. This practice was highlighted by Ofsted in January 2008 as part of a survey of good practice in Science teaching as follows, *"Departmental or subject Intranets were developing well. In some of the larger institutions visited, they were already very well developed and provided interesting and user-friendly information for students and staff. Most subject sites contained copies of syllabuses, schemes of work and assessments, together with deadlines and assessment criteria. The best contained summaries of key concepts, examination questions and mark schemes, links to useful websites and photographs, diagrams and video/TV clips"*.[21] Similar references were made by Ofsted in 2008 in relation to effective practice within a Sixth Form college, *"The business and economics department in a sixth form college used a fully interactive site of e-based learning resources. This included online text books, links to websites, student 'test yourself' questions with instant feedback, quizzes and a particularly innovative chat room known as 'ask the teacher'. The latter provided useful extra support for students. They emailed their homework to the teacher and received prompt, informative and detailed feedback"*.[22] Essentially, effective learning is more likely to arise from clear planning, relevant pace and challenge and high levels of study support. The above examples clearly detail not only *what* will be taught but also *how* it will be taught and this is a feature of the most effective Schemes of Work. It is easy to fall into a comfort zone where too many lessons revolve around a narrow range of teaching strategies and resources and the end result is lessons that hold no surprises for your students. To avoid this trap answer the following questionnaire and remind yourself of the wealth of teaching strategies that we might employ to not only build learning and understanding but to create opportunities for our students to practice and develop employability and functional skills.

Teaching strategies questionnaire

Take a moment to complete the questionnaire by ticking your responses and consider how far your Scheme of Work employs a sufficiently wide variety of teaching and learning strategies over time?

TEACHING STRATEGIES QUESTIONNAIRE				
Teaching strategies	Regular	Often	Rare	Never
Assignment				
Brainstorming*				
Buzz groups (paired work)				
Card games				
Case studies				
Computer Apps				
Craft practical work				
Database				
Debate				
Demonstration				
Design related tasks				
Discussion				
Display				
Exam past questions				
Experiment				
Feedback on lessons				
Feedback on learning				
Field trip / outdoor activity				
Flip chart presentations				
Games				
Graphic organisers				
Graphs and charts				
Group work				
Handouts				
Homework tasks				
Individual working				
Internet research				
Interviewing others				
Journal or blog				
Lecture				
Library research				
Listening to podcast				

Listening to music				
Mindmapping				
Note-taking				
One to one coaching				
Peer teaching				
Photo slide show				
Placement				
Portfolio building				
Poster creation				
Powerpoint presentation				
Presentation by learners				
Problem solving				
Project				
Question and answer				
Questionnaires				
Quizzes				
Reading textbooks				
Real objects				
Real work experience				
Role play				
Seminar				
Simulation				
Software programs				
Spelling test				
Spider diagram				
Spreadsheet use				
Starter activities				
Statistical analysis				
Survey				
Tabulating information				
Tests to time limit				
Timelines				
Tutorial				
Uploading to VLE				
Video / DVD watching				
Video film making				
Visits				
Visiting speaker				
Vocabulary glossary				
Websites				
Whiteboard and talk				
Word processing				
Worksheets				
Writing to time limit				
Writing essay				
Writing report				

*The National Epilepsy Association of Great Britain issued a press release in April 2003 stating that they have no objection to the term 'Brainstorming' and noted that the fundraising bear in the USA is called, 'Brainstorm'.

Planning for a variety of teaching activities overtime is important to help maintain interest and concentration. Oldham College received the top Ofsted accolade of five cross college 'outstanding' inspection grades in 2008 and in relation to teaching and learning the inspectors commented, *"Lessons have excellent pace and a strong focus on student participation and learners participate enthusiastically. Students are developing high skills of oracy and are thoughtful, developmental and reflective in pursuing their academic goals. A wide variety of teaching strategies are used to engage students and encourage their participation including discussion and debate, role-play, group and paired work, and student presentations. The sharing of good practice is firmly embedded".*[23] More recently in 2010 Kendal College received five Grade one inspection judgments and the inspectors commented, *"The best lessons are well-planned and purposeful, and lead to brisk, lively and imaginative teaching that enables all learners to make good and better progress".*[24] Hattie's research (see Chapter One) indicates that no single teaching strategy has a significant edge. Teaching strategies in general have an effect size of 0.60 against the threshold for learning effectiveness of 0.40. The key is to plan for variety because a variety of learning approaches will build learning. Rather than 'one take' to grasp a key topic the regular use of individual, paired and group tasks will offer 'multiple takes'. Ofsted regularly highlights that effective teachers focus not on the task but on the learning outcomes and react to student responses by, *"modifying and adapting lesson plans in the light of informal assessment of students' progress and understanding during the lesson".*[25] The 2012 Ofsted inspection criteria for schools elaborated this point, *"the extent to which the pace and depth of learning are maximized as a result of teachers' monitoring of learning during lessons and any consequent actions in response to pupils' feedback".*[26] Essentially read and respond to body language. Hattie has also indicated that 'space' to absorb new learning is important i.e. all student appreciate thinking and reflection time and more questions will arise if topics are revisited, *"students needed three or four exposures to the learning – usually over several days- before there was a reasonable probability they would learn".*[27] The aim is a continuum of learning. Regular recap at the start of lessons will check and build learning but apart from last week consider recapping a topic taught last month or even last term and assess how far key learning has been retained. Build review points into your Scheme of Work and set a firm expectation of revision and review. Feedback on learning, on a regular basis, is a powerful driver of personal improvement because it can deliver a shock – something you think you have taught well...? Consider one step back and three steps forward every lesson so that learning is firmly linked and interconnected.

Learning styles

Variety is also the answer to the vexed question of learning styles. Research published by Frank Coffield, Deputy Director of the Institute of Education, in 2004 highlighted that there is no scientific validity for the majority of learning style inventories typically used in our colleges and schools, *"some of best known and widely used instruments have such serious weaknesses (e.g. low reliability, poor validity and negligible impact on pedagogy) that we recommend that their use in research and in practice should be discontinued"*.[29] Different questionnaires give entirely different results. In particular the idea of labelling a student with a particular learning style and trying to match teaching to that learning style is flawed. Even if the learning style identified was valid learning in the same way would soon de-motivate and not address the development of wider skills and abilities. Variety is the answer because overtime all students will benefit. Coffield reserved his ire for VAKT in particular (Visual, Auditory, Kinaesthetic or Tactile learning) *"There is no scientific justification for teaching or learning strategies based on VAKT and tutors should stop using learning style instruments based on them. There is no theory of VAKT from which to draw any implications for practice. It should be a dead parrot. It should have ceased to function"*.[29] However, schools and colleges are not at fault in focusing on learning styles because many official organisations, including Ofsted, have extolled the benefits of learning styles. We have all to some extent admired the Emperor's new clothes. Learning styles, however, did permit a dialogue to be opened with students about how they like to learn and this is something of lasting benefit to rescue and build upon. Raising a dialogue at induction and during lessons around what is to be learned and how we learn is a useful step towards meta-cognition and building independent learning skills i.e. the students' role in learning. This issue is explored in full in Chapter Eleven.

Lesson Plans

Lesson Plans come in many different forms and layouts according to the nature of the programme and the curriculum. Individuals and course teams may devise their own lesson plans to suit their own learning situations but most colleges and schools have their own preferred standard templates. The key elements of an effective lesson plan can be captured on two sides of A4 – a title page and a planning grid.

Lesson plan title page

The title page should focus on the course and lesson information, aim(s), objectives and any learning support needs as follows:

- **Lesson Aim(s) –** the aims should be kept to a minimum and may often be just a single overarching aim. Each aim should start with the word, 'To' as in To understand... To provide... To develop... To appreciate...etc. Aims set a broad, overall statement of expected outcome for the lesson as a whole and are written as aspirations rather than measurable outcomes.
- **Specific Objectives or Key Questions –** the lesson aim(s) is followed by specific objectives or learning outcomes to break the overall aim(s) down into a series of short, precise, expected outcomes. This is normally achieved by continuing the prefix sentence, '*By the end of the lesson the students will be able to ...*' with a list of bullet points. Start each bullet point with a verb i.e. List....Write....Make...Debate...Saw...Draw...Bake...Prepare... The idea is to write a direction that is clearly measurable to ensure a firm link to assessment and to guide checks on learning throughout and particularly by the end of the lesson. A variation to this approach, with the aim of addressing differentiation, is to subdivide the objectives with the words, *all, most* and *some* i.e. *by the end of the lesson* ***all*** *students will be able to...* **most** students will be able to... and **some** students will be able to...? A further consideration is to replace specific objectives entirely with key questions. Here the teacher would state, *by the end of the lesson you should be able to answer:* A list of key questions can be then be presented which build in differentiation by ranging from concrete, basic questions to higher level questions. Staff can take as their guide the marking criteria for their subjects in terms of pass, merit and distinction criteria or Grade E as against Grade A. The key questions perhaps provide a sharper link to assessment during and especially at the end of the lesson. How far can the students

answer all of the key questions? Teacher training courses still lean towards formal objectives but innovative practice is always encouraged and so try posing key questions and make your own judgment as to whether they provide a better link to assessment.

Focus on learning

The writing of specific objectives is relatively straightforward but in practice there are pitfalls to be wary of. Specific objectives can encourage a task focused rather than a learning focused lesson i.e. the students have completed the task therefore objective fulfilled? Marzano reports, *"one fairly stable finding in the literature on goal setting is that instructional goals stated in behavioral objectives format do not produce effect sizes as high as instructional goals stated in more general formats...Perhaps they are simply too specific to accommodate the individual and constructivist nature of the learning process"*.[30] Effective teachers look beyond the task and ask themselves, *'how far have all the students understood'? 'What have they learnt'?* and more importantly, *'How will I know'*? Hattie ranks 'teacher clarity' of this type as eighth in his overall rank order of 134 influences on learning with an effect score of 0.75 significantly above the 0.40 threshold. Hattie emphasizes, *"teachers need to know the learning intentions and success criteria of their lessons, how well they are attaining these criteria for all students and know where to go to next in light of the gap between student's current knowledge and understanding and the success criteria of: "where are you going?", "How are you going?", and "where to next?"*.[31] The related subdivision of objectives into *all, most* and *some* adds more precision but also raises further difficulties. In particular how far can the learning challenge presented by any topic be accurately predicted? The aspects of new learning that individuals will find difficult will vary significantly and will emerge during and by the end of a lesson. Outstanding teachers closely monitor and react to the levels of understanding and student responses as the lesson unfolds. Defining what *all, most* and *some* should know in advance can promote low rather than high expectations and at worst pure guesswork. In particular, what should *all* know and understand about any topic as opposed to *most*? In practice the key is to address a hierarchy of learning through a 'big picture' lesson introduction and a questioning approach i.e. entering the lesson with a range of *key questions* from factual to challenging with the expectation that all will have a go. How far can all students answer the key questions by the end of the lesson? What are they finding difficult? Can it be presented in a different way? Can those who know explain it to those who do not? Moving with and following the learning is more important than 'covering' a fixed lesson plan.

Lesson plan grid

The second page of a lesson plan is most often in the form of a grid, as illustrated, to record the main learning and teaching activities. The grid below should be presented in landscape form to provide more space but it is presented here in portrait view for convenience. It is also a truncated table and clearly the columns should be extended to the full depth and width of the page.

Aspect	**Time**	**Teacher activity**	**Student activity**	**Resources**	**Wider skills / Notes**
Lesson Start • Lively and engaging appetiser • Recap of previous learning • Introduce 'big picture' objectives or key questions					
Lesson Development • Account / exposition of new learning • Regular Q&A • Mix of whole class, individual, paired and group tasks • Assess progress & stretch and challenge					
Lesson plenary • Summary and checking of learning • Bridge to next lesson & independent working / VLE					
Reflection / Student feedback					

The breakdown of the lesson as listed down the left hand column may be deleted, as wished. The headings have been entered to prompt a recommended sequence of learning and follow the steps of the Diamond Lesson Plan as presented in Chapter Six. However, you may adapt and adjust as wished.

The main columns of the lesson plan grid should be completed as follows:

- **Time** – enter the relevant starting time followed by the estimated time for the completion of each step of the lesson. Remember this is your estimation and the operative word is 'plan'. You do not have to keep to time. Rather be guided by the progress of the students and if need be carry an aspect of the lesson forward into the next lesson. Ofsted reflect this responsive approach in their published criteria for grade one lessons as follows: *"Lessons are thoroughly planned but this does not prevent effective use of unanticipated but productive opportunities that arise in lessons"*.[32] The purpose of the lesson is effective learning rather than rushing and cramming in another piece of information but overtime as you re-teach the same topic area you should end up with fairly realistic timings. However, do signal to your students (and to any inspector present) any alteration to your lesson plan and why so that they appreciate that you are in charge of the change rather than simply not noticing the passage of time.

- **Teacher activity** – list the key learning steps that you are planning to introduce. Remember that listening is one of the least effective means of learning and so avoid too much *'chalk and talk'* – over talking is one of the principal reasons why many lessons are ineffective because concentration spans are stretched too far and students drop off task. Consider lesson plans that regularly involve whole class learning, an individual task, a paired task and in a longer lesson a group task as well. This simple planning consideration will promote participation and avoid the trap of over talking. You should also record in this column how the task will assess learning to ensure a focus on learning rather than mere task completion. What are your key questions to check learning? How will you know by the end of the lesson that all students have met your minimum learning expectations and the more able have been stretched?

- **Student activity** – Against each heading in the teacher activity column list the associated learning activity. It might be listening and making own notes, watching a DVD and completing worksheet, discussion in pairs and arriving at a judgment, converting the data into a pie chart etc. A very limited range of activities in this column should make you reflect on how far you are making sufficient demands of the students. You may also include differentiation notes here with reference to extension tasks for the more able and extra support for the less able. Focus on the learning outcomes arising from the task because the outcomes provide the link to assessment.

- **Resources** – List the resources required to support the teaching and learning tasks identified. Any frequent repetition of whiteboard and handout should cause you to reflect and to consider the use of wider resources. The resources identified might prompt a dialogue with relevant learning support and technician staff or a reminder to book equipment etc. In particular consider the contribution ILT might make to reinforce and aid learning. Make it an aim to build student competency across the core Microsoft Office programs ™ i.e. Word, Excel and Powerpoint and Apple software within the creative field.

- **Wider Skills / Notes** – Employers and Higher Education need employees and students who have not only passed the relevant examination but also possess good functional, employability and personal learning and thinking skills. Most lessons will involve opportunities to practice and develop skills in research, working with others, ICT, using number, presenting, writing, oral presentations etc. Highlight any relevant skills development as part of your lesson objectives and ensure that your students appreciate the importance of good functional and employability skills as well as knowledge for their future careers. In addition consider any naturally occurring opportunities via the selection of topics, research tasks, group organization etc. to reflect equality and diversity good practice. Also capture any aspects of learning support in terms of the contribution of any learning support staff and/or any individual learning support needs necessitating special equipment or alterations to the classroom layout. This might also relate to meeting the needs of any English as an Additional Language (EAL) students.

- **Reflection / learner feedback** – Regular reflection is a key tool to improve teaching and learning. After a lesson consider what went well and what could be improved. Overtime this reflection will build an outstanding course of study by constantly refining the methods of teaching and learning. In addition capture and reflect upon any student feedback about aspects of the lesson / course they found difficult or enjoyable. This may be gained from question and answer, checks on learning, opinion surveys or focus groups outside of the lesson. In the Ofsted publication Excellent schools 2008, the following feedback technique was highlighted, *"teachers also regularly give students Post-its and at the end of the lesson, ask them to write down what went well and what could have been better and stick them on the door on the way out"*.[33] Also take advantage of any lesson observation schemes to gain evaluations of what worked and what could be improved. Feedback and reacting to feedback on your lessons occupies third place in Hattie's top ten list of major influences on learning with an effect score of 0.90 well above the 0.40 mean.

Individual Learning Plan (ILP)

In November 2004 the Ofsted publication,*'Why Colleges Succeed'* highlighted the importance of planning for individuals and not classes as follows: *"The learning and achievement of students are at the heart of teachers' planning and are the central purpose of all classroom/workshop activity. Teachers do not plan in a vacuum, but on the basis of a detailed knowledge of their learners' prior attainment and potential, acquired through initial assessment and induction and recorded in individual learning plans. Lesson plans become an active means of orchestrating the sequence of the proposed activities, according to the needs of the individuals within the group, but with sufficient built-in flexibility to be able to respond to the unexpected, should it occur. Differentiated approaches are planned for all students, not just the less able: Many lessons contain specific strategies for differentiation. Extension activities are provided for the more able students and extra support for the less able..."* [2] Similar criteria exists within the Ofsted 2012 inspection framework, as quoted earlier, and so this focus on the individual is clearly not a new feature of Ofsted inspections. All students should have an Individual Learning Plan (ILP) as a driver of progress and ultimately achievement. In most cases the ILP will be completed during induction and will be held by a Personal Tutor or Mentor and reviewed regularly with the student. The key feature should be to receive feedback on performance and to set challenging but achievable learning targets or goals i.e. personalisation: identifying individual barriers to progress and providing appropriate timely interventions and support as required. The monitoring of personal progress forms one whole part of the 2012 inspection criteria for Further Education as follows:

> *"Staff initially assess learners' starting points and monitor their progress, set challenging tasks, and build on and extend learning for all learners*
> *To make this judgement, inspectors will consider how well:*
> - *learners' additional support needs are quickly and accurately identified early in their programme through effective initial assessment, leading to appropriate planning and support throughout the duration of their programmes*
> - *staff work with learners to develop individual learning plans that are regularly informed by ongoing assessment*
> - *learners are set challenging short- and longer-term learning goals that are reviewed and updated regularly*
> - *staff assess learners' performance and progress, and monitor assessment practices to ensure they are timely, regular, fair, informative and reliable*
> - *planned assessment/assignment activities build on previous knowledge and extend learning for all learners".* [34]

Care should be taken to reflect upon the above criteria and how far it is addressed with clear procedures understood by all staff and students.

Effective feedback

Hattie's rank order of influences on student learning provides four key overlapping considerations in relation to feedback and goal setting:

Influence	Rank order	Effect size
Self report grades	1	1.44
Piagetian programmes	2	1.28
Feedback	10	0.73
Goals	34	0.56

The research on *'self report grades'* highlights that most student are sharply aware of their own progress and what they are finding difficult, *"high school students had very accurate understanding of their achievement levels across all subjects"* [35] but they often uncertain of what to do next to improve and may regard their ability as fixed rather than something changeable. The reference to *Piagetian programmes* stresses the importance of helping students to overcome learning frustration as they wrestle with and assimilate new and unfamiliar concepts. Feedback emphasizes the importance of building a learning dialogue to explore barriers to learning and task related improvement steps. The key is to focus on what the student(s) find difficult and to offer a pathway forward. Hattie summaries an effective feedback dialogue as follows, *"the major feedback questions are, 'where am I going (learning intentions/goals/success criteria, 'How am I going', (self-assessment and self-evaluation), and 'Where to next', (progression, new goals)".* [36] Finally goals should be challenging but coupled with building self belief, *"goals have a self-energising effect if they are appropriately challenging for the student as they can motivate students to exert effort in line with the difficulty or demands of the goal".* [37] Building trust and focusing on the completion of recommended improvement actions is the core the ILP process. ILPs vary significantly in terms of layout and content but an effective ILP should have four major sections:

- Biography – the individual, entry qualifications and career aims
- Initial assessment outcomes – identification of any support needs
- Learning targets – specification of measurable targets with timescale
- Learning outcomes – measurements of progress and difficulty

At its briefest it is possible to capture each section on one side of A4 and to print the ILP onto A3 paper and then fold into a folder style presentation. Additional pages and/or 'concern' notes can then be placed into the ILP for ease of filing. However, an electronic ILP is often the best solution because of the ease of updating and information sharing with relevant staff. In situations of largely one to one learning within some NVQ, ICT, Art and Design courses, Students with Learning Difficulties or Disabilities (SLDD) and vocational workshops etc then each teacher should hold an ILP for each student in their care and set individual targets for each lesson. The individual ILPs would replace the lesson plan in these situations because each student will be at different stages and perhaps engaged on different projects/ assignments. These can be completed and reviewed during one to one progress checks with each student in the lesson. The recording of reflective comments should be a standard feature of the last five minutes of each session by each student. This does not have to be a burden – short and to the point – but the comments will give the teacher a valuable overview of the progress being made by each individual and any further support and guidance each student requires to achieve their full potential. Any general issues should be addressed at the start of the next session. A teacher may choose to respond to a common difficulty by offering the relevant group of students some coaching support and likewise for an individual who expresses a particular difficulty. This approach should personalise the support provided and end the classic, unfocussed *'Are you OK'?* style of teacher question. Working to clear individual targets is the best strategy.

Applying learning taxonomies

Hattie placed 'Piagetian programmes' as second in his overall rank order of learning influences with an effect score of 1.28. This raises the importance of planning for learning i.e. an awareness of the hierarchy of learning and consideration of how best to assist students to learn. Jean Piaget (1896-1980) was a Swiss biologist who studied how children perceive the world, make sense of what they see and learn. He articulated four stages of cognitive and personal development from early childhood to adulthood:

- Sensor –motor
- Pre-operational thought

- Concrete operation
- Formal operations

The first two stages govern the early life experiences of a child as they explore and take in the world around them and the last two stages mark the transition from factual to abstract thought. This shift takes longer from some children than others. You may have noticed how a child at the cinema often needs to question the plot and to confirm the on-screen relationships and/or the sequence of events as they explore abstract reasoning. In terms of learning any new subject we first gain and digest the basic facts, vocabulary and information and then move into application and ultimately construct a conceptual framework. The concept of a hierarchy or taxonomy of learning has been explored and refined by many theorists and the dominant among them was Benjamin Bloom.

Bloom's taxonomy

Benjamin Bloom's Taxonomy of Educational Objectives was first published in 1956 and has been a mainstay of educational guidance ever since. Bloom (1913-1999) specified a hierarchy of cognitive development and in later writings also defined 'affective' (1964) and 'psychomotor' (1967) domains of learning.

Domains of learning

Cognitive	Affective	Psychomotor*
Knowledge Comprehension Application Analysis Synthesis Evaluation	Receive Respond Value Organise Characterise	Imitation Manipulation Precision Articulation Naturalisation

*Bloom was involved in this research but only gave a broad outline and the full development of the psychomotor taxonomy is most often attributed to R.H. Dave in 1967.

The cognitive domain is concerned with the development of thinking and intellectual skills, the affective domain with feelings and emotions and the psychomotor with physical skills. In each case there is a hierarchy from low order skills to high order skills. In essence a baker will know and be able to apply the theory of how and why the yeast makes the bread rise (cognitive), work well in team and develop a rapport with customers (affective) and be able to mix the dough and shape an attractive fougasse (psychomotor). All three skills areas are important to the baker's career but how far are all three taught and developed during a relevant training course? How skilled is the baker in all three domains of learning? A good Scheme of Work for Bakery and relevant Lesson Plans will include objectives and learning activities to build competency and skills across all three domains of learning. In writing your Scheme of Work and Lesson Plans consider how far you need to specify objectives across all three domains of learning and backtrack to the learning activities that would fulfill those objectives. If the lesson is learning a skill within a vocational workshop then the lesson plan should focus on student progression through the psychomotor taxonomy. However, remember that in a largely service sector employment world (76% of current UK economic activity) skills within the affective domain are of particular importance for all. To explore Bloom in more depth simply put Bloom's taxonomy into Google and you will find lots of helpful websites and detailed descriptions of each taxonomy.

Bloom revised

In recent years the changing nature of employment skills within the 21st Century 'knowledge' age and the significant growth in Service Sector employment has prompted a re-appraisal of Bloom's taxonomy. In 2000 Lorin Anderson and David Krathwohl published a revision of Bloom's cognitive taxonomy followed by Marzano and Kendall in 2007, *'The new taxonomy of educational objectives'*. Both revisions reorder and rename some steps as listed to improve the precision but in particular they redefine the higher order skills. Anderson and Krathwohl identify skills related to creativity as the highest point of cognitive development and Marzano and Kendall place an emphasis on high levels of intra-personal skills in terms of ability to reason and apply logic. Essentially more Spock than Kirk!

Bloom 1956	Anderson and Krathwohl 2000	Marzano and Kendall 2007
Knowledge	Remembering	Retrieval
Comprehension	Understanding	Comprehension
Application	Applying	Analysis
Analysis	Analysing	Knowledge ultilization
Synthesis	Evaluating	Meta-cognitive system
Evaluation	Creating	Self-system

The higher skill demands of employment in the 21st Century *knowledge age*, as detailed earlier, illustrate why a revision of Bloom's original taxonomy may be necessary. How far will your lesson and course planning address the development of 'soft skills' for the 21st Century economy? The revised taxonomy produced by Anderson and Krathwohl may be expressed within an attainment pyramid with the aim of rising from a base of lower order thinking and reasoning to the prized ability to add original ideas and to attain creativity.

Attainment pyramid

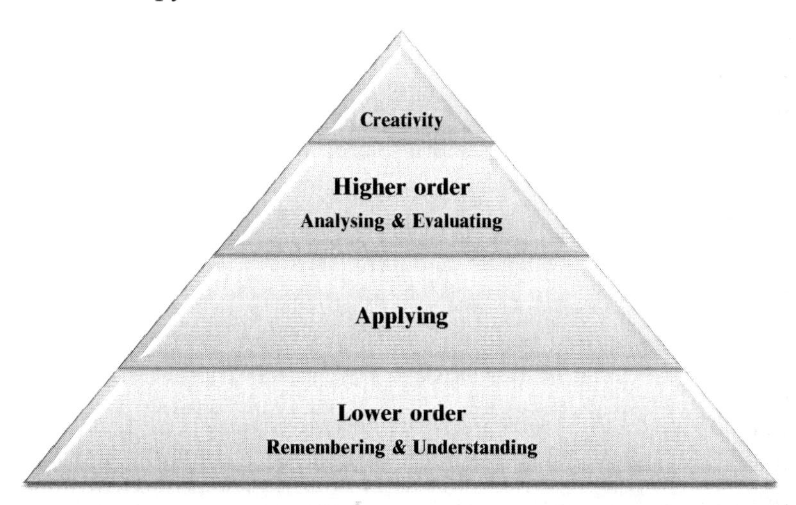

Structure of the Observed Learning Outcomes (SOLO)
The educational psychologist John Biggs is primarily associated with the development and publication of the five stage SOLO taxonomy in 1982. His taxonomy (developed in association with Collis) moves from 'pre-structural' learning characterized by misunderstandings or misapplications at the lower end of the scale to 'extended abstract' at the higher end and characterized by conceptual awareness. The focus

is on how well students understand and can evaluate and apply principles rather than simply recite facts or basic knowledge. The former is characterized as deep learning and the latter as surface learning. Our task as teachers is to teach to the 'gap' and in particular to provide students with the language and methods to analyse, evaluate and to construct meaning from what they learn. This is the prized ability of the effective teacher – the ability to recast information or to provide multiple examples until 'the penny drops'. It also underlines the importance of regular group or paired work to give students the opportunity to explore and question new learning.

Applying Bloom's taxonomy

The underlying consensus is that learning can be placed into a hierarchy moving from low order into high order reasoning. This hierarchy is reflected in the criteria and marking schemes provided by examination boards. Bloom's cognitive taxonomy may be attached to major qualifications goals as follows:

Bloom's taxonomy	Key Stage 3 Level	GCSE Grade	National Diploma	A-Level
Knowledge	4	D	Pass	D/E
Comprehension Application	5	C	Merit	C
Analysis Synthesis Evaluation	6/7	A*/A/B	Distinction	A*/A/B

Look at the published marking criteria for your course and discover how far a learning hierarchy exists. It is common for pass level questions to expect students to list, identify or describe whereas the higher marks are reserved for an ability to analyse, evaluate, compare. The following example is taken from the BTEC National Diploma specification for Animal Care:

Award	Criteria
Pass	***Describe*** common designs of kennels and catteries.
Merit	***Explain*** the differences in design of accommodation for specified breeds of cats and dogs
Distinction	***Cost*** and ***evaluate*** the equipment required for a specified kennel or cattery.

How do you plan for this differentiation in your lessons and the tasks you set? How do you lead your students from factual understanding, into application and finally into the higher order skills of analysis and evaluation?

Learning Portal

21st Century learning and the movement into the digital age raises a question mark over the effectiveness of the typical Scheme of Work grid as described and illustrated above. The Scheme of Work grid is not student friendly and does not lend itself well to presentation on a computer, tablet or smartphone screen and consequently the design of an electronic Learning Portal may be the answer in order to make firm links between the classroom and the Virtual Learning Environment (VLE). There are many advantages. Students who are recovering from illness in hospital or at home or away on work placements or field trips, or trips abroad or extended holiday will all be able to continue learning with minimum interruption. Equally cover for absent teachers is made much easier and in general independent learning anytime and anyplace will be fully supported. However, in too many schools and colleges the Virtual Learning Environment lacks structure and operates in isolation from the Scheme of Work and classroom. It is common to enter a VLE, click on a subject heading and find that all that exists to support learning is a blank space for the attachment of resources e.g. handouts, Powerpoint / Keynote, web site recommendations etc. Many staff do respond and upload resources but the result is all too often a random collection of folders rather than a guided pathway through useful topic linked resources. VLEs should avoid becoming repositories for files or random lists of website addresses or an electronic filing cabinet for replacement copies of lost handouts etc. The VLE should be the focal point to *drive* rather than support learning and this requires a more structured layout and an underpinning pedagogy to link the classroom and learning to the VLE. Ofsted 2012 criteria for Further Education makes several references to the importance of VLE support including, " *the promotion and development of independent learning skills, for example, through the use of a range of technologies, including a Virtual Learning Environment*".[38]

Example of an electronic learning portal

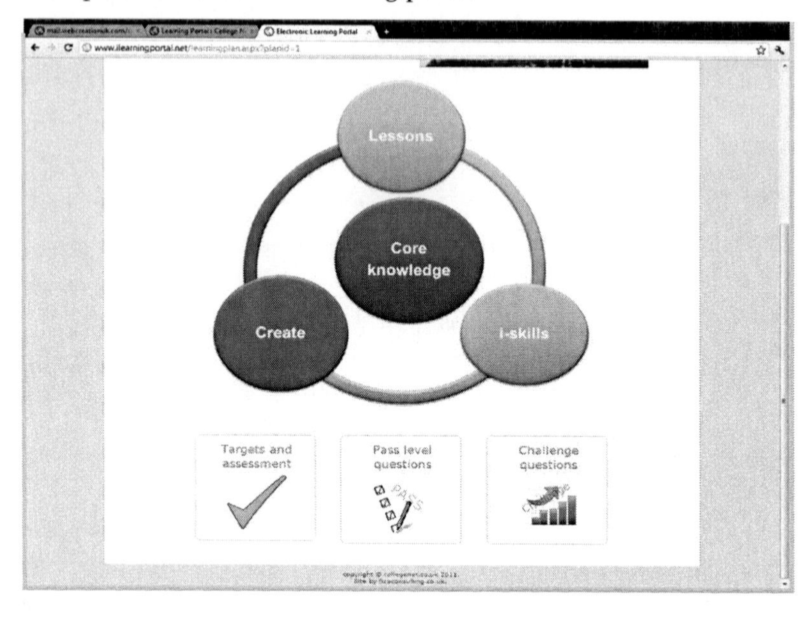

The above screenshot is faint so do visit Collegenet.co.uk to view this example of a learning portal. It is fully clickable and illustrates how key topics might be supported online with a range of resources but importantly linked to key questions to guide learning and independent research. An electronic portal of this type contains all of the features and more of a traditional paper based Scheme of Work and so perhaps it is time to move forward fully into the electronic era and embrace an online learning future. The textbook, 'The i-Learning Revolution: A new pedagogy also by Bradley Lightbody highlights how the use of the VLE can be fully integrated across teaching and learning within the new pedagogy of ***'Flipped Learning'***.

Enthuse and motivate

Full many a gem of purest ray serene
The dark unfathom'd caves of ocean bear:
Full many a flower is born to blush unseen,
And waste its sweetness on the desert air.

Gray's elegy written in a country churchyard (Thomas Gray 1716-71)

Many students arrive in our classrooms from unpromising circumstances but reveal a kernel of undiscovered or unremarked talent and ability. The challenge is to nurture and develop the ability of all students by providing an opportunity rich learning environment. Our core purpose is to stir curiosity, develop self belief, challenge but most of all to enthuse and inspire our students to achieve their personal best. Witness any young person who has a particular hobby, sport or social activity and they will devote hour after hour to the pursuit of karate, tap dancing, playing the clarinet, painting, building their Facebook profile, football, drama, dancing, maintaining a car, keeping topical fish, scouting, swimming etc. What drives them is an intrinsic interest in that particular hobby, sport or social activity. This intrinsic interest can produce sports stars, pop stars, inventors, writers, artists, actors and independent business success etc. The holy grail of teaching and learning is to trigger a similar intrinsic interest in learning and this is reflected in Lifelong Learning criteria, *"Implement appropriate and innovative ways to enthuse and motivate learners about own specialist are"*.[1] Ofsted's 2012 inspection criteria for Further Education includes, *"how well teaching and learning methods ..inspire and challenge all learners and enable them to extend their knowledge, skills and understanding"*.[2] Within the schools sector Ofsted's 2012 criteria raises a similar expectation, *"the extent to which teachers enthuse, engage and motivate pupils to learn and foster their curiosity and enthusiasm for learning"*[3] Many of our students lack personal goals and do not participate in any social and sporting activities. Consequently it is vital to raise their awareness of the opportunities open to them, to expand their horizons and to raise their ambitions. It is notable that Ofsted includes the judgment, *"how well leaders promote the ambition of high achievement for all learners"*[4] as part of the 2012 'outstanding' criteria for Leadership and Management and employs similar language within the schools inspection framework.

Motivational Influences

Individual levels of enthusiasm and motivation are subject to a wide range of positive and negative influences largely related to:

- Community influence
- Home influence
- Peer influence
- Personal influences

As early as age 10 these influences will have generated a positive or a negative attitude to learning (and/or life) and in the case of the latter present schools and colleges with a significant challenge to 'sell' the benefits of engaging in learning. The scale of this task was revealed in July 2008 by a Learning and Skills Council (LSC) survey of 16-19 student opinions on the importance of education, *"a staggering quarter of English teenagers believe that education is not important in achieving their goals…nearly half 47% would rely on being in the right place at the right time rather than work to secure the correct qualifications or skills required to reach their goals."*[5] It would appear that the National Lottery slogan,' it could be you' has been too successful and that too many young people are *'waiting to be discovered'* via programmes like the X Factor, Britain's Got Talent, Big Brother or by a modelling agency, a film producer, a record producer, or a football club. Our difficult task is to demonstrate via appropriate statistics and role models that qualifications remain the primary route to future job and personal satisfaction for the majority of the working population. An earlier survey by the LSC in May 2008 provides some hope that we could be successful, *"81% of teenagers find drive and ambition to gain qualifications and skills an attractive trait in a potential boyfriend or girlfriend. By contrast laziness is considered by far the biggest turn off among teenagers (49 per cent) followed by being uneducated (15 per cent) and lacking ambition (14 per cent)".*[6] Therefore our consistent message must be that effort brings rewards and that qualifications offer future success. The posters and destination information on our classroom and corridor walls should reflect this. Consider Professor Brian Cox who has become a household name in a highly successful television career and made Physics intelligible for the masses. He attended Hulme Grammar School in Manchester and forced himself to bounce back after gaining a disappointing Grade D in A-Level Maths but he went on to gain a First Class degree in Physics. How many Brian Cox's in terms of successful role models attended your school or college or can you identify in relation to your subject area? Holding high expectations, identifying role models and offering appropriate support can reverse the random disadvantages conferred by community, home, peers and personal image. This was the message the First Lady of the United States, Michelle Obama, delivered to children in the Elizabeth Garnett Anderson High School London 2nd April, 2009, " *I never cut class, I loved getting As. I liked being smart. I though being smart is cooler than anything in the world. You too, with these values can control your own destiny".*[7] Our aim is to project a learning culture that celebrates achievement and the joy of learning.

Community influence

How far do your pupils and students live in a community that has good facilities and is a bright, attractive place to live and where they feel safe? Some of our communities are blighted by vandalism, limited social and sports facilities and a sense of danger rather than safety. Living in a deprived community can significantly harm motivation and life chances because of negative role models, poverty, regular street crime and surviving rather than thriving households. In 2008 the World Health Organisation (WHO) stirred controversy when it reported that life expectancy in East Glasgow was a decade lower than life expectancy in Bangladesh or Gambia. The report entitled, *'Closing the gap in a generation'*, presented a stark assessment of the impact of unemployment, poor diets and sedentary lifestyles and set life expectancy for a male child in East Glasgow at 54 years but significantly 82 years if born only a few miles distant in the prosperous suburb of Lenzie. A poor community blights lives and can significantly reduce ambition and motivation. A research report commissioned by the National Association of School Masters and Union of Women Teachers (NASWUT) entitled, *'One more broken*

Window' investigated the negative impact of urban blight on learning, *"The manifestations of urban decay can easily impact upon pupils and their teachers. For example, the pupils attending schools situated in areas exhibiting symptoms of the broken windows syndrome may demonstrate poor behaviour in the classroom, have low self-esteem, little appetite for educational attainment and have little cultural and social capital to draw on. Conversely, their teachers may become disillusioned and frustrated with their limited ability to teach in a community where crime and incivility is rife".*[8] This report echoed earlier American research published by Wilson and Kelling in 1982 entitled, *'Broken Windows: the police and Neighborhood Safety'* which concluded that a downward spiral follows the first broken window, *"As buildings, streets, or even entire districts are allowed to become dirty, litter strewn and covered in graffiti, this gives rise to the perception that since no one else really cares about this area, "why should I?"*[9] This gave rise to the 'zero tolerance' policing culture in many American cities whereby low level crimes were targeted to reinforce good citizenship and a prevailing sense of law and order. One practical outcome of this research in the UK is immediate action by many councils to wash away graffiti as soon as it appears, to regularly remove litter and to quickly repair broken windows etc to arrest any copycat actions and a downward spiral. Many school and colleges have successfully adopted similar site maintenance policies to encourage a pride in the school and its buildings.

Indices of Deprivation

The relative standards of living between different communities in the UK are reported by the government in a 'deprivation index'. The overall UK index may be accessed at, www.communities.gov.uk. The current '*English Indices of Deprivation 2010,*' published in March, 2011 measured relative prosperity against seven standard domains:

- income
- employment
- health
- education
- access to services
- living environment
- crime

The rank order of the nine English regions from most deprived to least deprived is as follows:

North East
North West
London
West Midlands
Yorkshire and Humberside
East Midlands
South West
East of England
South East

The rank order reveals a north-south divide in prosperity with standards of living and educational attainment all significantly lower across our northern cities and major urban areas. An estimated five million people in the UK live within areas of high income deprivation although not all will be deprived. Pockets of affluence and deprivation exist side by side in all areas. London, perhaps provides the greatest example with the extremes of affluence and poverty only a short tube ride between. The regional data supports a significant correlation between impoverished communities and low rates of educational attainment, high rates of crime and anti-social behaviour. Across the English regions the following is the rank order of the ten most deprived districts in terms of low household incomes:

1. Liverpool
2. Middlesbrough
3. Manchester
4. Knowsley
5. Kingston Upon Hull
6. Hackney
7. Tower Hamlets
8. Birmingham
9. Blackpool
10. Hartlepool

The link between poverty and low educational achievement was unequivocally confirmed by a detailed statistical analysis of GCSE results undertaken by the Financial Times in 2011[10]. The data measured the performance of children registered for Free School Meals (FSM) as a signature of low income against their peers and revealed that they were 42% more likely to be in the bottom quintile for GCSE results. The highest correlations recorded between pupils registered for FSM and placed within the lowest quintile for GCSE results were 68% for Kingston-Upon-Hull closely followed by 66% for Newcastle-Upon-Tyne 66% and 64% for Knowsley in Liverpool. An associated deprivation map of England published by the Financial Times illustrated how underachievement was concentrated in the industrial urban areas of Northern England although Plymouth at 57% and Kent at 56% were also well above the national average. The following list is the rank order by percentage of pupils eligible for FSM within each region in 2010:

London 23%
North West 17.3%
North East 16.9%
West Midlands 16.6%
Yorkshire and Humberside 14.9%
East Midlands 11.4%
South West 9.5%
South East 8.6%

In terms of individual local authorities the highest percentage of pupils eligible for FSM was Tower Hamlets 55% and the lowest Wokingham 4.0%. In May 2012 a report entitled, 'Poverty in England' published by the Church Urban Fund provided a bleak assessment of the scale of underachievement, ill-health, unemployment and high crime levels within deprived communities[11]. The report named Toxteth in Liverpool as the most deprived district in the UK with 62% of children living in poverty compared to 6% in Camberley, Surrey which was named as the least deprived district in the UK. The correlation between disadvantaged communities and underachievement is beyond doubt and presents a national challenge to the education sector to help children to overcome the disadvantage of poverty. The most significant current research into the impact on poverty on learning is an on-going longitudinal study of a cohort of 3,000 children from pre-school to age 16 being conducted by the Institute of Education (IOE), University of London. The study entitled, *'Effective Provision of Preschool, Primary and Secondary Education'* may be accessed on the University of London website www.ioe.ac.uk. The cohort have entered High School but the primary stage has revealed marked differences in the levels of reading and writing skills between children from disadvantaged communities and their peers, " *higher levels of social disadvantage were a predictor of poorer outcomes…the challenges in raising attainment are greater for schools in areas of higher disadvantage.*"[12] A further IOE study published in June 2012 concluded that regardless of academic ability poverty impacted on progress and opened-up a significant achievement gap, "*a yawning gap in attainment between even the ablest children in the highest and lowest socio-economic groups…the reading skills of the highest performing English and Scottish 15-year-olds from disadvantaged families are, on average, more than two years behind those of the most able pupils from privileged backgrounds*"[13] This achievement gap was defined more broadly by research sponsored by the Joseph Rowntree Foundation in 2010, "*The gap in attainment between the poorest children and children from better-off backgrounds, already large at age 5, grows particularly fast during the primary school years. By age 11, only around three quarters of children from the poorest fifth of families reach the government's expected level at Key Stage 2, compared to 97% of children from the richest fifth*".[14] The limitations on life chances imposed by living in disadvantaged communities is starkly exposed by the website Comparefutures.org. This website permits comparisons to be made between the 'life chances' of being born and raised within different postcode districts. In terms of the chances of going to a top Russell Group university Kensington tops the poll with 30% of Sixth-Formers gaining a place compared to only 0.05 from Hull East. The impact of living within a disadvantaged community is significant because the environment of shabby streets and poorly maintained houses and a lack of green open spaces and sports and leisure facilities and high crime rates can damage self-esteem. It is possible for whole communities to feel neglected and to gain a sense of helplessness and this may enter our classrooms in terms of a significant number of students with low self-esteem and low personal expectations. President Obama addressed the issue of poverty and life chances in a speech direct to American school children 8th September, 2009, "*Maybe someone in your family has lost their job, and there's not enough money to go around. Maybe you live in a neighborhood where you don't feel safe, or have friends who are pressuring you to do things you know aren't right. But at the end of the day, the circumstances of your life – what you look like, where you come from, how much money you have, what you've got going on at home – that's no excuse for neglecting your homework or having a bad attitude. That's no excuse for talking back to your teacher, or cutting class, or dropping out of school. That's no excuse for not trying. Where you are right now doesn't have to determine where you'll end up. No one's written your destiny for you. Here in America, you write your own destiny. You make your own future"*[15] Obama raised the high expectation that each individual, regardless of circumstances, can achieve if they apply sufficient effort. This was the clear message of the Ofsted report, 'Twelve outstanding secondary schools' published in 2009,*"The 12 outstanding schools studied in this report defy the association of poverty with outcomes; they enable such young people to succeed and reduce their disadvantage.... The culture and norms inside the school can often be very different to those outside; as one headteacher put it: 'The street stops at the gate."*[16] This report details many successful strategies to address and mitigate socio-economic disadvantage.

Applying Maslow's Hierarchy

Abraham Maslow (1962) identified human needs in the form of seven key requirements for personal fulfilment as follows:

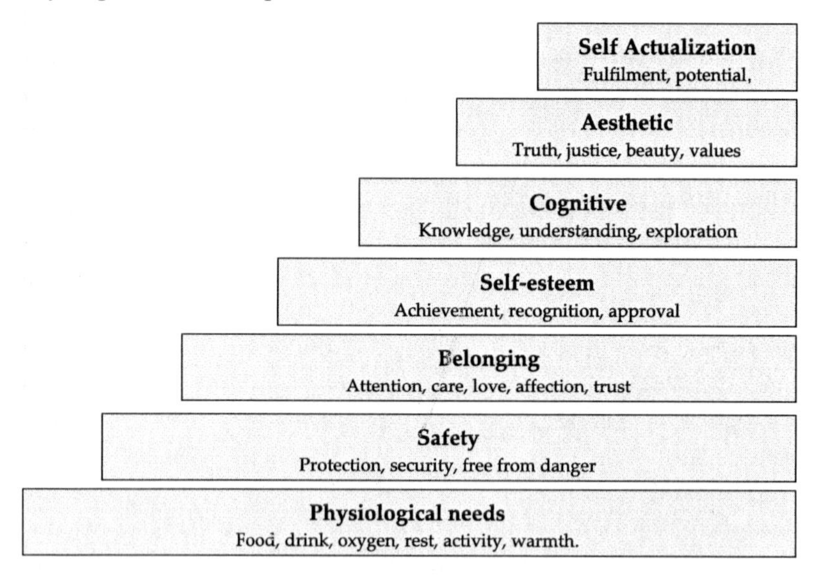

Deprived communities and deprived households often fail to satisfy the first four foundation steps and without this firm, secure base many pupils and students fall short of reaching and extending their cognitive abilities. Ofsted commissioned a major report into the impact of poverty on learning in 1993 only one year after its formation entitled, 'Access and Achievement in Urban Education'. The report painted a bleak picture, "*Beyond the school gates are underlying social issues such as poverty, unemployment, poor housing, inadequate health care and frequent breakup of families....poor levels of education and qualification among many parents complete a cycle of under-achievement which continues to affect the lives of their children. The community does not acquire sufficient numbers of people able to offer role models of educational success.*"[17] The report was renewed and updated in 2003 and arrived at very similar findings and dispiritingly showed no evidence of improvements in educational attainment within disadvantaged communities. In November 2011 the Ofsted Chief Inspector's report acknowledged the extent of the impact of poverty on attainment, "*Deprivation continues to be a significant factor influencing the quality of schools. .... the proportion of schools judged good or outstanding declines steeply as the proportion of deprived pupils at the school increases. A school serving the most deprived pupils in the country is four times more likely to be inadequate than a school serving the least deprived. At the other end of the spectrum 17% of the schools serving the least deprived pupils were outstanding compared with 7% of schools serving the most deprived communities. This variation in performance continues to have a significant impact on the life chances of many pupils, reinforcing inequality and reducing social mobility. Addressing this is one of the key challenges for the education system*".[18] The Chief Inspector of Ofsted Sir Michael Wilshaw addressed the need for action in a speech to the National College of School Leadership on 15th June 2012 and announced the appointment of a panel of experts to review the challenges and to make recommendations for improvements on the twentieth anniversary of the original report in May 2013. Sir Michael Wilshaw is personally aware of the challenges involved in raising attainment because he was the Headteacher of Mossbourne Community High School in Hackney a district with high rates of local deprivation reflected by the fact that some 40% of the pupils were eligible for Free School Meals. If we take advantage of the website Comparefutures.org it is possible to compare the postcode of the Chief Inspector's old school E58JY Hackney with the postcode of Holland Park secondary school W87AF in highly prosperous Kensington. The data reveals that the average entry to an elite university is 30% in Kensington as against 2% in Hackney and for Redbrick universities 31% as opposed to 12% respectively. The difference in attainment levels between the two postcodes is significant but during Sir Michael Wilshaw's time as Headteacher the GCSE pass rates for the national benchmark of five GCSEs grades A*-C soared above 80% making Mossbourne one of the highest performing schools in England. The Chief Inspector's recipe for success was essentially high expectations, zero tolerance, a 'can do' culture and raising ambition. Similar strategies also underpin the success of the London Challenge programme coupled with collaboration between schools to raise standards. The Challenge programme, established in 2003 attaches advisers, essentially coaches, to every school to review barriers to achievement and to suggest solutions and in particular to empower teachers to experiment and arrive at their own solutions. The impact has been significant with 30% of London's Secondary Schools judged 'outstanding' by Ofsted compared to a national average of 17.5%. London Challenge highlighted the importance of high expectations and this is also the approach adopted by the Teach First initiative which places graduates into some of our most challenging inner city schools.

Teach First

The Teach First programme (www.teachfirst.org.uk) is one of the most successful teacher training initiatives, within the schools sector. Teach First has successfully persuaded many high achieving graduates to try *teaching first* before considering or returning to other career paths. Ofsted have conducted an initial inspection and reported, *"the outstanding level of achievement of the four best trainees was so uniformly high across the range of standards that they were judged by inspectors to be amongst the most exceptional trainees produced by any teacher training route"*[19] *Teach First* places the trainees into challenging inner city schools and lists the skills required for success as follow:

- *"You'll need almost limitless supplies of energy, enthusiasm and optimism to tackle the inertia and disenchantment that characterise challenging schools.*
- *You'll need to be creative, brimming with ideas and capable of packaging and repacking ideas and concepts to capture the interest and imagination of students who, for whatever reason, have disengaged from education.*
- *You'll need self-discipline, and have the courage to confront failure and come back for more, because not everything you try will work.*

- *And you'll need thick skin – rhino thick. Be prepared to be challenged on everything you say or do and to engage your emotional intelligence to build relationships with people who feel you owe them a lot but may not feel they owe you anything in return.*
- *If you can offer all this, and combine it with awesome communications skills and a sense of humour – particularly the capacity to laugh at yourself – then you should find out more about applying to join Teach First. You could be just what we are looking for".* [20]

The level of challenge is not underestimated but the key to success is concerted whole team and school or college actions to arrest poor behaviour and to raise personal horizons beyond the confines of the local community.

Building a community profile

Consider building an overall socio-economic profile of your catchment area to inform initiatives to combat any significant evidence of deprivation. How does your local community perform in relation to others? The government website www.neighbourhood.statistics.gov.uk provides a summary of key social and economic indicators for every neighbourhood in England by postcode or local authority. In addition the annual School Performance tables for England provide an overview of GCSE and A-Level performance for every local authority. Go to www.education.gov.uk/performancetables/. If your college or school does serve a deprived community what measures can you take to build a greater learning capacity and/or to compensate for local disadvantage? In essence how do address the first four steps of Maslow's hierarchy?

Home influences

Some homes provide children with unqualified emotional support and personal encouragement during their formative years and others at the opposite extreme may involve psychological or even violent physical abuse. At ages 14-19, in particular, many students question their parents' or guardians' values and the result is tension in the home and a changing relationship that either helps or hinders learning. In addition some homes will confer a material learning advantage and others a material learning disadvantage as illustrated below

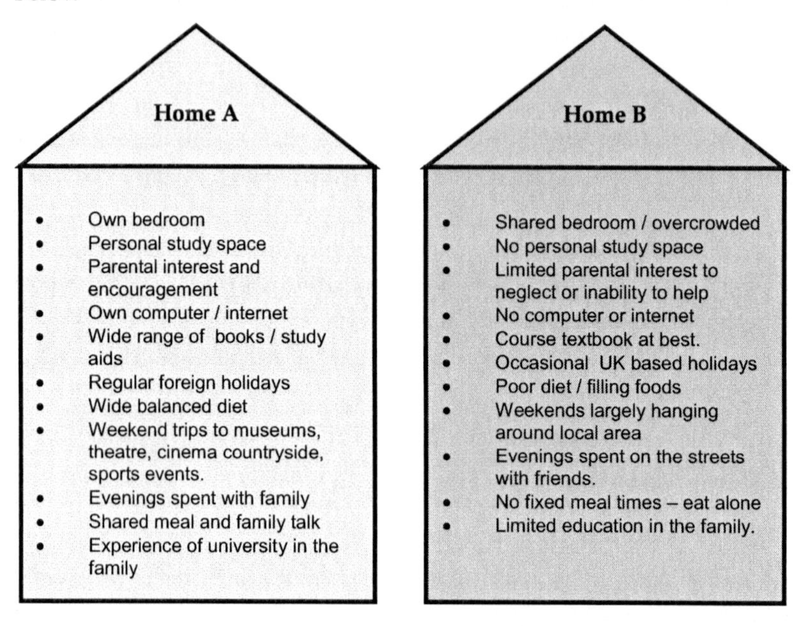

The above illustrations of Home A and Home B represent a broad generalisation because there are a host of exceptions and crossovers but they do illustrate the existence of significant home learning advantages or disadvantages. For instance, in 2012, 80% of UK households enjoyed internet access but within this overall percentage 97% of the richest homes had internet access compared to 46% for the poorest homes. However, research undertaken by Professor Waldfogel of the University of Columbia 2007-08 has concluded that the key home factor influencing effective learning is not material advantage or disadvantage but the level of parental support for learning and encouragement i.e. positive social attitudes and high levels of learning support may exist in any home regardless of material advantages. A home may be materially poor but emotionally rich and vice versa *"the biggest factor in the achievement gap is parenting style…it is a question of maternal sensitivity –warmth and nurturing…next in importance comes a factor more obviously related to income – home background that includes access to books and computers…taken together parenting style and the home learning environment explain between a third and a half of the gap in achievement between the poorest children and their middle class counterparts".*[21] Waldfogel's findings were underscored by research undertaken by Professor Stephen Scott at King's College London who concluded, *"Financial poverty is a factor but not a central one...it seems to be poverty of the parent-child experience that leads to poor child outcomes rather than poverty of a material kind"*.[22] Earlier in 2006 Lord Leitch in reviewing research evidence of underachievement in his report on World Class Skills reported, *"In turn, the strong links in the UK between the educational attainment of parents and their children means that the children of those who have not attained highly at school are also less likely to do well. This creates a cycle of disadvantage that locks generations of the same family into persistent poverty. This cycle needs to be broken by both raising aspirations and standards in all schools, and ensuring that adults have a real and effective second chance to improve their skills"*.[23] The negative or positive impact of parenting skills on achievement levels has been extensively documented by both the Institute of Education (IOE), University of London and the Joseph Rowntree Foundation (JRF). The most recent data, published in 2010 by the JRF highlights a performance gap of 54% in the attainment of five GCSEs at grades A*-C between the richest and the poorest households, *"Only 21% of the poorest fifth (measured by parental socioeconomic position) manage to gain five good GCSEs (grades A*–C, including English and maths), compared to 75% of the top quintile – an astonishing gap of 54 percentage points"*.[24] The differential performance is not only linked to parental support for learning but correlates with parental qualifications, *"significant characteristics such as family income, Free School Meals (FSM) and family Socio-Economic Status (SES) are less powerful predictors than parents' qualification levels."*[25] This conclusion by IOE researchers highlights that the higher the qualifications of the parents the richer is the support for learning in the home. More significant still is a higher correlation with the qualifications of the mother rather than the qualifications of the father, *"there were still very strong effects of mother's highest qualification level and the Early years home learning environment (HLE) on academic outcomes."*[26] Essentially educated parents tend to engage with their children much more often in a wide range of learning activities. The JRT qualified some of these activities in 2010 by asking parents, *"How often do you read to your child? How often do you tell stories to your child not from a book? How often do you play music, listen to music, sing songs or nursery rhymes, dance or do other musical activities with your child? How often do you teach your child numbers and counting? How often do you draw, paint or make things with your child? How often do you play sports or physically actives games* *outdoors or indoors with your child? How often do you play with toys or indoor games with your child? How often do you take your child to the park or to an outdoor playground?*[27] These rich interactions promote learning and earlier in 2007 the McKinsey report noted, "*the average child of professional parents has a vocabulary of 1,100 words and an IQ of 117. Whereas the average child of parents on welfare has a vocabulary of just 525 words and an IQ of 79. Unless schools intervene effectively to compensate for the impact of a poorer home environment, they stand little chance of closing the gap*".[28] The homes 'rich' in learning support consistently generate higher learning outcomes than homes 'poor' in learning support and this learning advantage is maintained the whole way through to GCSE level as shown by the following data from the JRT.

Attainment gap between poor and rich households 2010[29]

Stage	Poor home	Rich home
Key Stage 2 (Age 11)		
% reaching expected level	64.3	94.3
Key Stage 4 (Age 14)		
% reaching expected level	51.9	92.7
Key Stage 4 (Age 16)		
% attaining 5 GCSEs A*-C	33.2	84.0
% attaining 5 GCSEs A*-C including English and Maths	21.4	74.3

The parenting gap is not only in relation to supporting learning but in raising expectations of progression to university, "*Parental aspirations and attitudes to education vary strongly by socio-economic position (SEP), with 81% of the richest mothers saying they hope their 9-year-old will go to university, compared with only 37% of the poorest mothers. Such adverse attitudes to education of disadvantaged mothers are one of the single most important factors associated with lower educational attainment at age 11*".[30] In terms of international comparisons McKinsey in August 2008 published the following league table showing the difference between the average test scores achieved by 13 year olds in a maths test from homes with more than 200 books and those with fewer than 10. [31]

Country	% Gap
Saudi Arabia	29
Bahrain	40
Hong Kong	41
Jordan	58
Canada	62
Belgium	63
Japan	71
Netherlands	75
Australia	77
New Zealand	88
Singapore	88
U.S.	92
England	93

Although a fairly blunt measure the outcome shows a correlation between poverty and underachievement across all countries in the study but with England recording the greatest gap. In other words poverty was more significant to underachievement in England than in other countries. This impact of poverty in supressing achievement in England was confirmed by an Organisation for Economic Co-operation and Development (OECD) analysis published in April 2012, *"pupils in the bottom half of the OECD's socio-economic scale in England perform less well than their peers in the bottom half of the distribution across the OECD despite not being as disadvantaged"*.[32] There are no conclusive answers to this evidence but there is speculation than in other countries access to education is more highly valued and parents across socio-economic boundaries are more likely to push their children to work hard at school to escape poverty. In his review of influences on learning worldwide, John Hattie, Professor of Education, University of Auckland (see Chapter One) confirmed the significant influences of home and parental background. Against an average points score of 0.40 for influences on learning Hattie calculated *'home environment'* and *'parental involvement'* at 0.57 and 0.51 respectively; both above the 0.40 average. In relation to home environment Hattie also highlighted the significance of emotional support, *"achievement is more closely linked to the socio-psychological environment and intellectual stimulation in the home than to parental socioeconomic status indicators such as occupation and education"*.[33] The overall impact of the different home environments translates into a stark differential performance at GCSE level. In summer 2008, 75,000 students in receipt of Free School Meals took GCSE examinations and of those 31,647 or 42 per cent failed to achieve a single Grade C in any subject. This underperformance is repeated at A-Level. In 2008, 13,000 students achieved the significant benchmark of three grade As at A-Level but only 189 of those were in receipt of Free School Meals (FSM). After GCSE only 5000 students out of 75,000 eligible for FSM progressed into A-Level courses. Out of those only 40 in a typical year will gain a place in either Oxford or Cambridge. Poverty does limit life chances but the significant difference for achievement is not material advantage but the level of parental aspirations, emotional and learning support.

Engaging with parents or guardians

How does your college or school compensate for low or no learning support/encouragement in the home? Remember that a poor relationship at home might explain disaffected or passive behaviour in the classroom. Are counselling services advertised and promoted? Are careers services and HE guidance advertised and promoted? Are tutorial programmes planned to build personal confidence, and to raise self-esteem? In addition how does your school or college address the material disadvantages highlighted in Home B? Is there access to the internet, word processing and assignment support at school or college? Are there opportunities for enrichment including trips and visits outside the local area? Are residential courses in outdoor pursuit centres offered? Is study guidance offered? What is your strategy to engage with parents / guardians to help build learning support at home? When 16-19 learners were asked by LSC in July 2008, *"what if anything would help them stay on in education respondents stated that more support from their family would be a good start."* [34] The instinctive desire for parental affection and support at all age groups should never be under estimated and therefore parents or guardians should be regarded as allies to help promote enthusiasm and motivation for learning. This was the recommendation of Sir Alan Steer who chaired a major investigation into improving behaviour in our schools in 2005, *" It is extremely important that parents and carers are involved in their child's education and we applaud schools that undertake effective and proactive strategies to support this"*.[35] This conclusion was endorsed by the Ofsted report, 'Narrowing the Gap' published in April 2007 which drew upon the evidence of 37 Ofsted Area Reports and recommended, *"creative and flexible strategies to engage parents and carers, make them feel valued, enable them to give greater support to their son's education [focus on boys' underachievement] and help them make informed decisions about the future"*.[36] It is also an Ofsted expectation that there is effective communication with parents, *"Reporting learners' progress to parents, carers or sponsoring employers is important for learners under the age of 18. Inspectors will focus on the quality and accuracy of such reports and the effectiveness of the arrangements made by colleges to communicate with parents and employers. The college should consider the views of parents and employers when it judges the effectiveness of its reporting arrangements"*.[37] In August 2008 an analysis of A-Level results highlighted a North-South divide in pass rates with improvement in pass-rates only 2.3% in the North East compared to 6.1% in the South East between 2002 and 2008. One factor raised to explain the difference was a lower level of parental aspirations in many of our deprived northern communities. It is important to reach out to parents and to highlight the positive benefits of education. The Ofsted report, 'Twelve Outstanding High Schools' 2008 details the effective strategies of 12 schools serving highly deprived districts. In terms of parental engagement the report states, *"The outstanding schools are equally persistent at forging links with parents and the community. One of the challenges is to raise parental aspirations and ambitions for their children and themselves"*.[38] However, all too often progress evenings in our schools and colleges are poorly attended. Unfortunately some parents / guardians may have negative memories of their own time at school and feel intimidated by the whole process. Consequently consider linking the progress evening to a curriculum display, a demonstration of a range of crafts or sports, a drama presentation, a computer exhibition, a prize draw, or a motivating speaker ? Invite your Adult Education service to set up displays related to adult education opportunities, including taster sessions, to encourage enrolment. A parent or guardian may also become a student. Finally, remember that many parents / guardians who are keen to assist their son or daughter will often lack the knowledge of what best to do. A termly school or college '**Connect**' newsletter can be effective as a means of engaging with parents or guardians.

It might contain:

- career opportunities
- higher course information including university
- prompts to useful study aids / equipment
- indication of recommended independent study time
- timetable information
- holiday dates
- assessment information
- exam information
- college regulations and learner charter
- suggestions on how to assist their son or daughter
- adverts for adult education programmes
- contact details

A successful circular might only be four sides of A4 i.e fold A3 card to yield a title page, two inner pages and a back page to give a circular presentation. Note the reference to a Year Planner in Chapter Two and how this might be adapted to form a newsletter to parents or and / or guardians. If your college or school has Graphics Courses invite the learners to design an attractive title page and layout and be sure to include the names of the design team as a footer to give them positive recognition. The purpose is to gain, as far as possible, a learning push from home as well as a learning push from school or college. Ideally the school or college website could also have an electronic version and if parents' are online and have email addresses then a copy could be emailed. A more extensive version of the above was praised by Ofsted in an inspection of Alder Grange Community and Technology School in November 2006, *"the school is trialling as part of a national initiative, innovative ways of encouraging parents to be more involved in their children's education. The quality and content of the recently produced Parents' Handbook are exemplary".* [39]

Peer influences

Building confidence and increasing the self-esteem of young people is a significant challenge because many will associate with peer groups who do not value school attendance and learning i.e. Neets – Not in Education, Employment or Training. In 2011 21.9% of 16-24 year olds were classified by the Department for Education as Neets equating to 1.163 million young people – a record high. Neets are more likely to be convicted of crime and to serve prison sentences and to have higher rates of depression and suicide. More starkly Jon Coles, the Director General of Schools in 2009, highlighted a research study revealing that 15% of Neets were dead within ten years of leaving school with no qualifications. Many parents interviewed in relation to the rise of youth crime often state that they have lost control over what their son or daughter does. Research undertaken by The Prince's Trust and headlined on the BBC News 5th August, 2008 highlighted that two thirds of young people surveyed did not regard their parents as positive role models and tended to live separate lives from their parents with minimal contact. The pressure of the widespread macho culture on teenage boys should also not be underestimated. In some of our deprived districts gang membership is becoming a significant problem with pressure to join a gang or to risk becoming a victim. Therefore some children as young as 11 and 12 may have decided that school is not for them and will often cultivate an image of disinterest in education to mask underachievement and seek attention from their peer group by offering a challenge to authority. They may absent themselves from school at a significant cost to their personal futures and worse may become involved in petty crime with an end result of fractured home and community relations. This may trigger a downward spiral of taking a pride in criminal activity and accepting an ASBO as a badge of honour rather than shame. It is notable that 51% of young offenders have no qualifications compared to 15% of the population as a whole. The impact of peer group influences is more marked in boys rather than girls. A report commissioned by the Department for Education and skills (DFES) in 2007 into gender in influences in education concluded, *"Boys are more likely to be influenced by their male peer group which might devalue schoolwork and so put them at odds with academic achievement. It is argued that girls do not experience a conflict of loyalties between friends and school to the same extent as boys (Forde et al (2006) summarise theories of how boys try to maintain their sense of masculinity in a school setting. Boys feel compelled to conform to a dominant view of masculinity which conceptualises academic work as feminine and therefore being seen to work in school can be seen as a problem. In conflict with this identity, is the culture of school where academic achievement is the main criterion for judging the 'worth' of a pupil. In order to protect their self-worth and their masculinity, boys will commonly adopt four strategies: procrastination; withdrawal of effort and rejection of academic work; avoidance of the appearance of work; and disruptive behaviour".*[40] Compelling evidence of the above attitudes in action was provided in 2007 by a BBC life swap programme between the pupils of an average state school and a fee paying school. A striking difference related to peer group attitudes to homework. For the former it was something to be avoided and for the latter a challenge within a culture of peer competitiveness. Similar attitudes were noted by researchers from Roehampton and Birmingham universities in 2008 who reported that students who took an interest in learning were often negatively labelled by their peer group, *"the traditional swot is now referred to by a range of different names: boffin, boff, bod, spod, bodrick, keeno or nerd...fear of being labelled the class boffin colours pupils' attitudes to academic success".*[41]

Beyond peer influences on learning behaviour there are also the all-consuming teenage issues of friendships and selecting the 'correct' clothes, music and consumer durables of importance to their peer group. In general the post 1980 generation, *'Generation Y'* are reputed to exhibit a tendency to emphasise their 'rights' and 'choices' above a responsibility to the wider community or to accept social norms i.e. talking loudly on a mobile phone in a restaurant or a train is a right and not to be criticised, occupying a seat when someone older or infirm is standing is a right, shouting loudly in the street late at night when most of the neighbourhood is asleep is a right, sitting with feet on a chair is a right, dropping litter is a right etc. However, there is good news because despite the widespread public impression of rising crime the official Crime Survey figures for England and Wales 2012 show a further drop in overall crime figures of 4% from 2011 in a continuing downward trend from 2009. But within this general downturn young people face a greater risk of street crime than the general population. In 2011-12 one million young people aged 10-15 years were victims of crime with most in our urban areas. Over half of these recorded crimes some 566,000 were violent assault and the remainder theft of personal items. Young men were more likely to be both the perpetrators and victims of violent crime. The latter is a significant issue with some young men exhibiting a hair trigger against any perceived criticism no matter how mild. Unfortunately even a simple disapproving look may be sufficient to trigger a violent attack and has often resulted in parents and local communities losing control over behaviour on their streets. The extreme expression of this is the sad rise in knife crimes and a willingness by some young men to commit murder to maintain 'face'. The crime of murder no longer seems to be taboo but is regarded by some peer groups as an appropriate response to a perceived or an actual insult. In terms of risks the Ofsted 2012 inspection framework for schools includes monitoring, *"the extent to which pupils are able to understand and respond to risk, for example risks associated with extremism, new technology, substance misuse, knives and gangs, relationships (including sexual relationships), water, fire, roads and railways".*[42] Overall some young people exhibit a desire for immediate gratification and an inability to plan for the future and to accept the normal stepping stones of qualifications, job, promotion, rising income = future rewarding lifestyle. A key counter to this negative view of youth is for our schools and colleges to regularly celebrate success and to highlight the achievements of the overlooked majority of young people who make a positive contribution to society. Identify and list the many social, sports and community opportunities available for youth involvement within your area and build connections and place regular positive events into the college calendar to help build community cohesion.

Toxic childhoods

In 2006 the educational writer and researcher Sue Palmer published the book, *Toxic Childhood* which detailed the results of a three year study into how lifestyle changes may explain poor behaviour and low educational achievement. Palmer surveyed the opinions of 1,000 primary school teachers in relation to the following prompt question:[43]

How much do you think each of the following factors affects the learning of the children you teach?

Factor	% agreement	Description*
1. Too much TV	95	Unchecked access to TV, internet and computer games exposes young people to images of extreme violence and even personal danger.
2. Lack of sleep	92	An estimated two-thirds of children do not get enough sleep. Bedrooms are equipped with TV, computer, CD players, DVD players electronic games, mobile phones, and children arrive in school tired and unable to concentrate
3. Lack of talk at home	90	Decline of shared breakfasts and dinners and with them opportunities for family discussion and reinforcement of shared values and behaviour and limited vocabulary / confidence.
4. Poor parenting skills	89	Working parents with insufficient time or energy to interact with their own children. Too many hours alone with TV, games or sitters.
5. Family breakdown	86	Low self-esteem following family or parental break-ups. 70% of male young offenders come from 'broken' homes.
6. Lack of established moral code	84	A focus on 'my rights' overrides responsibility to wider society and basic good manners.
7. Poor diet	82	Increase in obesity, lethargy and hyperactive behaviour (sugar highs) from junk food.
8. Lack of outdoor play / exercise	80	Insufficient outdoor group play to build social norms, communication and co-operation or involvement in team sports with rules.
9. Pressure of targets	55	High anxiety is induced by regular exams, tests, targets and over demanding parents.
10. Celebrity culture	51	A demand for brand names and 'must have' behaviour i.e. immediate gratification. The 'bling bling' culture. The average child in the UK can apparently recognise 400 brand names by the age of 10.

*The descriptions are not direct quotation but summarise the research evidence.

Many of the above lifestyle factors are driven by peer values and are therefore difficult to shift and although the survey is based upon opinions of negative influences on primary school children it might be argued that these issues extend into teenage-hood. Collectively they may explain the low levels of concentration exhibited by some pupils and students in our classrooms and ultimately limited achievement. However, different studies produce different findings and a consensus on how far those factors, in combination, influence learning remains elusive. Hattie's rank order of influences on learning gives a low rank to most of these social influences e.g. watching too much television is ranked 137th out of 138 key influences on learning with an effect size of 0.18 far below the 0.40 significance threshold.

Personal Influences

Adolescence is difficult to navigate given media images of bodily perfection, uncertainty over future career plans, forming relationships and striving to establish a personal identity. The content of teenage magazines and social networking websites indicates that a significant number of 10-18 students will be more concerned about their self-image than learning. Consider the random allocation of nature:

- height
- weight
- hair
- teeth
- features
- sight
- accent
- skin

Some of the above may seem trivial areas of concern compared to students coping with learning difficulties, disabilities or medical conditions but even a minor blemish or perceived imperfection can result in a poor self-image and low personal confidence. A careless remark by a teacher, parent or peer can cause significant hurt. Evidence presented by the Children's Society to the 'Good Childhood enquiry in April 2008, included the statement, *"twenty-seven per cent of those aged 14-16 said that they often felt depressed…anxiety about appearance was mentioned by seven out of ten under-16s who said that they dieted some or all of the time"*.[44] In addition to nature's lottery staff need to remain alert to the possibility that many students may have had negative or challenging experiences of life.

- discrimination based on race, religion, gender or sexual orientation
- physical or psychological violence in the home
- medical condition
- break-up of a close relationship
- alcohol dependency and/or binge drinking
- pregnancy
- drug abuse
- victim of crime
- arrest
- detention
- parental divorce
- death of someone close
- bullying
- caring for an ill family member

Many young people will be struggling, and all often in silence, to cope with significant personal problems. A minority may be so unhappy that they self-harm or so depressed that they commit suicide. Figures released by the Samaritans in February 2012 indicate that the average suicide rate each year is 5,600 with men three times more likely than women to commit suicide. In 2007-08 there were 17 suicides of young adults in and around the town of Bridgend in Wales in an apparent rash of misplaced solidarity with dead friends. The growing Emo or *emotional* cult among many young people (characterised by wearing black clothes and black make-up) maintains a morbid fascination with death, self-harm and suicide as choices to be exercised to express inner sadness. Concern has been expressed in recent years by the growth in websites devoted to how to commit suicide. A study by the mental health group Young Minds in 2002 found that in a school of 1,000 pupils there were likely to be:

- 50 with serious depression,
- 100 in a distressed state,
- 20 with an obsessive-compulsive disorder
- 10 with an eating disorder.[45]

To address the above issues ensure that your college or school tutorial programme provides advice and guidance on how to gain support and help with personal worries and problems and promotes healthy lifestyles. Within the first few weeks of term all students should have an opportunity for one to one personal interviews to explore personal hopes and ambitions and to provide an opportunity for each student to express any personal anxieties. Remember that disaffected behaviour and low self-confidence can conceal significant personal difficulties. Are there sufficient role models and mentors? A student coping with a personal crisis or a poor self-image is more likely to drop out early or to underperform. A Learning and Skills Council (LSC) survey of learner satisfaction in 2008 reported that 15% of early leavers cited health problems, and 12% cited personal problems, pregnancy or difficulties with children or family commitments. What do your 'drop-out' surveys reveal? Therefore being alert to and intervening early to support 'at risk' students may ease their problems and improve retention.

A motivating environment

The common hallmark of outstanding colleges and schools is the maintenance of a motivational learning environment or culture that clearly fulfils the following Lifelong Learning criterion, *"Create a motivating environment which encourages learners to reflect, evaluate and make decisions about their learning"*. [46] How far can we stimulate a 'feel good' factor and present an 'opportunity rich' motivating environment that sets a tone and expectation of future personal success. Step into your college or school foyer with fresh eyes and what do you see? What happens in this building? Can you see:

- Photographs of senior management team and governors?
- Welcome statements?
- Exam achievements?
- Curriculum displays?
- Award and prize winners from last year?
- University entrance success ?
- Employment success?
- Learner representatives on college committees?
- Activities / enrichment opportunities for term ahead?
- Sporting fixtures?
- Social events / trips?

Look again but this time as a Black student, a Muslim student, a Sikh, student, a disabled student etc and how far do you feel welcomed and supported? As you walk down the corridor can you tell that you are entering different curriculum areas from the signs and notice board displays? If 'yes' then the college will have succeeded in raising initial motivational levels. Students will begin to feel a sense of pride in belonging to a bright, attractive, opportunity rich school or college community. This is basic subliminal advertising at work with the constant reinforcement of positive messages and images. Note how the stage hypnotist Derren Brown can plant suggestions into the unconscious mind and influence people's choices. Something you buy this weekend may well be the result of passing a billboard advertisement or simply an impulse buy resulting from an attractive in-store promotion. Clearly advertising works or manufacturers would not spend billions per year on billboards and TV advertising. What message or encouragement do blank empty walls provide? Wordsley School in the West Midlands re-modelled its reception to resemble the ambiance and comfort of a 'posh' hotel reception in order to remove the traditional barrier of the sliding glass window that confronts parents and pupils in many of our schools and colleges. It offers a highly positive image and raises a feel good factor; a sense of welcome for the visitor and for the pupils a pride in belonging. Kingsdale School in Dulwich roofed the open space between two buildings and created a huge, impressive atrium complete with full size trees. Nationwide many colleges have benefited from a major re-building programme that has finally ended the 'Cinderella' era for Further Education. Although sadly many colleges missed out when funding cuts prematurely ended the building programme. Many schools also benefited from the *Building Schools for the Future* programme and the rise of many impressive new academies in place of our dilapidated secondary schools. Most of our new school and college buildings are highly impressive in terms of architecture, space, light and colour and this by itself can be motivating but what about the individual and what about teaching and learning?

A learning culture

A 'visible' learning culture should permeate all aspects of the College or school's services and provision i.e. regular celebration of achievement but achievement in all fields. The purpose is to highlight opportunities for all – a portal to future personal success. Students who have clear future goals and develop a sense of self-worth and active citizenship are more likely to apply effort to succeed and to enjoy overall personal well-being. Consider the following quotes from 'outstanding' colleges:[47]

Kendal College

"All areas of the college radiate a strong subject identity, founded securely on real work experiences and this often results in vibrant, high-quality displays of learners work."

Loreto SFC

"A culture aimed at raising the aspirations and obtaining the best possible success for all learners is evident throughout the college. Students respond well within this culture and it encourages them to learn."

Holy Cross SFC

"Teachers meet frequently to discuss learning and this has led to a culture of continuous improvement… Staff value the supportive and collaborative culture and there is effective teamwork at every level."

Priestley SFC

"There is a strong culture of continuous improvement with a focus on supporting the learner to achieve. College managers monitor key performance indicators rigorously… Learners are very well supported by teachers and encouraged to aspire to a 'can do' culture of ambition and improvement. They are very well prepared for examinations. There is a strong culture of sharing good practice which is supported through well planned staff development activities."

Reaseheath College

"Leadership and management are outstanding. Leadership is inspirational and promotes very high standards in a positive and supportive culture that aspires to excellence".

Consider the following key elements of a visible learning culture and tick the columns as appropriate. As students move through the public spaces of the school or college from reception into specialist curriculum areas how far do they see the following visible evidence of a learning culture:

Aspect	Visible evidence	Yes	No
Raising horizons Mission, vision, values communicate clear direction and purpose	• Mission statement • Photographs of Principal and Governors • Photographs of senior managers • You said...We did... feedback • Listening college feedback post box • Newsletters to parents/carers		
High expectations Celebration of success in all fields and future career destinations	• Exam successes • Sporting successes • Destinations of past learners • Links to employers • Employment successes • University successes		
Celebrating diversity A sense of welcome, belonging and celebration for all	• Welcome statements • Cultural displays • Recognition of different traditions and festivals • Role model photographs • A safe, secure environment		
Whole person Personal enrichment opportunities, ECM and active citizenship	• Charity fundraising activities • Community / social links • Trips and visits out of college • ECM themed displays • Learner council / union displays • Enrichment opportunities		
Praise and awards Regular but earned praise and awards for learners and staff	• Photographs of staff award winners • Photographs of learner award winners • Best attendance prize • Learners of the month • Competition successes		

Actions and strategies linked to the above can build a feel good factor i.e. a sense of belonging and a common identity for all and help to reverse the impact of deprivation. Sometimes the actions are relatively simple but can have high impact i.e. a Sixth Form college in Sheffield displays a series of rotating messages on a large plasma screen including birthday greetings to named students. This is such a simple but powerful action which says you matter. The following quotation from a 2008 Ofsted review of Engineering highlights a rich praise and reward strategy, "*Successful centres celebrated the success of their learners. For example, 'value added lunches' were organised in one department to which parents and employers were invited and which were attended by the college principal. They were used to present awards for high attainment and achievement. In other colleges, learners' work was displayed prominently in corridors and on classroom walls; it contributed to department newsletters and sometimes to external literature. For example,* *learners' success in a motor racing competition was featured in the Institute of the Motor Industry magazine".*[48] Here is a further example of celebrating success, from land based colleges, as reported by Ofsted, *"Colleges gave high priority to celebrating student success and prizes awarded for livestock. This included external competitions and events, and special awards evenings, as well as recognition through newsletters and displays of trophies and shields,"*[49] Often it is the simple things that have impact. Sir Dexter Hutt who has built a reputation around turning around 'difficult' schools stated, *"we took photographs of every pupil who had achieved five or more A* – C GCSEs, framed them and displayed them prominently outside the main hall".* [50] Linked to the above are lessons that are presented with enthusiasm and passion for the subject as discussed in Chapter One. Students will respond well to a teacher who has clearly made an effort on their behalf. The following quotation is taken from the citation for Cathy McGowan, a Teacher of the Year 2012, *"the wall displays and layout leave no doubt that this is a welcoming environment dedicated to English Literature and to student achievement. A first year student commented, ' I love her classroom because it is so imaginative and I love all the phrases and quotes on the wall because they make me feel so special".*[51] If the subject or vocational skill clearly means something to the teacher then it is more likely to stimulate the interest of the students.

Visible senior management

An important element in the maintenance of a motivational environment is a visible senior management team who regularly 'walk' the college or school. The best impact is at the key points of the college or school day i.e. arrival, morning break, lunch time and afternoon break. Ofsted in its publication 'Why Colleges succeed' rated the motivational impact of 'visible' senior management highly, *"What is also a consistent feature in these colleges is the very 'hands-on' approach of senior managers to the college's core work which they make it their business to understand fully. Effective college principals are those who do not spend huge amounts of their time away from their institutions, but who are highly visible, talking with students, walking the corridors, making themselves accessible. The principal is highly visible around the college and senior managers are very accessible. The presence of the senior management around the college at key points during the college day is beneficial in maintaining the friendly and orderly atmosphere which characterises the college. College managers are readily accessible and respond quickly. The principal regularly visits each area of the college"*[52] Five years later in 2009 the same message was repeated in the Ofsted publication, 'Twelve outstanding secondary schools', in relation to the attitudes of principals, *"they prefer to be out in the school than in their office: 'management by walking about'.*[53] The 'visible' aim is not only to reinforce behaviour codes by correcting any poor behaviour encountered but to greet and welcome students and to convey the message that the students are valued and that the college is a place for personal advancement. This should be explicit in the College or School mission statement and from the vision articulated by the Principal and senior managers of the college or school. Ofsted 2012 criteria for both Further Education and schools includes the words 'ambitious vision' as part of the Leadership and Management criteria. The hallmark of the 'super-heads' serving some of our most deprived communities is to be visible – in the corridors, staffrooms, canteen, library – offering quick words of praise and encouragement to students and staff alike. Many Principals and senior staff aim to visit all major course groups within the first six weeks at college to welcome the students to the college and to reinforce behaviour codes but in particular to motivate with examples of the many opportunities for personal advancement. Some Principals, as part of their learner involvement strategy, offer a monthly 'tea with the Principal' and invite a selection of students from different courses to discuss their experiences. An effective learner involvement strategy can significantly boost student participation and sense of belonging and pride in the school or college. Phoenix High School in London serves White City a district among the 7% most deprived districts in the UK. The head teacher, Sir William Atkinson, was Knighted in the Queen's Birthday Honours List, June 2008 and explained the importance of the learning environment as follows, *"Our environment says you matter, you are high quality. It's important that the children get this message here especially as they might not be getting it at home…When dealing with kids whose prior experiences have limited their horizons, we have to inspire them. If they think they are losers, they mask those insecurities with all kinds of inappropriate behaviour."*[54] Sir Alan Steer the Government's Behaviour Tsar's policy was reported as follows, *"he believes it is important he should still take his place on the rota of senior staff checking pupils in each morning…it's a good way of tapping into their feelings. You can get a good idea of what is going on in the school just by listening".* [55] The Ofsted publication *'Why colleges Succeed'* published in November, 2004 highlighted the significance of a motivational environment as follows, *"Where a culture of learning exists, it invariably permeates the whole college and is self-perpetuating, being quickly adopted by new students…In these colleges, the principal and senior management team are successful in creating a culture where students are at the heart of the college's work. There is an unrelenting focus on students and their achievements, subscribed to by all staff….Communication and consultation with staff help to create a culture in which staff morale is high, staff feel valued and share a common purpose with their managers. This shared vision is a critical prerequisite for success."*[56] Nor is this importance of establishing a learning culture new. Consider the advice given in the Board of Education, *'Handbook of suggestions for teachers'* first published in 1904, *"The importance of their surroundings on children has been a commonplace of educational theory for centuries…by making the school rooms bright and attractive managers and teachers can do much to develop a sense of beauty and to cultivate good taste in scholars".* [57] Moving forward over a hundred years to 2010 we discover similar comments within an Ofsted college inspection report, *"All areas of the college radiate a strong subject identity, founded securely on real work experiences and this often results in vibrant, high-quality displays of learners' work.*[58]

Vocational Qualifications (VQ) Day

It is important to ensure parity of esteem between vocational and academic programmes. Too many of our young people gain a sense of failure because they are not succeeding with academic study. The TV presenter Bear Gryll (ex member of the SAS who climbed Everest at the age of 23), recalled his time at school , *"occasionally my name would be read out at the end of term as a GTF which stood for 'General Total Failure' ...deep down I think that gave me more determination to excel at climbing and karate".*[59] All too often we place an emphasis on academic skills and devalue vocational and wider skills and abilities. Awarding high status to A-Level and low status to the parallel vocational programmes is a national problem that harms motivation and hinders learning. A survey of students conducted for VQ Day 2012 revealed, *"more than three quarters of those studying A levels (76%) claim to have received little or no information on vocational options compared with the level of detail supplied for University applications and choices….The lack of vocational awareness among teaching staff is leaving thousands of students with limited choices for their future – a third of young learners polled (32%) stated VQs and vocational opportunities have never been presented to them as an option, while 77% were even discouraged from pursuing a vocational path.*[60] Our schools, colleges and media should take care to promote and celebrate achievements in Hairdressing, Catering and Brickwork etc just as strongly as the annual A-Level pass rates. The first national VQ day, organised by the then Learning and Skills Council (LSC), was held on 23rd July 2008 in the Royal Opera House, London to celebrate vocational achievements. The fifth national VQ day was held on 20th June, 2012. The overall English National winner and Learner of the Year 2012 was Dave Hughes who studied HND Graphics at Newcastle-under-Lyme College and now runs his own marketing company. He was selected from the nine regional 'Learners of the Year', one for each English region – there are parallel awards in Scotland, Wales and Northern Ireland.

Region	Learner	Programme
North East	Ian Henderson	Advanced L3 Management
North West	James Giblin	L3 Diploma Public Services
Yorkshire & Humber	Margaret Green	Int. Apprenticeship in Health
West Midlands	Dave Hughes	HND Graphics
East Midlands	Joseph Johnson	L2 Dip. Professional Cookery
East of England	Corrine Patmore	BTEC National Dip. IT
South East	Adam Bushnell	NVQ3 & ACA3 Bench Joinery
London	Rachel De Bose	AAT
South West	Chris Emery	NVQ3 Professional Cookery & Hospitality Supervision

Visit www.vqday.org.uk for more details.

However, it was notable that the VQ days passed with few, if any, mentions in the national TV or news headlines in sharp comparison to the annual jamboree that accompanies the release of A-Level results every August. Even within colleges many teaching staff are unaware of the existence of VQ day. What is your school/college strategy to combat this national indifference to vocational success? Who were the vocational high achievers in your school and college and did the local and national media celebrate their achievements? Perhaps VQ day should be renamed National Qualifications day (NQ) and moved into August when all achievements A-Level and vocational should be released to the media on the same day. The establishment of a separate VQ day falls into the trap of maintaining rather than bridging the academic / vocational divide.

World Skills (worldskills.org)

World Skills is essentially the Olympics for vocational courses with students able to compete for Bronze, Silver and Gold awards across 45 vocational areas – anything from Brickwork to Hairdressing. The organisation was founded in 1946 in Spain by Jose Antonio Elola Olas to promote the benefits of vocational education when he was General Director of the Spanish Youth Organisation. The first competition in Spain proved so successful that in 1950 it became an international event and it is now held every two years. The last World Skills championships were held in London October 2011, involving 57 competitor countries, and four British students won prestigious Gold medals:

World Skills Gold medal winners

Name	Skill	College
Philip Green	Bricklaying	Belfast Metropolitan
Shane Trevitt	Plumbing and Heating	Leeds College of Building
Christopher Berridge	Stonemasonry	Bath College
Kirsty Hoadley	Visual Merchandising	East Berkshire College

The overall top ten countries in the medal table (ranked by total medal points) were as follows with the UK in fifth position:

1. Korea
2. Japan
3. Switzerland
4. Brazil
5. United Kingdom
6. France
7. Finland
8. Chinese Taipei
9. Australia
10. Austria

How far does your college promote the World skills championships and celebrate the achievements of our students?

City and Guilds Vocational Rich List [61]

The City and Guilds vocational rich list highlights the success that can flow from a vocational career. All those listed started off their careers as students on vocational courses and among them are the following household names:

Dame Vivienne Westwood,
Delia Smith,
Rolf Harris
Gary Rhodes,
Alan Titchmarsh
Billy Connolly,
Sir Alex Ferguson,
Stella McCartney,
Eric Clapton,
Vidal Sassoon,
Sir Jackie Stewart,
Alexander McQeen,
Deborah Meaden,
Jamie Oliver,
Nicky Clarke and
Alan Shearer.

However, in terms of wealth the most successful vocational top ten are:

No.	Name	Business	Background	£ Wealth
1	Laurence Graff	Diamonds	Apprentice jeweller	£2 billion
2	Sir Anthony Bamford	JCB Plant	Apprentice engineer	£1.95 billion
3	John Caudwell	Phones4U	Apprentice engineer	£1.6 billion
4	Trevor Hemmings	Property development	Apprentice bricklayer	£1.03 billion
5	Sir Terry Matthews	Hotel Development	Apprentice engineer	£950 million
6	Sir James Dyson	Vacuum cleaners	Design student	£760 million
7	Yianis Christodoulou	Hotel Development	Apprentice jeweller	£500 million
8	Jim McColl	Engineering consultancy	Apprentice engineer	£435 million
9	Steve Morgan	Redrow Homes	Civil engineering student	£430 million
10	John Bloor	Property developer	Apprentice plasterer	£425 million

A related display may raise horizons plus the awareness that good Functional Skills were a large part of their success. Therefore building and improving Functional Skills as well as vocational skills and knowledge are important. Overall there is no simple answer to raising student enthusiasm for learning. What acts as a trigger for one student may not for another student. The answer lies in schools and colleges pursuing multiple strategies.

21 steps to building motivation

As a starting point consider the following 21 steps to improving motivation. How far are these steps currently evident within your own curriculum area or the college or school as a whole?

STEP	EXAMPLE
1. A learning culture	Celebrate success with corridor and classroom displays related to achievement, sports, awards, destinations, exam results, role models, curriculum, future employment.
2. Celebrating diversity	Ensure all feel welcome with relevant welcome notices, recognition of different cultures, languages, traditions and festivals.
3. Fun inductions	Induction activities not just for course information but fun team activities to build group bonds, friendships and self esteem within an upbeat, fresh start atmosphere.
4. Personal targets	Clear capture of individual strengths and areas for improvement in an ILP with challenging but achievable targets. Remember the targets are the minimum prediction and with hard work...?
5. Home connections	Course newsletter to parents/carers with information on how they can help their son or daughter succeed plus invitation to first progress evening.
6. Active progress evenings	Attract parents/carers to progress evenings with a curriculum display, adult education learning fair/stalls (parents/carers might enrol in an evening class or leisure pursuit), music or drama presentation, visiting speaker on careers/university entrance/local employment opportunities, advice and guidance on buying a computer/using the internet, competition with a prize, a buffet etc.
7. Learning to learn	Specify the 'tools' they are going to need to study successfully, how to organise their files and model and direct how complete and present each learning task.

8. Big picture learning	The use of Year Planners or similar student study guidance booklets to translate the Scheme of Work into user friendly bite-size chunks of learning and give learners precise guidance on what to learn and how to study. Ideally develop an online Learning Portal.
9. Challenge tasks	A monthly challenge task i.e. a problem, a puzzle or a case study to resolve with a prize for first three correct answers. Set challenge appropriate to the course level. Use your digital camera (with permission) to post winners on your notice board.
10. Success in six weeks	A series of short, focussed graduated tasks over the first six weeks up to October Half Term to give all a sense of progress and satisfaction. All to succeed and meet first ILP targets.
11. Formative assessment	Explicit how to improve improvement guidance on all work accompanied by standard marking sheets showing marking criteria as appropriate.
12. Differentiated questioning /task	Graduated questions on worksheets and varied questioning techniques that permit all to provide answers and to gain praise and a feel good factor from participation and correct answers.
13. Variety of activity	Lessons with quick-fire appetisers, short, sharp presentations, differentiated active learning techniques, lots of visuals.
14. One to One	Identifying some sessions to be largely devoted to one to one support rather than every lesson being dominated by whole class teaching. Identifying times in the Scheme of Work when the class will be engaged in a major assignment or group tasks and give 'coaching' support to each individual.
15. Listen	Planning time to listen, review and discuss learning and progress within lessons. Sufficient checks on new learning are built into lesson plans.
16. Group identity	Use regular random pair and group formation strategies to build friendships and group bonds and especially across gender and ethnic divides. Encourage peer working and peer support. A sense of belonging is a stronger motivator.
17. Events	Plan events to look forward to a quiz, wacky challenge day, a sporting competition, celebrate diversity with relevant cultural events, key charity events/fundraising, mark national occasions and anniversaries, a trip out, a residential team building weekend etc

18. Role models	Linked to future employment prospects and/or university courses, invite in role models, visiting speakers or past students. Script it for them – get the positives you want.
19. Recognition	Ensure progress is recognised by displaying work, a letter of praise home, a personal letter from the Programme Manager, a letter from the Principal, a letter from the Chair of Governors, attachment/adoption of a particular governor, a framed certificate of achievement, an awards night, display on progress evenings for parents/carers to see. A visit by the Principal. Overall reverse the discipline chain and have a praise chain! Works for staff too!
20. Praise and reward	Awards evenings, prizes for a variety of categories not just academic achievement, regular verbal praise in classroom and corridors, quick one to one praise for something well done at beginnings or ends of lessons. Student of the Month!
21. Online support	Online forums, blogs, email links with tutors and managers to raise questions and get answers. Online extended learning support to promote independent learning and to offer a platform of support for the least able.

Talking of motivation

Kim Smith of Gateshead College has devised a challenge programme for her Uniformed Public Services (UPS) students to keep them motivated and on their toes. The annual 'Wipeout' contest takes place over six weeks with a theme for each week as indicated.

The contest starts with a fitness challenge that links directly to the standards of the Physical Fitness unit of the course programme and involves competing against Royal Marine Commandos. The Charity fundraiser challenge permits each team to take-over the college for a day to run their own charity collection event for a charity of their choice. The team that raises the most money wins that particular heat. Next the teams compete in a General Knowledge quiz which also covers their course units in Politics, Citizenship and Diversity. This is followed in Week Four with a series of mental agility problem solving tasks and in Week Five the College Catering students host a Bushtucker Trial with blind food tastings including some army ration packs. Finally, in the last week of the contest the teams demonstrate their expertise in drill on the parade ground. Kim Smith has devised a really inspiring competition which tests course information and stretches the students to deliver their best. What might you devise for your students as a challenge competition to build a bond between your students and for a sense of enjoyment? Might you establish inter-programme challenge competitions across your college? Overall the above 21 steps should not only improve motivation but provide the tools and clear awareness of what and how to study. Once students feel in control over their own destiny and gain a sense of progress we are more likely to trigger an intrinsic interest in learning and as Michelle Obama discovered, learning can be cool.

Equality and Diversity

"We hold these truths to be self-evident, that all men are created equal, that they are endowed by their Creator with certain unalienable Rights, that among these are Life, Liberty and the pursuit of Happiness".

(United States Declaration of Independence 4th July 1776)

The above words are one of the most famous statements on equality and summarise very succinctly the rights of individuals to be free and equal. However, as the Americans and all nations have discovered it is one thing to pass a law but another for people to live by it and to treat others equally regardless of their race, gender, disability, religion, sexual orientation, transgender identity and / or age. Within the United States it was not until 1865 that slavery was abolished but whereas Black Americans gained their freedom many White Americans refused to acknowledge Black Americans as equals and enforced segregation. Prior to the passage of the Civil Rights Act in 1964 it remained legal in many U.S. States to maintain 'Whites' only bars, restaurants, shops, theatres, housing, hotels, schools, buses, trains, toilets etc. In 1957 a contingent of the elite 101st Airborne Division was required to escort the first Black students into Little Rock Central High School, Arkansas to enforce a Supreme Court ruling that White only schools were unconstitutional. Many employers would also openly refuse to employ a Black person and within the military Black and White soldiers served in separate units with the Black units largely restricted to labour duties. Within South Africa the segregation of the Black, Asian and White populations was not formally ended until 1994. This recent history of discrimination on the basis of someone's race is just one form of discrimination. The battle for equality is also a major battle for women, homosexuals, the disabled, the religious, transsexuals and the elderly. All of those groups face discrimination on a regular basis within the United

Kingdom and to a much greater extent in many other countries and so the promotion of equality and diversity is a major and significant task for all schools and colleges. Our significant aim should be to enact Life, Liberty and the pursuit of Happiness.

The Equalities Act 2010

The Equalities Act received its Royal Assent 8th April 2010 and took effect from 1st October 2010. The Act introduced a single **equality duty** in relation to seven specified aspects of personal identity:

- Gender
- Race
- Disability
- Age
- Trans-gender
- Belief
- Sexual orientation

Each one of the above personal identities confers **'protected characteristics'** and outlaws any related direct or indirect discrimination. The Equalities Act introduced a single overarching legal framework to replace the many separate equality laws passed in England over the last 40 years. The major laws subsumed by the Equalities Act were:

Ethnicity

- Race Relations Act 1976
- Crime and Disorder Act 1998
- Race Relations Amendments Act 2000
- Race Relations Amendment Regulations 2003

Gender

- The Equal Pay Act 1970
- The Sex Discrimination Act 1975
- The Gender Recognition Act 2004
- The Equality Act 2006

It should be noted that in the UK women first gained the right to vote in 1918 but then only for women aged over 30 and it was not until 1928 that women were granted the same right to vote as men i.e. 21+ The universal right to vote at age 18 for both men and women was introduced in 1969.

Disability
- The Disability Discrimination Act 1995
- The Disability Discrimination Amendment Regulations 2003

Religion
- The Employment Equality Religion or Belief Regulations 2003
- The Equality Act 2006
- The Racial and Religious Hatred Act

Sexual Orientation
- The Employment Equality Sexual Orientation Regulations 2003
- Equality Act 2007
- Civil Partnerships Act 2004
- The Criminal Justice Immigration Act 2008

Age
- Employment Equality Regulations 2006

Transgender
- Sex Discrimination Act 1975 Gender Reassignment Amendment
- Gender Recognition Act 2004

The Equalities Act is highly comprehensive and ranges from everyday practical rights like the right to breast-feed in public places, access to all public buildings for the disabled, to the more complex areas of employment rights and the outlawing of any evidence of discriminatory practice in private as well as public institutions. Belief also embraces the right not to believe and equally protects humanists and atheists from discrimination.

The Equality Strategy 2010

In December 2010 the Government responded to the passage of The Equalities Act by publishing an Equality Strategy to carry forward the provisions of the Act. The Strategy acknowledged that the significant issue was not the passage of the law but influencing and altering people's attitudes and perceptions to equality and diversity. The strategy document provided examples of some of the equality challenges facing Britain.[1]

Examples of equality challenges for the UK
Decades after equal pay laws were passed, women are paid over 12 per cent less than men across a range of sectors, increasing to 22 per cent when part-time workers are included The factors behind the gender pay gap are complex. Outdated expectations of women's jobs and family roles, occupational segregation and traditional approaches to job design, coupled with a lack of flexibility in our systems of maternity and paternity pay and difficulties in finding flexible childcare, all contribute.
Some ethnic groups have unemployment rates three times higher than white men.
Muslim men have the lowest employment rates compared with those of other major faiths or no faith.
Children who are perceived as 'different', such as disabled children, experience more bullying than others.
Over 70 homicides in England and Wales between 2007 and 2008, and 2009 and 2010 were charged as resulting from racially or religiously aggravated, transphobic or homophobic or disability-related hate crimes.
Despite disability discrimination legislation, around a third of disabled people experience difficulties in accessing goods or services, including health services. The employment rate of disabled people in Great Britain is far lower than the overall working-age population: 48.4 per cent compared to 72.2 per cent. Within that, some groups face even greater barriers to work, for example only 6.4 per cent of adults with learning disabilities who use social services are in work.
The chances for children in lower income families of being socially mobile are lower in the UK than most international counterparts. By the age of seven, children with a higher social class background, but low assessed ability, overtake those from a lower social class background with high ability.
People are living longer, but men and women in the highest socio-economic group can expect to live up to seven years longer than those in the lower socio-economic groups.
Although infant mortality rates are at their lowest ever, black Caribbean and Pakistani babies are twice as likely to die in their first year than Bangladeshi or white British babies.
Persistent inequalities exist for some groups. For example, under 10 per cent of Gypsy and Traveller pupils attain five GCSEs or equivalent at A*-C grades including English and maths compared with over 50 per cent for the average population.
Black Caribbean pupils are three times more likely to be permanently excluded than the school population as a whole.

Clearly although Britain has made significant changes over the past fifty years many people still experience discrimination, face limitations or simply have their life chances reduced because of what rather who they are.

Ofsted equality and diversity criteria

The provisions of the Equalities Act 2010 are reflected within Ofsted criteria for Schools and Further Education with the identification of possible 'at risk' groups.

> *"disabled pupils, as defined by the Equality Act 2010, and those who have special educational needs*
> - *Boys*
> - *Girls*
> - *groups of pupils whose prior attainment may be different from that of other groups -those who are academically more or less able*
>   *-pupils for whom English is an additional language*
>   *-minority ethnic pupils*
>   *-Gypsy, Roma and Traveller children*
>   *-looked after children*
>   *-pupils known to be eligible for free school meals*
>   *-lesbian, gay and bisexual pupils*
>   *-transgender pupils*
>   *-young carers*
>   *-pupils from low income backgrounds*
>   *-other vulnerable groups".* [2]

In all cases schools and colleges should monitor progress and provide additional support as necessary to ensure that each pupil / student reaches their full potential. The list of 'at risk' groups for Further Education is extended to include:

> *"older learners*
> *learners of different religions and beliefs*
> *ex-offenders*
> *women returners*
> *teenage mothers".*[3]

The focus of the Ofsted criteria for schools is on addressing individual needs, narrowing the achievement gap, supporting disabled pupils and combating bullying. In relation to the latter schools should be alert to a rise in online bullying via social network sites. Ofsted criteria for Schools emphasises the need to safeguard all pupils *"pupils' behaviour towards, and respect for, other young people and adults, including, for example, freedom from bullying and harassment that may include cyber-bullying and prejudice-based bullying related to special educational need, sexual orientation, sex, race, religion and belief, gender reassignment or disability".*[4] The significant drive is to boost achievement in relation to the 'narrowing the gap' national agenda, *"how well gaps are narrowing between the performance of different groups of pupils in the school and compared to all pupils nationally".*[5] Within Further Education the Ofsted criteria for equality and diversity is more extensive than the criteria specified for schools. The aspects common to both sectors are action on bullying and the 'narrowing the gap' agenda. However, it is notable that within the FE Inspectors' Handbook the criterion is worded as a firm expectation that improvements are being made, *"Achievement gaps are narrowing between different groups of learners".*[6] In addition to this Further Education teachers, unlike their school counterparts will be judged on how well, *"staff use materials and teaching methods that foster good relations and are sensitive to and promote equality of opportunity"* and similarly *"how well staff maximise opportunities in sessions and all learning contexts to promote equality of opportunity and awareness of cultural and linguistic diversity".*[7] This focus on the integration of effective equality and diversity measures within FE classroom practice is reflected in the grading criteria for 'Teaching, Learning and Assessment': [8]

Grade One – Outstanding

> *"Equality and diversity are integrated fully into the learning experience. Staff manage learners' behaviour skilfully; they show great awareness of equality and diversity in teaching sessions."*

Grade Two – Good

> *"Equality and diversity are promoted and learners' behaviour is managed well, although some work is still needed to fully integrate aspects of equality and diversity into learning".*

Grade Three – Requires improvement

"The promotion of equality and support for diversity in teaching and learning is satisfactory".

Grade Four – Inadequate

"Staff show insufficient understanding and insufficiently promote equality and diversity in teaching sessions."

The Grade Three criterion is perhaps not very illuminating and also contradicts the overall descriptor, 'requires improvement'. In the 2009-12 inspection framework Ofsted imposed a 'limiting grade' on equality and diversity within the Further Education sector to prompt greater and faster action to 'narrow the gap' and to ensure positive actions following the passage of the Equalities Act. The limiting grade was dropped from the 2012 inspection framework but Colleges need to be alert to the above criteria because weak practice will almost certainly deny the award of a Grade One for Teaching, Learning and Assessment' . This is significant because the award of 'outstanding' for Overall Effectiveness is dependent upon a Grade One judgment for Teaching, Learning and Assessment and so in essence a limiting grade is still in force. Finally, a further difference between the Schools and Further Education sectors is the significance placed on equality and diversity in the Leadership and Management grade, *"Leaders and managers actively promote equality and diversity, tackle bullying and discrimination, and narrow the achievement gap"*[9] This direction forms a significant judgment within the Leadership and Management criteria and note the focus on *'actively promote'*. The inspection focus is on 'active' equality and diversity initiatives rather than 'passive' compliance i.e. the possession of policy statements that meet statutory requirements. How far does your equality and diversity policy and/or strategies make a difference and how do you know? Also be aware that judgments on bullying and discrimination relate to staff as well as students and that there must be clear evidence of monitoring the progress of 'at risk' groups and evidence of intervention if targets are missed.

Core equality and diversity focus

Within schools and colleges there are three key factors which influence not only progress but also progression:

- Gender
- Ethnicity / Race
- Disability

The evidence that these factors influence achievement and life chances is very well documented and consequently all schools and colleges should have strategies to ensure that, as far as possible, all relevant pupils / students experience the support, encouragement and additional assistance needed for success in their study programmes.

Gender

At the last census held on 27th March 2011 the UK population was recorded as 63.1 million with 56.1 million living in England and Wales. In terms of gender the population of England and Wales is 28.5% million female and 27.6 million male. However, whereas the population is evenly balanced between male and female citizens their life chances are not. Consider the following data published by the Equality and Human Rights Commission for 2010-11 on the percentages of women across different aspects of public life and employment:

Where are the women?[10]

Members of Parliament 22%
Member of Cabinet 17%
Members of House of Lords 22%
Directors of FTSE 100 companies 12%
Local Authority chief Executives 23%
Senior ranks in the Armed Forces 1%
Senior Police Officers 17%
Senior Judges 13%
Civil Service senior managers 29%
Head Teachers Secondary Schools 35%
Principals FE Colleges 33%
Health Service Chief Executives 31%
Editors of national newspapers 9%
Directors of National Museums and Art Galleries 26%
Chief Executives of National sports bodies 25%

The issue for young women in the 21st Century is not qualifications but gaining promotion at work and rising through the 'glass ceiling' to the top positions across our major professions and industries. The issue for young men is academic underperformance and the need to improve their personal skills to compete for jobs in the Service Sector dominated 21st Century economy. The Industrial Age has gone and with it the many thousands of unskilled jobs that required brawn rather than brain power.

Stereotypical career choices

The impact of peer and media influences on young men and women results in stereotypical subject and career choices and this starts very early. Visit a toy shop like Toys-R-Us and notice how the Girls' aisle is dominated by toys linked to Babycare, Beauty, Fashion and Housework with all the toys largely presented in shades of garish pink. Visit the Boys' aisle (yes there are separate aisles) and note that the boys' toys are linked to Sports, Jobs, Warfare, Cars and Trucks. Even Lego kits conform to this gender bias with Lego's newest product the 'Friends' sets aimed at young girls and featuring five highly groomed female figures to place within a beauty shop, cafe, gymkhana setting etc. Simply buying a bicycle leads you to light-weight pink bikes for girls often with tassels projecting from the handlebars and for the boys chunky, heavy bikes all in dark greens and blacks. Since when was ironing an enjoyable pastime? It is notable that the girls are offered toy ironing boards to play with but not boys. Girls are offered all manner of soft cuddly toys to nurse whereas boys are offered Action Men figures, Wrestlers and Superheroes etc. Media images regularly reinforce that some jobs and activities are for girls and some are for boys via images in newspapers, magazines, TV adverts, drama and films. Next time you are watching a television programme observe the jobs held by the characters and reflect on the images e.g. who is doing the DIY, the ironing, repairing the car, cooking the dinner, changing a baby's nappy, etc. This gender bias flows into subject choices and ultimately creates a distorted employment market.

A-Level subject choices by gender summer 2011

Consider the A-Level subjects selected by young men and women

Summer 2011 as published by the Joint Council for Qualifications. The percentages given are all for female entries but clearly some arithmetic will give you the reverse.

Male majority	Towards neutral but majority all female	Female majority
Chemistry 47%	German 58.5%	Sociology 74.5%
Geography 46.4%	Critical Thinking 57.1%	Art & Design 73.4%
Politics 42.6%	Biology 56.6%	Psychology 72.9%
Design & Technology 42.2%	Classics 55.5%	Communication Studies 72%
Business Studies 40.7%	Media 54.1%	English 70.4%
Mathematics 40%	General Studies 52.8%	French 68.9%
Music 39.8%	History 51%	Religious Education 68.2%
ICT 39.1%		Drama 67%
Physical Education 34.8%		Spanish 66.9%
Economics 32.1%		Law 60.4%
Further Maths 31.2%		
Physics 20.8%		
Computing 7.5%		

Joint Council for Qualifications 2011 www.jcq.org.uk/national.results/alevels/

The boys lean towards maths, science, business and ICT/Computing whereas the girls lean more towards the Social Sciences, English, Arts and Languages. This gender bias feeds through to university degree courses.

Rank order of degree choices by gender

Top five female degree choices	Top five male degree choices
Medicine	Engineering
Veterinary Science	Computer Science
Education	Architecture
Languages	Mathematics
Social Studies	Physical Sciences

Source: Higher Education Statistics Agency (HESA) 2009

The same issue is perhaps more starkly revealed in the selection of apprenticeships.

Apprenticeships by percentage female 2008

Apprenticeship	% female apprentices
Electro-Technical	1
Engineering	3
Construction	1
Automotive	0
Retail	69
Business Administration	81
Health and Social Care	92
Childcare	97
Hairdressing	92

Source Trades Union Council (TUC) 2008

The end result of this educational journey is entry into the employment market and within the employment market all too often the occupations gained by women are low paid, part-time and with limited promotion prospects compared to male employment. This is illustrated by the following data from the Office for National Statistics for 2008 and refers to actual numbers in employment.

Category	Male employment	Female employment
Managers & Senior Officials	3,008,523	1,581,207
Professions	2,154,509	1,621,643
Associate Professional and Technical	2,123,110	2,178,908
Skilled Trades	2,971,519	249,641
Personal Services	397,260	2,034,793
Sales & Customer Services	745,543	1,482,032
Machine Operatives	1,830,471	253,012
Administrative & Secretarial	701,626	2,638,131

Source Office for National Statistics (ONS) 2008

Within the above data there are some glaring extremes e.g. 465,000 male Engineers as opposed to 35,000 female, 598,349 Production Managers as opposed to 49,868 female, 253,000 IT Managers as opposed to 61,478 female and in reverse 81,000 female Social Workers as opposed to 22,000 male, 471,000 female Nurses as opposed to 57,000 male and finally 454,000 female Cleaners as opposed to 152,000 male. What is the gender division of your subject or course programme? What are the destinations of your pupils / students? How do you promote careers for boys in Hairdressing and careers for girls in Construction or boys into Sociology and girls into Physics etc? How do you 'educate' parents and guardians about the career options? Do your leaflets, brochures, corridor and classrooms display appropriate case studies and photographs of relevant role models? When was your last gender equality initiative and how successful was it? Ofsted are not so much interested in your commitment to equality as your actions. Our goal is not 50/50 enrolment as a measure of success but simply ensuring that career opportunities are clearly advertised and open to both sexes to help counter the significant social and media stereotypes of male and female occupations. Every year The Financial Times publishes a list of the 100 most influential women in European Financial markets. The magazine 'Management Today' are into their 12th year of publishing the 35 most influential female managers under 35 to monitor and Forbes regularly refreshes its top ten list of the world's most influential women. Simple references to relevant male and female role models can make a significant difference to aspirations. Why not approach an appropriate local or national role model to give out prizes at your next awards evening? Are relevant biographies in your library, are passages quoted in your handouts and are there photographs and case-studies on your classroom walls? Women in general may also face discrimination in terms of their role in society. Some men hold the conservative view that men are the breadwinners and women are housekeepers and mothers. Within some ethnic groups this tendency is even more pronounced and the life chances of some young women may be severely restricted to the point of forced marriages. All schools and colleges should not shrink from questioning 'cultural' behaviours that conflict with the rights of the individual. Overall, young women need to be encouraged to be ambitious and to aim for the top and young men need to question sexist attitudes that denigrate women as the 'weaker' and/or 'glamorous' sex.

Academic progress

Women outperform men at every level from nursery school through to university Girls have an earlier disposition towards language and social development which confers a learning advantage throughout life. *"Findings from the longitudinal study, Effective Provision of Pre-School Education which followed a cohort from age 3 to 7, indicated there were significant gender differences in young children's intellectual and social behavioural development at entry to pre-school. Girls generally showed better social development than boys, especially in cooperation/ conformity and independence and concentration. Girls also showed higher attainment on all cognitive outcomes. Girls made greater gains in pre-reading, early number concepts and non-verbal reasoning than boys over the pre-school period. The researchers also found that the pre-school home learning environments differed for boys and girls. Significantly more girls' parents reported activities such as reading, teaching songs and nursery rhymes".*[59]

Female GCSE and A-Level students now routinely outperform their male peers:

GCSE Grades A*-C 2012

Female 73.3%
Male 65.4%

Within this data the award of A-A* is also dominated by young women with 26.5% gaining a Grade A or A* as opposed to 19.8% of their male classmates.

A-Level A*-B Grades 2012

Female 54.7%
Male 50.2%

When Grade A-A* at A-Level is isolated the percentages are 27% female and 25.8% male. Within BTEC vocational programmes in 2012 girls also outperformed boys. The results for BTEC Business Studies revealed 28% of girls achieved a Distinction compared to 17% of boys and in male dominated programmes like Construction 18% of girls achieved a Distinction compared to 7% of boys and in Engineering the percentages were 28% against 16%. This dominance is maintained at university level with 49.2% of women now progressing into university compared to 37.8% of men. In terms of achievement the Higher Education Policy Institute (HEPI) has reported that 63.9% of women gain an upper second or first class degree classification compared to 59.9% of men. The general consensus on male underachievement concludes that young men often adopt a more casual attitude to the quality and presentation of their work, exhibit poor time management skills and lack effective study and organisational skills in comparison to young women. In 2008 researchers from Roehampton and Birmingham universities concluded that boys operated to short term goals and rejected conformity to school rules in favour of the approval of their peers. Street Cred is not doing your homework. It is notable that 80% of children permanently excluded from schools are boys because of their higher tendency to question and to challenge rules and regulations. However, they also exhibit significant underachievement and therefore does the underachievement produce the challenge? Boys tend to be more immediate and perform best to short term goals rather than to future rewards and welcome active participation. There is some evidence to suggest that boys perform less well in extended coursework tasks than girls but will dominate in revision tests and multiple choice exams that directly test knowledge. How does your school or college respond to the challenge of engaging boys in learning? Are there clear behaviour rules and boundaries? Is there sufficient competition and challenge? Do you model the outcomes expected and show exemplars? Do you provide clear and precise instructions with deadlines? Do you build and develop relevant study and Functional Skills? Do you praise and reward effort? Do you demonstrate the point, purpose and applications of what is being studied to build motivation?

Ethnicity

The United Kingdom is a multicultural nation with the rise of a much more diverse population over the past fifty years following immigration from Commonwealth nations and after 1973 the European Union. We are all citizens of Europe and have the right of settlement and employment in any European country. The further expansion of the European Union in 2004 has altered traditional patterns of immigration with a notable surge in Polish immigrants in particular. The rank order of ethnicity in terms of relative sizes of populations is as follows:

White
Indian
Pakistani
Mixed heritage
Black Caribbean
Black African
Bangladeshi
Chinese

Data from the most recent census March 2011 has yet to be released but is unlikely to alter the rank order. Britain remains a predominantly white country (92%) despite the often emotive language used by some parts of the media. Each ethnic group reflects separate waves of immigration into the UK in response to advertised job vacancies. The first significant example of this was the arrival of S.S. Empire Windrush into Tilbury Docks, London on 21st June 1948. The Windrush carried 492 Jamaican immigrants drawn by adverts to help resolve Britain's post war labour shortages for bus and tube drivers in London. In subsequent years similar advertising across Asia attracted many immigrants to employment in the textile mills of Yorkshire and the North West and to manufacturing employment in the Midlands. More recently Eastern European workers have responded to adverts to fill labour shortages in the agricultural districts of the East of England. Within the White population the most significant immigrant group are the Irish also drawn by the many higher job opportunities in England. Lord Taylor of Warwick, the son of Jamaican immigrants and the first Black Conservative peer, entitled his memoirs, *No Blacks, no Irish and no Dogs'* in a reference to the common sign posted in the windows of guests houses in 1950s England. The punk rock star John Lydon aka Johnny Rotten of Irish heritage also selected the same title for his autobiography. The appeal and availability of different job opportunities has resulted in significant regional variations in the settlement patterns of ethnic minority groups. London has the highest ethnically diverse population followed by the West Midlands and the lowest regions are South West and North East.

Linguistic diversity

In terms of linguistic diversity in January 2008 815,450 school children or 12.5% of the school population did not speak English as their first language. Within Primary schools the average percentage is higher at 14.3%. This is a sharp rise from 10.5% in 2004 and reflects the arrival of Eastern European immigrants. For Secondary schools the average percentages are 10.6% and 9.5% respectively. Within England the borough with the highest number of pupils with English as an Additional Language (EAL) is Slough with 51.8% in the primary sector and 39.7% in the secondary sector. Within London the borough with the highest number of EAL pupils is Tower Hamlets with 76.9% in the Primary sector and 70.3% in the Secondary sector. Overall, some 240 languages are spoken in our schools with the most significant language groups as follows:

Language	Number of pupils	% of all pupils
Punjabi	102,570	1.6
Urdu	85,250	1.3
Bengali	70, 320	1.1
Gujarati	40,880	0.6
Somali	32,030	0.5
Polish	26,840	0.4
Arabic	25,800	0.4
Portuguese	15,560	0.3
Turkish	16,460	0.3
Tamil	15,460	0.2
French	15,310	0.2
Yoruba	13,920	0.2
Chinese	13,380	0.2
Spanish	10,000	0.2
Not specified	175,680	2.7

Source www.dcsf.gov.uk January 2008

What is the linguistic diversity within your school or college? How far is this diversity welcomed and reflected? What are the related support needs and how are they addressed? How do you ensure that all groups and individuals achieve their full potential? It used to be quite common to equate an inability to speak English with a lack of intelligence. Many very able and well educated adult or child immigrants often found themselves placed into low ability classes simply because they could not speak English. It was also common to withdraw pupils or students from most of their mainstream curriculum to receive additional English lessons. The outcome was a very slow acquisition of English because the students never heard English spoken in context and their academic development was also disrupted because they missed too many mainstream lessons. Waheed Safi arrived in the UK as a refugee from Afghanistan in 1995, speaking no English, but in summer 2008 he passed A-Levels in Physics, Chemistry, Maths and Further Maths, all at Grade A, at Uxbridge College and progressed to Oxford University to read Engineering Science. Photographs and case studies of Waheed and similar students on notice boards can raise high expectations? Dual language nations like Canada have aptly demonstrated that full immersion brings rapid results and variations of this are increasingly the policy in the UK i.e. classroom integration coupled with bilingual support rather than withdrawal.

Academic performance by ethnicity

There are significant differences between the academic performances of different ethnic groups. Chinese heritage pupils are the highest performing ethnic group in all subjects at all levels followed by Indian heritage pupils. In summer 2008 Howard Loh, aptly demonstrated the academic dominance of Chinese heritage students by gaining seven grade As at A-Level. This was matched by George Lee in summer 2011 with Grade As in French, Spanish, General Studies, Maths, Further Maths, Critical Thinking and Physics. In Summer 2012 the identical twins Jai and Krishan Patel passed five A-Levels each at grades A*-A and accepted places at London University and Cambridge respectively.

Percentage 5 GCSEs A*-C by ethnicity (including English and Maths) 2011

MINORITY ETHNIC	PERCENTAGE
Chinese	78.6
Indian	74.4
Bangladeshi	59.7
Dual heritage	58.5
White	58.2
Black African	57.9
Pakistani	52.6
Black Caribbean	48.6
Traveller / Roma	10.8%

www.education.gov.uk 2011

All of the groups have significantly improved their pass rates by an average of 14% since 2007. The most improved groups are

Bangladeshi and Dual heritage students who have both overtaken White students in the rank order. The dominance of Chinese and Indian heritage children is evident from as early as the end of Key Stage One when at age seven they outperform all other ethnic groups in the 3Rs Reading, Writing and Arithmetic. This dominant position is maintained the whole way through the school system to A-Level and beyond. A significant factor underpinning their success is high parental aspirations and homes that strongly promote effort and learning. However, poverty is also a significant factor and some ethnic groups endure higher than average rates of very low incomes or unemployment. In March 2008 Dr. Steven Strand of Warwick University published the outcomes of a longitudinal study into ethnic minority underachievement commissioned by the then Department for Children, Schools and Families (DCSF) and identified three general factors to explain underachievement, low aspirations by parent(s), negative attitudes to learning and insufficient independent learning and effort to complete homeworks. However Strand confirmed that poverty rather than ethnicity has the greatest impact on learning outcomes. Consequently when the above data is adjusted to measure the performance of pupils eligible for Free School Meals (FSM) White pupils drop to the bottom of the table just above Traveller / Roma heritage pupils. However, the latter numbers are too low for statistical reliability and likewise for 'Looked After' pupils who also significantly underachieve. However, a sharp reminder that individual effort and determination can negate background was provided in Summer 2012 by Shelby Holmes from a Traveller heritage background. Shelby gained a place at Oxford University following the award of Grade A*s in English Literature, Religious Studies and a Grade B in History despite a school attendance figure of 69%. Her mother had left school at age 10 and her father at age 14 and she studied while also running stalls within a travelling fairground. A further example from Summer 2012 of individual effort overriding disadvantage was provided by the identical twins Kirstie and Zoe Green of Thorne near Doncaster. The twins each gained Grade A*-As in English Literature, Religious Education and History and were accepted for places by Cambridge University –they were the first students from Doncaster to achieve places at Cambridge in 30 years. The scale of White underachievement was revealed in a statistical analysis undertaken by the Financial Times in 2011. [11] The data revealed that White pupils from low income homes dominated the lowest quintile in Secondary schools. This evidence of underachievement by White pupils was confirmed by a Department of Education Statistical Release February 2012, *"For White British boys eligible for FSM, 26.0 per cent achieved 5 or more A*-C grades at GCSE or equivalent including English and mathematics GCSEs, compared with the overall national level of 58.2 per cent – an attainment gap of 32.2 percentage points".* [12] In comparison the performance of Black Caribbean pupils (registered for FSM) does not dip as sharply in Secondary School and their average GCSE pass rate of 33.2% is 7.2% above their White peers. The Principal of West Nottinghamshire College, Asha Khemka OBE has launched an initiative to support White working class students because of her observation, *"significant numbers of white working-class young people don't really have a strong family infrastructure behind them. We find they are from three or four generations of worklessness and a poverty of aspiration. There are high levels of teenage pregnancy and low levels of progression to higher education".*[13] Khemka's conclusions reflect formal academic research and in particular the lack of a strong family infrastructure and low aspirations in many white working class homes. In contrast most Indian and Chinese heritage students enjoy extended family support which places a high value on education as a pathway to future success and personal fulfilment. Indian and Chinese homes typically promote educational achievement, reward good progress and often have family members who have attended university and can offer study support and guidance but most of all they raise an expectation of future progression to university or professional employment. Within other ethnic groups and especially White British those values are most often associated with Middle Class homes and most Working Class children do not receive the same level of push or emotional and academic support to work hard at school and to take a pride in academic success. This 'push' is however, fairly universal across Chinese and Indian communities regardless of poverty or wealth. Consequently schools and colleges should be alert to not only the 'at risk' factor associated within ethnicity but also to home backgrounds and should ensure that internal assessment and final examination data is analysed for underachievement by ethnicity and home backgrounds. What actions might you take to assist struggling students? In addition what does your progression data reveal and especially applications, as well as actual progression to university in terms of differential rates of progression? The underachievement by

Black Caribbean students within our schools raises particular concerns because their underachievement remains high not just within the data for low income households but across all income groups. In other words the generally observed correlation between higher prosperity and higher achievement does not appear to apply to the same extent within the Black Caribbean community. The achievement gain is marginal rather than significant. In addition, Black Caribbean pupils are over represented in school truancy and exclusion data. In considering the low performance of Black Caribbean children Strand highlighted concerns in relation to low expectations and a failure to settle at school. There are two significant issues, in relation to Black boys, which may help to explain their lower than average performance: absent fathers and racism.

Absent fathers

Some thirty years ago the dominant social debate in Britain was about the decline of the extended family and the rise of the nuclear family but today the debate has shifted to the decline of the nuclear family and rise of the single parent household. According to www.statistics.gov.uk Asian children are least likely to be raised in a single parent household (10%) but the percentage jumps to 22% for White households and to 48% for Black Caribbean.[14] In 2010 the Black M.P. David Lammy stated that 44% of Black African and a significant 59% of Black Caribbean children were being raised in single parent households.[15] Overall the number of single parent households has more than doubled since 1979 from 1.4 million to 3.2 million. In nine out of every ten cases the single parent is female and all too often the father plays little or no part in the child's life. Lammy himself was raised by his mother and he praised her hard work and sacrifices, after his father walked out and never returned home when he was aged 11. The lack of meaningful contact with a father is the issue rather than divorce or separation because this may be beneficial in terms of a more stable home. Care must also be taken not to demonise men because the lack of contact is often not the father's choice and organisations like 'Fathers for Justice' regularly campaign for greater access to their children following divorce. However, for adolescent boys, in particular, the absence of their father is often interpreted as rejection. The significant issue is the loss of a male role model to guide them through adolescence and in particular the many challenges and negative temptations encountered on our streets. In 2007 Tony Sewell the Chief Executive of the Charity, Generating Genius expressed his concern and emphasised the importance of the father/son relationship, " *the role of the father was one of guidance, giving his son love as well as discipline. He provided the safe guidelines which his son understood which kept aggression in check. Today in many parts of South London black children who have a father living at home are often the exception rather than the rule. The consequence is that too many young men find themselves looking for security not in the safe arms of Dad but in those of an older gang leader"*.[16] David Lammy has also expressed his concern that the lack of a male role model promotes low self-esteem and leads to a more rebellious and negative lifestyle, " *All the research tells us that children who grow up without strong relationships with their fathers are:*

more likely to get into trouble at school and to suffer from depression
more likely to smoke, drink and take drugs
more likely to go on to become parents themselves as teenagers
more likely to drop out of education and end up on benefits
more likely to go to break the law and end up in prison". [17]

Sewell and Lammy are not alone in raising concerns about the high percentage of absent Black fathers. Diane Abbot M.P., Trevor Philips Chair of the Equality and Human Rights Commission and David Cameron have all made similar remarks. Of greater significance Barack Obama robustly addressed the issue of absent Black fathers in a speech on Fathers' Day 16th March 2008, *"too many fathers are MIA, too many father are AWOL, missing from too many lives and too many homes. They have abandoned their responsibilities, acting like boys instead of men and the foundations of our families are weaker because of it"*.[18] It was view Obama had earlier expounded in his book, The Audacity of Hope. However, the issue of absent fathers is not simply a 'Black' issue because the trend is upwards across all ethnic groups with a third of households expected to be single parent households by 2015. This trend is significant because single parent households tend to be poor households. 72% of children raised in single parent homes experience significant poverty because the majority of single parents are not in employment. This is the real issue because poverty can significantly limit life chances. Colleges and Schools need to plan for additional support. Attention should be focussed on raising ambitions, holding high expectations, building self-esteem, issuing and upholding clear behaviour codes, resisting negative peer group influences, offering helpful 'how to' study guidance, highlighting male role models and offering advice to the parent on how to support their son or daughter to learn and offering access to a hardship fund as appropriate. However successful learning is a partnership and our students have to accept their responsibilities to learn and to make an effort to succeed. This was the theme of President Barack Obama' s address to the 100th anniversary celebration dinner of the National Association for the Advancement of Coloured People, 16th July 2009. Obama not only told parents to switch off the television and put away the X Box but urged all children to have greater ambition, *"your destiny is in your hands and don't you forget that. That's what we have to teach all of our children! No excuses. No excuses....I want them to be aspiring to be scientists, engineers, doctors and teachers and not just ballers [basket ball players] or rappers. I want them aspiring to be a Supreme Court justice. I want them aspiring to be President of the United States".* [19]

Racism

Direct racism is a significant blight for many ethnic groups with open abuse still common. Physical assault remains a regular and significant threat for many young Black and Asian people and at its most extreme murder. This danger was starkly illustrated by the murder of Stephen Lawrence, a Black Sixth Form student, in South London on 22nd April 1993. The subsequent failure of the police investigation to arrest and prosecute the prime suspects was the subject of an enquiry Chaired by Sir William McPherson in 1999. The McPherson report made 70 recommendations for improvement of how racist incidents are reported and investigated and in particular concluded that the police investigation was flawed and 'institutionally racist'. The murder of Stephen Lawrence was unfortunately not an isolated occurrence. Since Stephen's death there have been a further 71 racist murders with 39 Asian victims, 25 Black, 4 White British and 3 White East European. The casual and alarming nature of racism on our streets was starkly revealed by a Panorama documentary in October 2009 when two undercover Muslim reporters one man and one woman, posing as a married couple, were sent to live on a Bristol housing estate. Within an hour of moving-in stones were thrown at them and they endured aggressive racist abuse from young children as well as adults. The male reporter was punched, on his second day, by one of his new neighbours because he was a 'Paki' and invited to walk on the road because he might be run-over. Black and Asian people are regular victims of open hostility. However, whereas direct racism is visible and can be monitored and combated it is indirect or even unintentional racism that is harder to identify and overcome. Indirect racism is the gradual acceptance of stereotypes i.e. the development of a collective institutional or group opinion and culture that governs reactions and even instinctive responses. This issue was first identified as a major factor in promoting low expectations of ethnic minority children in the Swann Report, Education for All of 1985, *"A well-intentioned and apparently sympathetic person may, as a result of his education, experiences or environment, have negative, patronising or stereotyped views about ethnic minority groups which may subconsciously affect his attitude and behaviour towards members of those groups ... We see such attitudes and behaviour as a form of 'unintentional' racism"* [20] What is the stereotype of Black boys? Black boys are often linked with a 'challenging' macho rap culture which often celebrates gangs, gun culture and misogyny. Do we unconsciously absorb this stereotype and apply it to all Black boys? Darren Nelson a concierge and one of a group of ten adults invited by the Equality and Human Rights Commission to share their experiences commented, *"when people see a black guy wearing casual urban clothes, they think: 'that geezer must be in a gang, he's a bit of a hoodie'. I"d say these stereotypes have actually got worse because of the rise in drug use and gang violence: people are even more intimidated by groups of black guys hanging around now"*.[21] A further member of the group Pete Turner a musician commented, *"I know that when I walk into a room the first thing that someone's going to see is a black man. I'm a black Mancunian man, but before that I'm Pete, that's it"*. [22] Do we see the person and judge the person or does your mind unconsciously flick to a negative stereotype? In 2011 the Prime Minister David Cameron criticised Oxford University for its low level of Black students. The entry statistics revealed his concern. In October 2010 only 20 out of 2,617 British students enrolled by Oxford were Black a drop from 27 in 2009. In addition, a total of 21 Oxford Colleges made no offers to Black students. However, there is no doubt that the pool of eligible students is sharply in favour of White students. In 2009 29,000 White students achieved the Oxford entry benchmark of three Grade As at A-Level compared to 452 Black students. However, the percentage success rate of those Black students who do apply is still low in comparison to White applicants. In the case of Cambridge

University in 2010 11% of Black applicants were successful as against 27% for all applicants. How many positive images of Black boys or men have you seen in newspapers, billboards, TV adverts, films, books, plays, museums, libraries, TV programmes, music etc ? The next time you see an image of a Black person pause and look. Is the Black person in a professional or a manual job? Is he or she cast as the villain or the hero? Is he or she in prison or selling drugs or stealing a car? All too often the Black person is in a negative role rather than the role of the top politician, the Chief Executive of a company, the Senior Police Officer, the Surgeon, the Lawyer etc. Those Black people also exist. Visit the website www.100greatblackbritons.com and consider how many images of them appear on TV, in newspapers or in your textbooks, handouts, classroom and corridor displays as appropriate to your subject? The Oke quadruplets from Woolwich South-east London, Tolu, Tayo, Tobi and Tosin made press headlines in summer 2008 when they all successfully passed their A-Levels and all have since progressed to university including Cambridge. A simple case study with photographs on a notice board is very powerful. Look in the children's section of a good bookshop and count how many Black and Asian faces there are on the book covers as opposed to White faces? It is said that the inclusion of a Black president in the TV programme 24 paved the way for Americans to elect Barack Obama because it raised the concept and made it acceptable. This unintentional racism is often linked to research into the halo effect i.e. liking and approving of someone from a single positive impression. It is said that interview panels make up their mind in terms of instant like or dislike of a person within 3 seconds of their entry into the interview room. A positive halo is perhaps triggered by a confident walk, an engaging smile, a firm handshake, discovering the applicant also supports your football team, a witty remark etc. A universal positive halo attaches to attractive people and babies – they will receive our best smile and feel our personal warmth. Likewise our society awards a positive halo to tall men and the well dressed as opposed to short men and the poorly dressed. In relation to race how far do we attach a positive halo to White and a negative halo to Black? List as many words as you can associated with the word Black. How many are positive words? What are our positive and more importantly negative halos? Do we instinctively assign positives and negatives to the people we pass in the street? Do you think it is possible that our body language and level of eye contact might betray an unconscious negative or positive approval as a person walks past? Within our schools and colleges how far do ethnic minority groups feel a positive halo i.e. a sense of welcome, that they belong and at its simplest level that they are liked. Hattie provides an interesting anecdote, *"My colleague Russell Bishop moves around classes asking students, " Does your teacher like you?" and so many ethnic minority students (in New Zealand) say no but the white students say yes! When teachers are shown the results of surveys (including this question) they are often astonished-primarily because they assumed that the relations were positive..."*[23] A negative halo towards an individual or an ethnic group can translate into low expectations and placement into lower sets. If unchecked and unquestioned it is easy to slide into inadvertent institutional racism based on perceptions rather than performance. A significant clue that some ethnic minority students feel a lack of support is evidenced by the rise in attendances at Saturday 'supplementary schools' within ethnic communities across the UK run by community volunteers. There are estimated to be 5,000 'Saturday' schools or 'Learning Clubs' active in the UK ranging from a few students to hundreds in attendance and offering tuition in GCSE, and A-Level as well as more general learning assistance. Given that attendance is voluntary such schools clearly fulfil a need and perhaps the need is as simple as 'belonging.' Diane Abbot M.P commented on their recipe for success as follows, *" what all of these schools have in common are highly motivated black teachers, involved parents, strong discipline and boundaries and a celebration of the children's cultural identities".*[24] Rather than a paper charter of rights and entitlements perhaps our diversity strategies need to be active and visible – actions speak louder than words. Prior to the introduction of the Disability Discrimination Act it used to be common in our schools and colleges for someone to 'walk' the school or college with a wheelchair to test how far the buildings and facilities were accessible to a wheelchair user. Why not 'walk' your school or college but looking through the eyes of a Black or Asian student? What evidence of Black or Asian people do you see in leaflets, posters and displays in the foyer, corridors, classrooms, library, book choices, newspaper choices, periodical choices, canteen and seating areas? What sign of Black and Asian people are there in lesson handouts, textbooks, recommended websites, case studies and within Lesson Plans and Schemes of Work? How far are the interests, languages, customs, diet and festivals of different ethnic groups provided for and/or celebrated in your college or school? How did your School or College mark Black History month last year or Eid-ul-Fitr or Diwali or Chinese New Year or Holocaust memorial day etc? How far does the curriculum, social and sports opportunities, work placements, visiting speakers, trips out of college, admin staff, teaching staff, senior management and governors all reflect different ethnic groups? How far do your students identify with your school or college and feel a sense of community, shared values and ultimately enjoyment.

Religion

Religious faith is often intertwined with ethnicity and it is a fundamental part of personal identity. Britain is officially a religious country with the Church of England as the formal religion of the state. The term Christian is a very broad label and encompasses the major schism between Protestant and Catholic faiths and within the protestant faith many separate churches with variations of religious belief and practice. Britain, unlike many other countries, has never developed a secular constitution with a separation between state and religion. Our Head of State, the Queen, is also Defender of Faith i.e. the Protestant faith. This reflects our past history of religious conflict and the passage of the Act of Settlement 1701, which confirmed England as a Protestant nation and stated that the Monarch '*cannot be nor ever marry a Roman Catholic*'. Prince Charles is known to favour the title Defender of the Faiths to reflect multi-faith Britain and there has been some speculation of a repeal of the Act of Settlement which remains the law of the land.

Religious schools

As Britain is not a secular state religious schools are state funded. There are 7,000 state-maintained religious schools in England and Wales and the significant majority are Christian. There are for example only five Muslim state-funded schools despite the importance of religion within the Muslim community. There is a rising demand for more religious schools, particularly Muslim, and this raises a significant debate about the dangers of segregation. The experience of Northern Ireland is that segregated education coupled with segregated housing contributes (produces?) to community strife.

However to deny requests for more schools for ethnic minority groups would be discriminatory and the other alternative of withdrawing state funding from Christian schools is highly unlikely although possible. Schools and colleges have a major role in play in acknowledging that separate communities do exist and that outside of school or college pupils and students from different communities may have few opportunities to mix. Ideally we should seek partner schools and colleges as the basis for regular staff and student exchanges and joint activities, sports and celebrations. In general consider how far dress codes, food choices, holiday dates, festivals and celebrations etc reflect different religious observances. You may find dates for the key festivals for all major religions by visiting http://www.bbc.co.uk/religion/tools/calendar. This website also holds a wealth of information about each major faith group.

Learners with Learning Difficulties or Disabilities (LLDD).

Disability comes in many forms and may be present from birth or the result of an accident or debilitating medical condition. There are approximately ten million disabled people in the UK of which 6.8 million are of working age 16-65. In terms of school-age children there are an estimated 770,000 children under sixteen years coping with a disability. Disability is a significant barrier to employment and to gaining qualifications. In 1995 the Disability Discrimination Act (DDA) now a part of the Equalities Act 2010 placed a legal duty on employers and all public institutions including schools and colleges to outlaw discrimination and to ensure full access to services. Prior to the passage of the DDA it was often common for employment, educational and social opportunities to be routinely denied to the disabled because of actual or perceived barriers of access or support. Poor physical access to cinemas, theatres, sporting events, shops, pubs, restaurants, concerts, gardens, museums etc largely confined the disabled to their homes and turned them into second class citizens. The result is lower than average educational qualifications and lower rates of employment for disabled young people. 23% of the disabled have no qualifications compared to 9% for the general population. However, with appropriate support there are many success stories like David Holt who is wheelchair bound and coping with Cerebral Palsy but in summer 2011 achieved three Grade As at A-Level (Psychology, Law and English Language) and progressed to

Queen Mary University, London. Ofsted's 2012 criteria for Schools raises a requirement for close monitoring of progress , *"how well disabled pupils and those who have special educational needs have achieved since joining the school"*.[25] The measure of progress is firmly based against the entry skills and abilities as clarified by the following statement by Ofsted, *"while many pupils with special educational needs are not precluded from attaining as well as or better than their peers, for those groups of pupils whose cognitive ability is such that their attainment is unlikely ever to rise above 'low', the judgement on achievement should be based on an evaluation of the pupils' learning and progress relative to their starting points at particular ages and any assessment measures held by the school, but should not take account of their attainment compared to national benchmarks"*.[26] There are no similar direct references to the progress of Learners with Learning Difficulties or Disabilities (LLDD) within the Ofsted criteria for Further Education but they are a part of the 'all groups' criteria. Managers, however, are charged with responsibility for ensuring that the disabled have full and equal access and relevant support.

Numbers of disabled people within the working population 2008

	All 16-64 years	**16-24 years**	**25-34 years**	**35-49 years**	**50-64 years**
Number disabled	6,860,000	659,000	975,000	2,337,000	2,890,000

Learning difficulties

Autism is a significant learning difficulty that manifests itself as a restless inability to concentrate and an absence of normal social awareness. Some of the key symptoms are:

- fidgeting / restlessness
- difficulty in remaining seated
- easily distracted
- difficulty in sharing and taking turns
- often blurting out answers to questions
- difficulty in following instructions
- difficulty in concentrating on a task
- often moving from one incomplete activity to another
- often talking excessively

- often interrupting others
- often not seeming to listen
- often missing directions
- chronic procrastination

Autism is an umbrella term for a range of Autism Spectrum Disorders (ASD) including Attention Deficit Hyperactivity Disorder (ADHD) or simply Attention Deficit Disorder (ADD) and Asperger's Syndrome. The diagnosis of Autism is at an all-time high and may be linked to a genetic disorder which affects how the brain imprints and links information. Some form of Autism affects 166 children per 10,000 or basically 1% of the child population and 7% of the population as a whole. Autism is five times more common in boys than girls and is often accompanied by problems with oral and written communication. Students with Autism can significantly disrupt learning in the classroom because of restlessness and an inability to remember routines and instructions. The condition can be managed with appropriate drugs therapy and the attachment of a specialist support worker. It is often not appreciated that Autism is for life and that all students should have a transition plan for adult life. In general, consider how far your college or school has open access and appropriate support for learners with learning difficulties and / or disabilities.

Embedding equality and diversity checklist

The Ofsted report, 'Race Equality in Further Education' published in 2005 provided guidance and examples of effective actions to embed equality and diversity across the curriculum and wider provision. The key areas of specified good practice related to:

- data analysis
- initial assessment and support
- EAL / ESOL support and development
- celebration of diversity
- inclusive curriculum
- assessment monitoring and action
- tutorial support
- recording of racist incidents

The following checklist reflects the above aspects and the standards expressed in the Ofsted Inspectors' Handbook, the Equality and Human Rights Commission and the Lifelong Learning standards for teaching and learning. To score enter a tick for full agreement, a question mark for partial agreement or a cross for no agreement against each statement. Reflect on your answers and review your existing strategies and policies to ensure that, as far as possible, all students in your college or school receive your best support.

No.	score	Question
Personal actions		
1		Are you conscious of your own ethnicity and cultural identity and aware that what is a norm for you (or in your workplace or friendship group) may not be for someone else?
2		Do you avoid language, images, metaphors, similes and jokes that might give offence to a woman, a man, a Muslim, someone who is gay, disabled or does not drink alcohol, a Christian etc ?
3		Do you monitor the chat and comments of your students in the corridors and classrooms and correct any potentially or actual discriminatory language, gestures or behaviour?
Course promotion		
4		Do you have a range of student photographs from different backgrounds on any relevant pages of your College internet and Virtual Learning Environment (VLE)?
5		Do you have a range of photographs of students, case-studies and role models on any relevant publicity stands for careers events to challenge stereotypical career choices?
6		Do you have a range of images of students, case-studies and role models on any relevant publicity leaflets and across the prospectus to challenge stereotypical career choices?
7		If there are under-represented groups on your course have you discussed and undertaken an initiative to improve recruitment?
8		Are there sufficient staff in your teaching team from different backgrounds to reflect the college and wider population?
Planning		
9		Does your Self-Assessment Report present evidence of progress made in embedding equality and diversity and analysis of relevant data?

10			Does your Quality Improvement or Development Plan include smart targets for embedding equality and diversity?
11			Do you look at each major topic of your Scheme of Work and select case-studies, examples, illustrations, role models, visiting speakers, trips, materials, DVDs, websites that reflect different backgrounds, a diverse society and future employment in a global economy?
12			Do you provide your students with a copy of the Scheme of Work to encourage independent learning and with clear 'how to study' guidance?
13			Do you send a newsletter to parents or guardians each term with details of how they can help their son or daughter to achieve their potential plus dates of parents' evenings, trips etc.
14			Do you have parents' pages and relevant support and information for parents on your Virtual Learning Environment (VLE)?
15			Do you offer support for students from low income homes who may not have a computer, broadband access, textbooks or sufficient study space at home etc to successfully achieve?
16			Do you plan dates of examinations, coursework submissions, assessments, parents evenings, careers evenings, trips, visiting speakers etc around the dates of key festivals and faith events?
17			Do you check for the existence of good practice in equality and diversity in the relevant work place for any students going on a work placement?
18			When writing a lesson plan do you look at the topic through the eyes of a woman or man, a Sikh, a Muslim, a disabled person etc and consider whether there are any wider aspects of sensitivity or best practice to build student awareness ready for employment in a diverse society? If so do you add a relevant lesson objective?
19			Do you have a personal profile of each student that informs you of their personal identity and home background as a basis for differentiation, support and equality and diversity promotion?
Environment			
20			Are your classrooms, workshops, equipment, resources accessible by all?

21			Do your curriculum displays, role-models, case-studies, students' work, student prizes and success stories on your classroom and corridor walls reflect students from different backgrounds?
Lessons			
22			Do you start lessons with a regular starter activity that may reflect diverse backgrounds in terms of topic, individuals, places etc?
23			Do you express clear objectives or pose key questions that range across Bloom's taxonomy and may include relevant equality and diversity issues linked to the topic or future employment?
24			Do you select regular recap activities appropriate to the students and course level e.g. to stretch more able, to check for students underachieving, to offer support in pairs, to offer elements of competition to motivate, to build confidence and promote speaking?
25			Do you pose questions across Bloom's taxonomy from basic to challenging to stretch all students to their potential and ensure all participate?
26			Do you regularly employ random pairs and random group memberships to help students to bond and to guard against the appearance of sub-groups or isolated class members?
27			Do you select or prompt subject matter for group and paired tasks that reflects relevant equality and diversity issues or the students' cultural backgrounds and encourages consideration of a diverse society?
28			Are the images in your textbooks, handouts, worksheets, DVDs and Powerpoint slides across different backgrounds?
29			Do you make positive remarks and build rapport about different aspects of cultures, traditions and festivals so that all feel respected equally?
30			Do you praise linguistic diversity and the ability to speak more than one language?
31			Do you support English as an Additional Language (EAL) students and students from underachieving backgrounds who may all find the technical and specialist language in your lesson a barrier to progress?
32			Do you intervene and correct any inappropriate language and gestures or evidence of bullying or intolerance?

33			Do you express high expectations for all in terms of exams and future career options?
34			Do you provide boys especially with clear 'how to' guidance, deadlines, study skills assistance, organisational skills to improve coursework performance in particular? Do you encourage the ambition of girls?
35			Do you provide all with the support they need in Functional Skills to successfully match the course standards?
36			Do you regularly display students work on the VLE or wall displays and ensure overtime that all students receive recognition?
37			Do you regularly involve all students in the lesson in terms of participation in Q&A, presentations, research etc?
38			Do students who need additional support in the lesson receive it and do you jointly plan and set and monitor targets for the relevant students?
39			Are student opinion questionnaires on what the students enjoy and what would improve their lessons and/or course/college collated by ethnicity and gender?
Assessment			
40			Does your initial assessment identify entry skills, entry standards, career ambitions and set challenging but achievable targets for each student?
41			Do you review and discuss subject targets as expressed in each student's Individual Learning Plan?
42			Do you monitor internal assessment outcomes by gender and ethnicity and offer any additional support as required?
43			Do you monitor progress lesson by lesson and intervene with one to one or other support perhaps a 'study buddy' or support packages on the VLE etc to help overcome any blocks to progress?
Tutorial			
44			Does your tutorial programme build awareness of different cultures, faiths and traditions and address issues of abuse, discrimination and harassment?
45			Do activities build personal, spiritual, moral, social and cultural understanding?
46			Do all students receive one to one guidance and support and the opportunity to express difficulties and to receive appropriate support?
47			Do you monitor the students' take-up of enrichment and sports activities to

			encourage intermixing across the College and is there a sufficient range of activities across different interests?
48			Do those with a faith receive sufficient support in terms of resources and key dates in their calendar?
49			Are there regular competitions and prizes between tutorial groups and different courses to gain a wider mix of students?
50			Do you analyse 'non completers' by gender, ethnicity and disability over more than one year to check for any patterns and support issues?
51			Do you monitor discipline records and exclusions over more than one year by gender, ethnicity and disability to check for any patterns and support issues?
52			Do you log any racist incidents and take appropriate action?
Community			
53			Do you have links to any appropriate community groups and as a source of visiting speakers and/or mentors?
54			Do you have links to any appropriate employers and as a source of visiting speakers, placements, visits, mentors?
55			Do you have links to any appropriate charities and as a source of visiting speakers, mentors and visits?
56			Do you have links to any appropriate universities and as a source of visiting speakers, mentors and visits?
57			Do make contributions to your local community or the wider world community via links, fundraising, projects or special activities? With Skype there is no need to get the minibus out!
58			Do you or preferably your students mount displays in the public spaces of the college and/or library to celebrate key festivals and events?
Achievement / Progression			
59			Do you analyse achievement data by ethnicity, gender and disability and introduce initiatives to help any underperforming groups?
60			Do you analyse destination / progression data by ethnicity, gender and disability and introduce initiatives to help any underperforming groups?

It is a misnomer to regard effective equality and diversity as treating everyone the same yet this is a common response by many in our society i.e. *I treat everyone the same*. Life is unequal and we need to assist those who through no fault of their own face discrimination and/or significant barriers to achievement and progression. Consequently some groups do need our additional support and help to ensure equality of opportunity and ultimately to offer all, as far as possible, *Life, Liberty and the pursuit of Happiness.*

Assessment for Learning

"Using assessment for learning increased student engagement and doubled the speed of learning. Students learned in six months what they would have taken a year to learn in other classroom".[1]

Professor Dylan Wiliam, Deputy Director, Institute of Education, University of London

Assessment for Learning (AfL) rather than Assessment of Learning reflects an approach to teaching and learning than should be at the core of all lessons. In essence AfL is the effective development and application of formative assessment based on the observation that students learn best when they are participants in their own learning rather than passive recipients. The current focus on Assessment for Learning arose from the work of the Assessment Reform Group (AGR) formed in 1989 to spearhead research and development into effective assessment. The AGR commissioned an investigation into the impact of formative assessment in the classroom led by Professors Paul Black and Dylan Wiliam of King's College, University of London. In 1998, their publication, *'Inside the Black Box: raising standards through classroom assessment'*, synthesised evidence from 250 academic research projects on formative assessment. Black and Wiliam compared the effectiveness of each research project by allocating each one an 'effect size', *"The formative assessment experiments produce typical effect sizes of between 0.4 and 0.7 ....A gain of effect size 0.4 would improve performances of pupils in GCSE by between one and two grades. A gain of effect size 0.7, if realised in the recent international comparative studies in mathematics would raise England from the middle of the 41 countries involved to being one of the top 5".* [2] Black and Wiliam concluded, *"We know of no other way of raising standards for which such a strong prima facie case can be made on the basis of evidence of such large learning gains"*[3] The term Assessment for Learning (AfL) was coined to counter the widespread interpretation of assessment as a summative procedure i.e. a test or a piece of written work to be submitted, marked and graded. Whereas AfL is a formative procedure i.e. a developmental process of regular checks on learning in 'real time' to uncover and correct misunderstandings as they arise lesson by lesson. The Ofsted 2012 inspection framework for Further Education includes the criterion, *"how effectively learning is monitored during sessions, including where learners are receiving additional learning support"*.[4] The Grade One 'Outstanding' criteria for schools 2012 extends this further with not only regular checks on learning during lessons but evidence of effective interventions, *"Teachers systematically and effectively check pupils' understanding throughout lessons, anticipating where they may need to intervene and doing so with notable impact on the quality of learning"*.[5] What actions and interventions do you make in relation to formative assessment outcomes?

Assessment for Learning model

The Assessment for Learning model has significant implications for the role of the teacher and how students' progress is assessed. In relation to the former the switch is from lessons focussed on 'imparting information' to lessons that check how far students understand and can apply the information. In relation to the latter the switch is from offering grades and percentages to explaining how to improve. In the report 'Why Colleges Fail,' published in 2004, Ofsted noted, *"A common feature of a number of unsatisfactory lessons was the failure of teachers to make regular checks on students' learning and their determination to continue with the planned work even when the students clearly did not understand it"*.[6] Essentially effective teaching should produce learning. There is no gain in moving forward to the next topic if some or most students are still struggling with the current topic. The role of a teacher is not simply to impart information for students to record but to help all to understand and assimilate new learning. If teachers ignore evidence of misunderstandings and advance to the next topic the unspoken message to the students is; 'you should be able to understand this, at this pace and if you can't then this places a question mark over your ability'. Black and Wiliam highlighted the danger of demoralising students: *"Pupils who encounter difficulties and poor results are led to believe that they lack ability, and this belief leads them to attribute their difficulties to a defect in themselves about which they cannot do a great deal. So they 'retire hurt', avoid investing effort in learning which could only lead to disappointment, and try to build up their self-esteem in other ways. Whilst the high-achievers can do well in such a culture, the overall result is to enhance the frequency and the extent of under-achievement. The positive aspect is that such outcomes are not inevitable. What is needed is a culture of success backed by a belief that all can achieve".*[7] Students who struggle to make progress may quickly associate school or college with failure and in consequence adopt the survival strategy of either playing the class clown or lapsing into challenging behaviour and/or absenteeism. Ofsted commented on this link to poor behaviour in 2001, *"Often, they displayed a 'don't care' bravado in an attempt to mask their learning difficulties. Too often they were entirely preoccupied with their standing within the peer group and, rather than attempt to gain recognition through achievement, chose to seek it by other means".*[8] All students will find some aspect of new learning difficult and therefore teachers need to develop a learning culture that invites questions and helps all students to have the confidence to say, 'I don't understand...? Can you repeat…? I'm not sure how…? Learning should be deepened and consolidated by a range of learning activities designed to reveal and resolve misunderstandings as they arise. Black and Wiliam's research has also highlighted that the issue of marks and grades is of limited value because it simply informs a student whether their work is above average, average or below average. The more significant information for all three groups is guidance on how to improve. Professor John Hattie's analysis of major influences on learning (see Chapter One) identified formative feedback as one of the most effective strategies teachers could implement,*"the most powerful single moderator that enhances achievement is feedback. The simplest prescription for improving education must be "dollops of feedback" — providing information how and why the child understands and misunderstands, and what directions the student must take to improve"*. However, Hattie continued, *"The incidence of feedback in the typical classroom is very low, usually in seconds at best per day".*[9] This is the challenge of Assessment for Learning – how do we routinely build feedback and clear checks on learning into our lessons? In 1999 the ARG published an endorsement of Black and Wiliam's research in *Assessment for Learning, Beyond the Black Box* and highlighted five key Dos and Do Nots in relation to effective practice:

"The research indicates that improving learning through assessment depends on five, deceptively simple, key factors:

- *the provision of effective feedback to pupils;*
- *the active involvement of pupils in their own learning;*
- *adjusting teaching to take account of the results of assessment;*
- *a recognition of the profound influence assessment has on the motivation and self -esteem of pupils, both of which are crucial influences on learning;*
- *the need for pupils to be able to assess themselves and understand how to improve. At the same time, several inhibiting factors were identified. Among these are:*
- *a tendency for teachers to assess quantity of work and presentation rather than the quality of learning;*
- *greater attention given to marking and grading, much of it tending to lower the self-esteem of pupils, rather than to providing advice for improvement;*
- *a strong emphasis on comparing pupils with each other which demoralises the less successful learners;*
- *teachers' feedback to pupils often serves social and managerial purposes rather than helping them to learn more effectively;*
- *teachers not knowing enough about their pupils' learning needs".*[10]

The above points are a succinct summary of the key action points for effective Assessment for Learning practice and key areas of concern.

10 principles for Assessment for Learning

In 2002 the Qualifications Curriculum Agency (QCA) endorsed the above guidance and in association with the ARG published ten guiding principles to govern the development of Assessment for Learning across the school curriculum

1. Effective planning
A teacher's planning should provide opportunities for both learner and teacher to obtain and use information about progress towards learning goals. It also has to be flexible to respond to initial and emerging ideas and skills. Planning should include strategies to ensure that learners understand the goals they are pursuing and the criteria that will be applied in assessing their work. How learners will receive feedback, how they will take part in assessing their learning and how they will be helped to make further progress should also be planned.
2. How students learn
The focus of learning has to be in the minds of both learner and teacher when assessment is planned and when evidence is interpreted. Learners should become as aware of the 'how' of their learning as they are of the 'what'.

3. Central to classroom practice
Much of what teachers and learners do in classrooms can be described as assessment. That is, tasks and questions prompt learners to demonstrate their knowledge, understanding and skills. What learners say and do is then observed and interpreted , and judgements are made about how learning can be improved. These assessment processes are an essential part of everyday classroom practice and involve both teachers and learners in reflection, dialogue and decision making.
4. Key professional skills
Teachers require the professional knowledge and skills to: plan for assessment; observe learning; analyse and interpret evidence of learning; give feedback to learners and support learners in self -assessment. Teachers should be supported in developing these skills through initial and continuing professional development.
5. Sensitive and constructive
Teachers should be aware of the impact that comments, marks and grades can have on learners' confidence and enthusiasm and should be as constructive as possible in the feedback that they give. Comments that focus on the work rather than the person are more constructive for both learning and motivation.
6. Fosters motivation
Assessment that encourages learning fosters motivation by emphasising progress and achievement rather than failure. Comparison with others who have been more successful is unlikely to motivate learners. It can also lead to their withdrawing from the learning process in areas where they have been led to feel they are 'no good'. Motivation can be preserved and enhanced by assessment methods which protect the learner's autonomy, provide some choice and constructive feedback, and create opportunity for self-direction.
7. Promotes understanding of goals and criteria
For effective learning to take place learners need to understand what it is they are trying to achieve – and want to achieve it. Understanding and commitment follows when learners have some part in deciding goals and identifying criteria for assessing progress. Communicating assessment criteria involves discussing them with learners using terms that they can understand, providing examples of how the criteria can be met in practice and engaging learners in peer and self assessment.
8. Helps learners to know how to improve
Learners need information and guidance in order to plan the next steps in their learning. Teachers should: pinpoint the learner's strengths and advise on how to develop them; be clear and constructive about any weaknesses and how they might be addressed; provide opportunities for learners to improve upon their work.
9. Develops the capacity for self-improvement
Independent learners have the ability to seek out and gain new skills, new knowledge and new understandings. They are able to engage in self-reflection and to identify the next steps in their learning. Teachers should equip learners with the desire and the capacity to take charge of their learning through developing the skills of self-assessment.
10. Recognises all educational achievement
Assessment for learning should be used to enhance all learners' opportunities to learn in all areas of educational activity; it should enable all learners to achieve their best and to have their efforts recognised.

The QCA principles collectively placed an emphasis on learning i.e. what the students need to know and how well they know it. Hattie words it as follows, *"Where are you going?", "How are you going?" and "Where to next?".* [11] The Vision 2020 Report published in December 2006 and commissioned by the then Department for Education and skills (DFES) defined Assessment for Learning in similar terms.

Vision 2020 Assessment for Learning responsibilities	
Teacher	**Pupil/Student**
• Establish where pupils are in their learning • Clarify where pupils should go next – define learning goal • Help pupils to achieve the learning goal	• Understand the standards of performance expected of them • Pupils monitor the quality of their performance against that standard • Pupils understand what they need to do to improve their performance.

Vision 2020 made five key developmental recommendations to carry forward assessment for learning:

1. *"Engineering effective discussions and questions and tasks that elicit evidence of learning.*
2. *Providing feedback that moves learners forward*
3. *Clarifying and sharing learning intentions and criteria for success*
4. *Activating pupils as the owners of their own learning*
5. *Activating pupils as resources for one another".*[12]

The above five recommendations were firmly based on Wiliam's research and form the core of effective Assessment for Learning practice. After several pilot schemes a national Assessment for Learning strategy was launched 2008-11 by the then Department for Children, Schools and Families (DCSF). The strategy initially targeted Key Stages 2 and 3 with a budget of £150 million to embed Assessment for Learning into the nation's classrooms. One of the specified aims reflected Hattie's words and the Vision 2020 guidance *"every child knows how they are doing, and understands what they need to do to improve and how to get there. They get the support they need to be motivated, independent learners on an ambitious trajectory of improvement".*[13] The strategy involved the development of a new assessment tracking initiative entitled Assessing Pupil's Progress (APP). However, the QCA was dissolved in 2010 and following concern about the burden of additional recording the Department for Education invited schools to decide their own approach rather than developing and imposing a standard national scheme. The method of implementation was the issue rather than the benefits of Assessment for Learning.

Lifelong Learning Professional Standards

Within the Lifelong Learning Post 16 sector, professional standards were set by Lifelong Learning UK which is now an integral part of the Learning Skills Improvement Service (LSIS). The standards are specified within six separate domains and Domain E relates directly to Assessment for Learning as follows:

Lifelong Learning Professional Standards **Domain E Assessment for Learning**	
They are committed to: ES 1 Designing and using assessment as a tool for learning and progression. ES 2 Assessing the work of learners in a fair and equitable manner. ES 3 Learner involvement and shared responsibility in the assessment process. ES 4 Using feedback as a tool for learning and progression. ES 5 Working within the systems and quality requirements of the organisation in relation to assessment and monitoring of learner progress	
EK 1.1 Theories and principles of assessment and the application of different forms of assessment, including initial, formative and summative assessment in teaching and learning.	EP1.1 Use appropriate forms of assessment and evaluate their effectiveness in producing information useful to the teacher and the learner.
EK 1.2 Ways to devise, select, use and appraise assessment tools, including, where appropriate, those which exploit new and emerging technologies.	EP 1.2 Devise, select, use and appraise assessment tools, including where appropriate, those which exploit new and emerging technologies
EK 1.3 Ways to develop, establish and promote peer- and self-assessment.	EP 1.3 Develop, establish and promote peer- and self-assessment as a tool for learning and progression.
EK 2.1 Issues of equality and diversity in assessment.	EP 2.1 Apply appropriate methods of assessment fairly and effectively.
EK 2.2 Concepts of validity, reliability and sufficiency in assessment.	EP 2.2 Apply appropriate assessment methods to produce valid, reliable and sufficient evidence.
EK 2.3 The principles of assessment design in relation to own specialist area.	EP 2.3 Design appropriate assessment activities for own specialist area
EK 2.4 How to work as part of a team to establish equitable assessment processes.	EP 2.4 Collaborate with others, as appropriate, to promote equity and consistency in assessment processes.
EK 3.1 Ways to establish learner involvement in and personal responsibility for assessment of their learning.	EP 3.1 Ensure that learners understand, are involved and share in responsibility for assessment of their learning.
EK 3.2 Ways to ensure access to assessment within a learning programme.	EK 3.2 Ensure that access to assessment is appropriate to learner need.

EK 4.1 The role of feedback and questioning in assessment for learning.	EP 4.1 Use assessment information to promote learning through questioning and constructive feedback, and involve learners in feedback activities.
EK 4.2 The role of feedback in effective evaluation and improvement of own assessment skills.	EP 4.2 Use feedback to evaluate and improve own skills in assessment.
EK 5.1 The role of assessment and associated organisational procedures in relation to the quality cycle.	EP 5.1 Contribute to the organisation's quality cycle by producing accurate and standardised assessment information, and keeping appropriate records of assessment decisions and learners' progress.
EK 5.2 The assessment requirements of individual learning programmes and procedures for conducting and recording internal and/or external assessments.	EP 5.2 Conduct and record assessments which adhere to the particular requirements of individual learning programmes and, where appropriate, external bodies.
EK 5.3 The necessary/ appropriate assessment information to communicate to others who have a legitimate interest in learner achievement.	EP 5.3 Communicate relevant assessment information to those with a legitimate interest in learner achievement, as necessary/ appropriate.

The Lifelong Learning criteria amplify the original QCA ten principles of Assessment for Learning and in particular emphasise the importance of peer and self-assessment.

Ofsted inspection criteria

The 2012 inspection criteria for both Schools and Further Education promotes a major focus on effective assessment activity as the key to securing individual progress. The criteria for Further Education were introduced with the following statement *"A rigorous and informative assessment process is essential to successful learning, as is the support learners receive"*. Two key criteria govern judgements on assessment activity within Further Education;

> *"staff initially assess learners' starting points and monitor their progress, set challenging tasks, and build on and extend learning for all learners"*

> *"learners understand how to improve as a result of frequent, detailed and accurate feedback from staff following assessment of their learning".*[14]

The first relates to accurate and motivational target setting and the second to the quality of feedback and guidance on 'how to improve'. Both are significant concepts within Assessment for Learning good practice. The importance of target setting is detailed in greater depth in Chapter Two in relation to the development of effective Individual Learning Plans (ILP). The role of feedback in promoting learning, as detailed by Ofsted, relates not just to the quality of the feedback but to how far the students understand the feedback and how to improve their work.

"inspectors will evaluate:

- *the extent to which learners understand their progress towards their learning goals and what they need to do to improve,*
- *how well learning objectives are understood by learners and progress is recorded in feedback to learners,*
- *the feedback on learners' work, such as the accuracy and consistency of marking, and the correction of spelling, grammatical errors and inaccuracies,*
- *learners' understanding of what they have to do to improve their skills and knowledge, which is checked and reflected in subsequent tasks and activities.*[15]

Similar criteria are a feature of the inspection criteria for Schools with both progress and feedback the focus of inspections:

"the extent to which the pace and depth of learning are maximised as a result of teachers' monitoring of learning during lessons and any consequent actions in response to pupils' feedback"

"how well pupils understand how to improve their learning as a result of frequent, detailed and accurate feedback from teachers following assessment of their learning". [16]

The Ofsted Chief Inspector's Report published November 2011 commented on the poor implementation of Assessment for Learning as the primary reason why too many colleges failed to move beyond 'satisfactory', *"The poor assessment of students was at the heart of why many of these colleges had failed to improve. Students' progress was not closely monitored by their teachers, leading to declining achievement, and managers were typically too slow to spot these problems. Errors in initial assessments led to students taking unsuitable courses. Once on the courses, teachers' use of assessment was not sharp enough to ensure appropriate challenge and progress. Too often teachers neither identified nor responded to students' literacy needs".*[17] Ofsted's criteria and inspection judgements effectively state that effective teaching produces learning and this should be apparent by the end of an individual lesson as well as at the end of a whole course of study.

Core good practice

Despite robust research evidence underpinning the benefits of Assessment for Learning it has been disappointingly slow to take-off. It is fourteen years since the publication of *Inside the Black Box* and ten years since Professor's Hattie's research findings confirmed the significance of formative feedback. In 2008 Ofsted published an evaluation report on the impact of Assessment for Learning and discovered inconsistency and uncertainty among teaching staff in terms of implementation, *"In five of the schools, effective assessment for learning had contributed to pupils' outstanding achievement and transformed their learning. Where assessment for learning had had less impact, the teachers had not understood how the approaches were supposed to improve pupils' achievement. In particular, they used key aspects of assessment for learning, such as identifying and explaining objectives, questioning, reviewing pupils' progress and providing feedback without enough precision and skill. As a result, pupils did not understand enough about what they needed to do to improve and how they would achieve their targets. Teachers did not review learning effectively during lessons; opportunities for pupils to assess their own work or that of their peers were infrequent and not always effective".*[18] Clearly where Assessment for Learning was implemented successfully it raised achievement but in the majority of cases the core good practice was insufficiently embedded within classroom practice. The core good practice that teachers should focus upon was reinforced and elaborated by Dylan Wiliam at The North of England, Education conference held in the Royal Armouries, Leeds 4th-6th January 2012. Wiliam's listed five key drivers of Assessment for Learning:

> *"1. Clarifying, sharing and understanding learning intentions*
> *2. Engineering effective discussions, tasks and activities that elicit evidence of learning*
> *3. Providing feedback that moves learners forward*

4. *Activating students as learning resources for one another*
5. *Activating students as owners of their own learning"*

Wiliam is very generous with his conference materials and you may view and download his conference papers and Powerpoint presentations from his website www.dylanwiliam.net. In essence the five underpinning concepts may be summarised as clarity, questioning, feedback, peer-support and meta-cognition. Let's consider each one in turn in terms of strategies and application.

Clarifying, sharing and understanding learning intentions

Lessons can go wrong at the very start because teachers feel obliged to deliver the lesson objectives in 'teacher speak' i.e. '*by the end of the lesson you will be able to...*' followed by some precise objectives. Clearly all teachers should be able to write clear behavioural objectives and to plan their lessons to achieve them but reading a list of objectives to the class tends to have limited impact. Chapter Seven discusses the importance of 'big picture' lesson introductions whereby the learning intentions are made explicit but in a way that students can grasp and understand. Paraphrase and seek to motivate your students with an overview of why they should enjoy the lesson and what you expect them all to learn. Translate your formal objectives into a series of key questions that they should be able to answer with some suggestions for stretch and challenge. Build the learning partnership and a learning dialogue by asking what they know about the topic already and by establishing what they do not know. Hattie's research indicates that students in general, *"already knew at least 40 percent of what the teachers intended them to learn"*.[19] As the lesson unfolds confirm the basic facts or concrete information that all should grasp and the higher levels of information application, analysis and evaluation to work towards. Ensure the level of challenge matches the course level by reference to the relevant examination board marking criteria for pass, merit and distinction or grade E compared to grade A (and now A*) at A-Level and share the criteria with the students. Provide examples of exemplar assignments or answers and pass level standards to illustrate the gap and aim to teach to the gap. Ensure key vocabulary that may be common to you is discussed and confirmed with the students e.g. analyse, evaluate, describe and indicate lower and higher order reasoning skills. Hattie expressed it as follows, "*teachers need to know the learning intentions and success criteria of their lessons, know how well they are attaining these criteria for all students and know where to go to next in light of the gap between students current knowledge and understanding...*"[20] In terms of setting assignments or homework ensure that all members of the relevant subject team agree the success criteria so that there is consistency of guidance and marking. Share the marking criteria with the students so that they appreciate how marks will be won or lost. Ofsted has highlighted that the absence of standard assessment criteria is a common problem in some failing schools as follows, "*Marking was an aspect of teaching where what pupils needed and what they received diverged starkly. In all the schools inspected, without exception, the marking of pupils' work varied between extremes in quantity, promptness, regularity and helpfulness. In most of the schools, there was excessive variation of practice even within the same subject department. There was insufficient scrutiny of practice and debate about this in the school. Often, helpful whole-school policies existed but they rarely informed departmental practice to the extent that pupils could see a common pattern to the way their work was marked. For example, pupils were at times given marks or grades, according to criteria of which they were made aware, in one subject but not in another; or one teacher wrote clear, constructive comments which told pupils how to improve their work, while others merely ticked. Pupils received prompt feedback from some teachers but their work went unseen, or at least unacknowledged, by another for a long time*".[21] It is not unusual to find that within a course team staff mark to different standards or methods. Some might mark out of 20, some might issue a percentage while others might issue a grade. In addition, some might issue no marks or grades at all (this is recommended Assessment for Learning practice) and write improvement points only. Some might correct spellings and grammar and perhaps deduct marks whereas others might ignore mistakes. If assessment is to be effective then a consistent standard needs to be agreed and *shared with the students.* In practice each assignment should be accompanied by marking criteria. Otherwise students may gain the impression that no standard exists beyond the whim of the individual teacher. Consequently the best practice is for the whole staff team to maintain common standards including a commitment to the building and correction of Functional Skills as expressed in the Further Education Ofsted Inspectors' Handbook 2012, "*the feedback on learners' work, such as the accuracy and consistency of marking, and the correction of spelling, grammatical errors and inaccuracies".*[22] This criterion re-butts the oft repeated myth that teachers should not correct spellings and grammar etc. Sensitivity is important to avoid demoralising a student (so don't circle every mistake) but at the same time most students are unaware of their mistakes and they cannot improve until their mistakes are highlighted. Simple misspellings on job or university application forms are sufficient to convey a negative impression of the applicant regardless of exam success. All teachers are first and foremost teachers of English and wider Functional Skills. The clarity and sharing of learning intentions and related marking criteria will advance learning more rapidly because the students will have clear standards to work against and of greater significance they can start to self-mark and identify their own areas for improvement.

Engineering effective discussions, tasks and activities that elicit evidence of learning

It is through discussion and answering questions that learning takes place. Students, in any lesson, will lose concentration and will regularly fall into 'micro sleeps' as they tune in and tune out as the lesson unfolds. It should never be assumed that in a class of twenty students all twenty have absorbed every aspect of a presentation and simultaneously understood each learning point. Even if all were fully alert and concentrating for all of the time there will always be some who were puzzled by some or even all of an explanation or demonstration but do not feel confident enough to voice their uncertainty. Consequently when teachers ask the classic question, 'do you all understand?' few if any students volunteer otherwise. Some students may also think that they *do* understand but in actual fact they have misheard or misunderstood the explanation or demonstration. Teachers must draw their students into a learning dialogue and raise the expectation that they should expect to have questions and uncertainties because they are engaged in new learning. Why should they know it? It is important to establish an *'it's OK to be wrong'* culture because the students are grappling with unfamiliar concepts or procedures. An effective teacher will regularly scan body language for signs of uncertainty and will pause to take questions and to ask questions to check learning and build discussion. Asking questions and using different forms of questions to encourage discussion is a significant skill and this is explored in

Chapter Eight. However, one key point to absorb is that research evidence presented by Black and Wiliam indicates that most teachers offer insufficient thinking time for students to answer questions. The mean time in a research study between teachers asking a question and then intervening to prompt an answer was only 0.9 seconds! Imagine you've asked a question and now time 10 seconds on your watch. It seems like forever doesn't it? Yet that is only 10 seconds. Do you have the nerve to wait 10 seconds or more for someone to answer your question? Researchers at Stanford university recommend a 'wait time' of 4-5 seconds for a factual response and 8-10 seconds for a more demanding conceptual answer. Teachers do not like silences but forget that students need more thinking time to absorb the question and to consider their answer. One teacher in the study noted, *"increasing waiting time after asking questions proved difficult to start with due to my habitual desire to add something almost immediately after asking the original question. The pause after asking the question was sometimes painful"*.[23] When teachers waited and gave more thinking time the following benefits were observed:

- *"Answers were longer*
- *Failure to respond deceased*
- *Responses were more confident*
- *Pupils challenged and added to or improved the answers given by other pupils*
- *More alternative explanations or requests for clarification were made"*.[24]

Provoke discussion with the greater use of open questions, longer thinking time and paired dialogues to help students express and share possible answers to key questions with a partner. Invite their opinions. Raise a 'culture' that their opinion or view is wholly valid if they can defend it. Draw into a dialogue using the Socratic techniques discussed in Chapter Eight and help the students to explore their own thinking and to arrive at conclusions. The overall gain is full engagement rather than a few more able students dominating the answers. To avoid a few able students dominating Q&A apply a 'no hands' policy whereby the teacher selects who will answer and in doing so can apply differentiation by seeking factual responses from some students and more evaluative extended answers from more knowledgeable students. In essence students will advance rapidly when teachers build and extend discussion in the classroom to check learning and to respond in **'real time'** to correct any misunderstandings or uncertainties.

Providing feedback that moves learners forward

The traditional approach to feedback used to be the classic red pen underlining of errors, with a percentage mark and perhaps a vague summary comment along the lines of, 'could do better'. The problem was how do you do better? One of the key principles of Assessment for Learning is not to give any marks or grades and especially not in the early weeks of a new course. It is recommended that marks and grades are reserved for summative assessment because otherwise students focus on the grade or mark and ignore the improvement guidance. This concept is not new. The Board of Education Handbook for Teachers, first published in 1904, provides the following guidance,*"the essential point, however, is that the child should understand what is wrong and know how to correct it. This can never be secured if the teacher's revision goes no further than merely marking every mistake, without regard to its relative importance, and handing the exercise back to the child without comment."*[25] All students on a new course will need time to absorb the standard of working and to make the transition perhaps from GCSE into higher level courses or even a repeat of the same level. Many students may have underachieved at GCSE and formed low opinions of their ability and a low mark will compound this and perhaps de-motivate and reinforce a sense of failure. Providing each student with how to improve guidance provides a clear action agenda to follow. Whereas presenting a student with a succession of marks at a bare pass level reinforces negatives with no way forward. Black notes that during trials of Assessment for Learning techniques one pupil awarded 4 out of 10 asked the teacher, *"how is that going to help me get better?"*[26] Low marks with no improvement guidance may generate frustration and the frustration may in turn cause students to give up, *"The worst scenario is one in which some pupils get low marks this time, they got low marks last time, they expect to get low marks next time, and this is accepted as part of a shared belief between them and their teacher that they are just not clever enough. Feedback has been shown to improve learning where it gives each pupils specific guidance on strengths and weaknesses, preferably without any overall marks"*.[27] Providing *'ways to improve'* guidance opens up a positive dialogue and a focus on the aspects students find difficult. The dialogue can reveal that others share the same difficulty. This is an important realisation because it gives students the confidence to speak-up and to seek improvement guidance. Hattie emphasized that teachers should establish, *"an environment where error is welcomed and fostered – because we learn so much from errors..."*[28] Ofsted's 2012 inspection framework for Further Education clearly endorses the importance of effective feedback and it is worth repeating the significant criteria, *"the extent to which learners understand their progress towards their learning goals and what they need to do to improve"* and *"learners' understanding of what they have to do to improve their skills and knowledge, which is checked and reflected in subsequent tasks and activities"*.[29] Likewise within the Schools' sector Ofsted specifies, *"how well pupils understand how to improve their learning as a result of frequent, detailed and accurate feedback from teachers following assessment of their learning"*.[30] Clearly there is an expectation that effective feedback is embedded as standard everyday practice rather than exceptional 'outstanding' practice. The Sutton Trust which regularly conducts and reviews educational research published *'The Teaching and Learning Toolkit'* in July 2012 and firmly recommended 'feedback' as a 'very high impact for low cost' strategy. Their review of the benefits of feedback stated, *"Providing effective feedback is challenging. Research suggests that it should:*

- *be specific, accurate and clear (e.g. "It was good because you..." rather than just "correct").*
- *compare what a learner is doing right now with what they have done wrong before (e.g. "I can see you were focused on improving X as it is much better than last time's Y...").*
- *encourage and support further effort (getting a balance between support and challenge).*
- *be given sparingly so that it is meaningful as too much feedback can stop learners working out what they need to do for themselves.*
- *be about what is right more often than about what is wrong (e.g. "This section is excellent because..." or "I thought this was the best way because...").*

Wider research suggests the feedback should be about complex or challenging tasks or goals as this is likely to emphasise the importance of effort and perseverance as well as be more valued by the pupils. Feedback can come from other peers as well as adults". [31]

There is an emphasis here on 'effort' i.e. students are given improvement steps to implement but there must be encouragement and checking to ensure that the effort has been made. The well know author and educationalist Geoff Petty promotes 'medal and mission' i.e. providing the student with two or three things that were well done (medal) and making two or three points for improvement (mission). Another common strategy for pre-entry and entry level courses is to standardise on '*two stars and a wish*' so that the students, and especially less able students, have only one key improvement point to act upon. You might also consider *hot and cold marking*. Here you mark a student's work by using a red highlighter pen (hot) on particular words or passages or sections that impress and blue (cold) on parts that could be improved. This reverses the normal association of red with errors. Clearly you need to be cautious with the ratio of red to blue or you will achieve the reverse of what you intend. Highlight in blue only one or two selected aspects of improvement to focus upon and seek a commitment to act on the improvement suggestions. One strategy is to use the 'carry forward' technique whereby the students list the improvement guidance at the top of their next piece of work and hopefully demonstrate that they have applied the guidance. To be effective the improvement guidance needs to be worded in precise steps rather than vague prescriptions so that the student is in no doubt of the actions to improve. Pro-formas can be designed to capture the feedback. Consider a Personal Action Steps for Success (PASS) pro-forma as a method of addressing positive feedback.

PASS – Personal Action Steps to Success

To strengthen action on feedback consider branding your improvement guidance under the **PASS** banner:

Personal
Action
Steps to
Success.

Reproduce the pro-forma on A4 card and invite your students to make it the first page in their ringbinders.

PASS **Personal Action Steps to Success**			
Date	Action	Completed	Initials

Use the Pass pro-forma to drive learning and effort by your students by specifying regular actions to follow-up or consolidate aspects of new learning. A teacher may specify a 'Pass' action for the class as a whole during or at the ends of lessons or for an individual in response to an observed learning difficulty or question. It can also promote differentiation because the actions suggested for a high achieving student will be to stretch and challenge whereas for a low achieving student to ensure that they meet the minimum course standard. This 'real-time' focus on learning during lessons is very powerful because ultimately students who ignore the Pass actions will have to acknowledge that they have not helped themselves to learn. We immediately counter the *'I'm no good at...'* argument because we have evidence that improvement steps have not been enacted. Avoid specifying bland generic actions in favour of concrete achievable steps for improvement. As far as possible invite the student to think through what the best action steps might be and to articulate what they are finding difficult. The act of being listened to is empowering and prompting a student to nominate their own improvement actions will have even greater impact. Some of the actions might encourage peer support by inviting the student to look at how ? laid out or completed the task. In each case it is about stretching each student to achieve his or her full potential with appropriately demanding actions. If wished the Pass concept can also be applied to a single assignment with the marking criteria on one side and on the reverse space for self-assessment against the criteria, space for teacher comments and an agreed future Pass action(s) list. Finally the Pass action list (completed for each assignment) should be stapled, by the student, to the next homework or assignment to demonstrate that the actions have been addressed. Overtime by pursuing this technique we refine and further refine the performance of each student towards mastery and higher than expected learning outcomes.

Activating students as learning resources for one another

Learning from one another is very powerful. Black and Wiliam's research indicates, *"students often accept from one another, criticisms of their work that they would not take seriously if made by their teacher"*[32] and in observed peer discussions, *"when students received help from each other they asked for repeated explanations until they had understood"*.[33] More recently, in July 2012, The Sutton Trust has confirmed peer tutoring as a *'high impact for low cost'* strategy and describes the strategy as, *"A range of approaches in which learners work in pairs or small groups to provide each other with explicit teaching support. In cross-age tutoring an older learner takes the tutoring role and is paired with a younger tutee or tutees" ... In Reciprocal Peer Tutoring, learners alternate between the role of tutor and tutee. The common characteristic is that learners take on responsibility for aspects of teaching and for evaluating their success"*.[34] Sometimes the social embarrassment of asking the teacher for further help or for the student to admit that they have not understood the teacher's explanation hinders progress. Most of us during our schooldays will have asked older siblings, parents or friends for help with homework when we were stuck. Girls in particular will often engage in co-operative learning whereas boys tend to be more solitary in their approach to study. Assessment for Learning seeks to build co-operative learning as a regular part of the classroom in the hope that it will spill outside of the classroom but in particular because it will deepen learning. If we regularly place students in pairs and groups (ensure a high achieving student in each group) to discuss and compare what they know and understand and to enter into reciprocal teaching it will deepen and confirm their own learning. The low achieving students will gain a new perspective and perhaps an explanation in words or examples they can grasp and the high achievers, will consolidate their understanding. Black and Wiliam noted, *"by articulating one's understanding high attainers are forced to make richer and more profound links to their existing knowledge, thus strengthening long term retention"*.[35] Equally some learning misunderstandings on both sides of the discussion might be revealed and corrected because the students feel more confident to raise questions about something others are expressing uncertainty about. A key strategy is to introduce regular peer assessment whereby students swap scripts and provide feedback to each other against standard assessment criteria. Equally we can provide opportunities for peer sharing and teaching by 'jigsaw' group tasks, 'hotseat' question and answer sessions, class presentations, online forums, swapping study tips, presenting useful resources etc. Essentially we establish that students can and should learn from one another rather than the teacher being the source of all information and learning. Hattie highlighted this issue with the observation, *"teachers enter classrooms and see students as recipients rather than producers of teaching and learning"*.[36] Teaching and learning is a partnership and we must take care to build independence rather than dependence. Many active learning techniques of this type are presented in Chapters Eight, Nine and Ten.

Activating students as owners of their own learning

Professor Tim Brighouse the former Chief Education Advisor to London Schools endorsed the importance of formative assessment and ipsative or self-assessment techniques,*"practising formative and ipsative assessment – that is measuring the pupils' understanding of the next step in their own learning and ensuring they act on it while trying to improve on their own previous best"*. [37] The aim is to raise self-awareness of personal progress (often referred to as 'meta-cognition') and the setting of targets and raising the concept of personal best. Hattie has identified 'self-reported grades 'as holding the highest rank in his overall rank order of 138 key influences on learning, *"students were very knowledgeable about their chances of success"* but he also raised the associated danger, *"they may only perform to whatever expectations they already have of their ability"*.[38] It is highly important to challenge ideas of fixed ability and to constantly remind students that ability is not fixed but a product of effort. The significance of effort was identified in 1991 by research undertaken by Anders K Ericsson, Professor of Psychology at Florida State University. Ericsson studied the success factors underpinning world class expertise across most fields of academic, musical, artistic, and sporting success and looked for a common factor and found it. The answer was 10,000 hours. The world class experts in our midst were not born with a higher brain function or a physical advantage but rather devoted a minimum of 10,000 hours of effort to practice, develop and refine their skills or knowledge. As the notable Spanish Violinist Pablo de Sarasate (1844-1908) stated, *'For thirty-seven years I've practiced fourteen hours a day, and now they call me a genius'*. [39]

A taxonomy of assessment

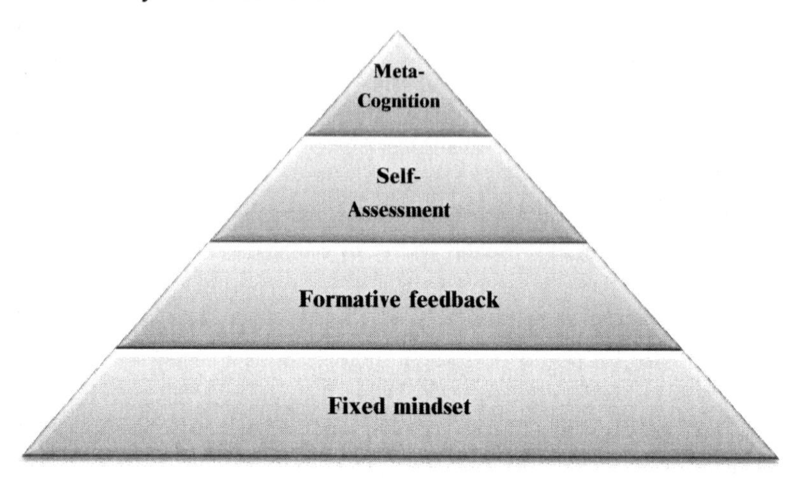

Lev Vygotsky (1896-1934) was a psychologist in the Moscow Institute of Psychology during the late 1920s. Vygotsky postulated the theory of the Zone of Proximal Development (ZPD) which essentially addressed the fundamental difference between *'can do'* and *'can't do'*. In other words self-belief. Vygotsky articulated that the inner voice of *'can't do'* was a significant barrier to learning especially when students expressed opinions like, *'I'm no good at maths, I can't do maths'*. Vygotsky addressed this fundamental issue of self-belief by offering the positive proposition of *'can do'* and *'can do with help'*. It is a simple construct but one that if applied can empower students to accept that their ability is not fixed but moveable with help. This reasoning was significantly extended by the work of Professor Carol Dweck of Stanford University in 1987 with controlled experiments in relation to effort and intelligence. Dweck identified the tendency of many students to ascribe their low progress in a given subject to an innate inability to understand maths or science or English etc. rather than a measure of time and effort applied. Dweck defined two predominant attitudes in relation to achievement, *Fixed IQ* and *Untapped potential*. Those who fall into the 'Fixed IQ' mindset believe that it is all in the genes i.e. a fixed ability whereas those with an 'Untapped potential' or a 'growth mindset' are open to the idea of seeking support and applying effort to succeed. Dweck recommended that teachers praise effort and the time invested rather than ability or intelligence i.e. not so much 'oh you are really clever' but rather, 'you must have worked really hard on this'. Dweck's guidance was confirmed by the most recent PISA international study of student achievement. In 2011 PISA tracked the most successful students from disadvantaged backgrounds in relation to successful progress in science lessons and observed that the common characteristic was 'resilience'. The successful students maintained higher rates of attendance and *"the more self-confident students are, the greater their odds of being resilient….Some 75% of resilient students believed they can give good answers to test questions..."* [40] The most recent research published by the University of Edinburgh in August 2011 identified over 600,000 aspects of gene activity that contribute to cognitive ability. The study by Professor Ian Dreary concluded that genes account for 50% of our cognitive ability and nurture 50%. The evidence points to a common cognitive threshold or capacity to learn which subsequent environmental influences can either expand or degrade. The conclusion that IQ may not be fixed is also strengthened by the so called Flynn effect named after Professor James Flynn of Otago University, New Zealand. Flynn charted evidence of a steady rise in IQ levels over the last century. The evidence came to light because IQ tests are norm referenced and Flynn observed that the companies involved were resetting the norm level for each generation to give consistent variables. In theory each generation was becoming more intelligent and this gave rise to two propositions: either selective breeding of the human population or improvements in learning. The generational difference is around 15 points and it is speculated that the greater exposure of children to television, radio, advertising, books, games, computers, quizzes and perhaps greater familiarity with the style of tests is steadily increasing cognitive ability and this higher cognitive ability is inherited generation by generation. In other words we are all, on average, more able than our forefathers. IQ is essentially a broad rather than a precise indicator of ability and it is opportunity, motivation and self-belief that can make the difference. Essentially our schools and colleges should be 'opportunity rich' to stretch and develop thinking and personal experiences beyond any limitations of home or community. In particular schools and colleges have to 'sell' that achieving exam success is not about being 'clever' but about effort. Hattie's research states in relation to motivation, *"the notion that increasing achievement is a function of our efforts and interest is critical to our success"*. [41] President Obama in speaking to American school children 8th September 2009 also directly urged American children to apply effort to succeed, *"At the end of the day, we can have the most dedicated teachers, the most supportive parents, and the best schools in the world – and none of it will matter unless all of you fulfil your responsibilities. Unless you show up to those schools; pay attention to those teachers; listen to your parents, grandparents and other adults; and put in the hard work it takes to succeed. And that's what I want to focus on today: the responsibility each of you has for your education. I want to start with the responsibility you have to yourself. Every single one of you has something you're good at. Every single one of you has something to offer. And you have a responsibility to yourself to discover what that is."*[42]

The assessment pyramid offers a summary of the stepping stones of personal advancement. Firstly all teachers need to challenge the 'fixed mindset' by providing clear 'formative feedback' which details 'how to improve'. Once students apply the improvement guidance and hopefully gain higher marks they will also gain in motivation and steadily apply more effort. This positive mindset can be strengthened by introducing self-assessment and peer assessment against marking criteria to deepen awareness of how marks are won or lost. Finally, as confidence expands the students should begin to question their own progress and to identify and apply their own improvement actions and ultimately gain meta-cognition i.e. self-aware of own ability and able to set and achieve own learning goals. To successfully advance up the pyramid means promoting a learning culture where all appreciate that to learn is beneficial and that effort will bring results. Some classroom cultures denigrate learning and in some cases students may be chastised as 'boffins' or 'boff' by their classmates for their participation as highlighted in Chapter Three. There is nothing new here because in times past the terms 'swot' or 'teacher's pet' were used in a similar derogatory way. Teachers need to firmly act to outlaw this form of learning sabotage by speaking to the worst offenders on a one to one basis and to regard it as evidence that they are struggling and need support. The fact that someone labels one of their classmates as a 'boffin' is evidence of their own negative self-assessment i.e. judging their own ability in relation to the 'boffin'. Offer support to such students in a doctor / patient style discussion i.e. concern that they might be struggling, what they find difficult and how you might help. Thereafter find something positive about their work to praise and seek to draw them into an analysis of what aspects of the subject or topic they are finding difficult. Within the lesson regularly pause to invite self-assessment using fast techniques like mini whiteboards, traffic light cards / dots, thumbs up or down, post-it notes etc to identify any mistakes or misunderstandings. As far as possible correct any misunderstandings immediately and re-teach any key aspects for the class as a whole or offer small group or one coaching support while the class are engaged in tasks. In this way learning can step forward very rapidly because once the students know that the focus is 'learning' they will be encouraged to volunteer what they do not understand. Students are always self-assessing. They know if they are stuck or if they understand. The key is getting them to share their self-assessment with you. At the end of the lesson pass around some A5 feedback slips or simply Post-It notes. Invite students to complete sentences like, *'I'd like more help with....' I found X difficult because...' Can you explain more about...'* See Chapter Ten for more suggestions of this type. Hattie emphasised that gaining feedback from students is the most effective driver of progress, *"feedback was most powerful when it is from the student to the teacher...when teachers seek or at least are open to feedback from students as to what students know, what they understand, where they make errors, when they have misconceptions, when they are not engaged – then teaching and learning can be synchronised and powerful".*[35] Feedback opportunities offer the students some sense of control over what they are learning and an easy method of asking for help. It can be as simple as posting their questions into a question box by the classroom door while leaving. Incorporate answers into the next lesson plan or for individual queries provide one to one support while the rest of the class is engaged in a task. Alternatively adopt a self-assessment grid for students to reflect upon and judge and their own progress as follows.

Judgement	Self-assessment	Pass actions	Completed
✓	I am confident I understand...	I will extend my learning by...	
?	I have a few questions about...	I will seek answers by...	
X	I need more help with...	I will re-learn this by...	

This encouragement to self-assess will build meta-cognition because as students reflect on their progress against the course standards they will hopefully take actions to close the gap. The Sutton Trust recommended metacognition strategies in July 2012 as *'High impact for low cost'* and confirmed research conclusions that *"Meta-cognitive approaches have a consistently high levels of impact with meta-analyses reporting impact of between seven and nine months additional progress"*. Once students feel a sense of personal progress they may be sufficiently motivated to read and work ahead and hence the quote from Wiliam (start of chapter) that Assessment for Learning, *doubled the speed of learning.*

PACE – Performance, Attendance, Class work and Effort.

Whereas **Pass** is directed at improving formative assessment **Pace** is its companion for summative assessment. Most schools and colleges have well established summative assessment systems and all will probably report upon the four Pace headings albeit in different ways. The Pace headings focus on the key measures of student progress as follows:

Performance
Attendance
Classwork
Effort

The term **'performance'** relates to formal, summative test or exam outcomes i.e. formal graded assignments or tests. The term **'attendance'** relates to each individual's percentage attendance. The term **'classwork'** or coursework, if preferred, relates to progress within routine classwork, homework and assignments as distinct from a formal graded test or assessment performance. The term **'effort'** relates to the amount of effort being put into personal study but this may be altered to 'extended learning' (perhaps for adult students) to mean the same thing but in a less challenging way. To implement PACE each course team should agree a grading scale. Perhaps the most straightforward is an A to D grading scale:

A = Excellent
B = Good

C= Satisfactory
D= Unsatisfactory

Common marking criteria

Next each course team needs to agree the criteria for the award of each 'Pace' grade i.e. excellent in a test might be 80%+ or matching a list of criteria. Pace can be captured on one side of A4 to allow for ease of comparison and can easily be created in Word™ or Excel™ and placed on a Virtual Learning Environment (VLE) for ease of access and updating by all staff. The following example of a Pace record form for a class can be swiftly completed by entering the assessment grades A-D against each named student. Appropriate ethnic origin coding and targets may be entered alongside the student names to check for any differential performances and to prompt early interventions as required. The completed record permits an 'at a glance' overview of the progress being made by each student and how far each student is consistent in their formal test performances as against routine classwork and coursework. Some students might achieve well in a formal test (performance) but less well in routine classwork and vice versa. In addition low grades for attendance and/or effort might explain a low overall assessment record.

CLASS PACE RECORD

Performance, Attendance, Coursework and Effort

Course		Subject	
Teacher		Date	

Student name	P	A	C	E	comments

A= Excellent, B= Good, C= Satisfactory, D= Unsatisfactory

The above PACE record can be held by each teacher for their own lesson but for Personal Tutors the approach is to present an assessment overview for each student and consequently the form is personalised as follows:

TUTORIAL PACE RECORD

Performance, Attendance, Coursework and Effort

Course		**Student**	
Tutor		**Group**	

Autumn Term

Subject	**P**	**A**	**C**	**E**	**comments**

A= Excellent, B= Good, C= Satisfactory, D= Unsatisfactory

To complete the form simply repeat the above table down the page for Winter and Summer terms or alter to Term One, Term Two etc. It should be possible to fit on one side of A4 for clarity and again provide an 'at a glance' overview of progress.

Traffic Light assessment

Finally the traffic light system is a possible refinement to add to the PACE record forms. Simply replace the grades A-D with the traffic light colours Green, Amber and Red. In Word™ or Excel ™ colour each 'Pace' cell appropriately with Green for good or better, Amber for satisfactory and Red for unsatisfactory. Once completed this has high visual impact in terms of where the support actions are required.

Assessment for learning activities

Chapters Seven, Eight, Nine and Ten incorporate a wide range of practical activities to put Assessment for Learning into action. The focus is to design lessons that move away from a 'chalk and talk' focus on the 'transfer' of information to most of the lesson time revolving around discussing, analysing and interpreting the information. The result should be lessons which place more responsibility on the shoulders of the students to reflect upon and to question their own learning and ultimately to engage in regular independent learning.

6 Diamond lesson plan

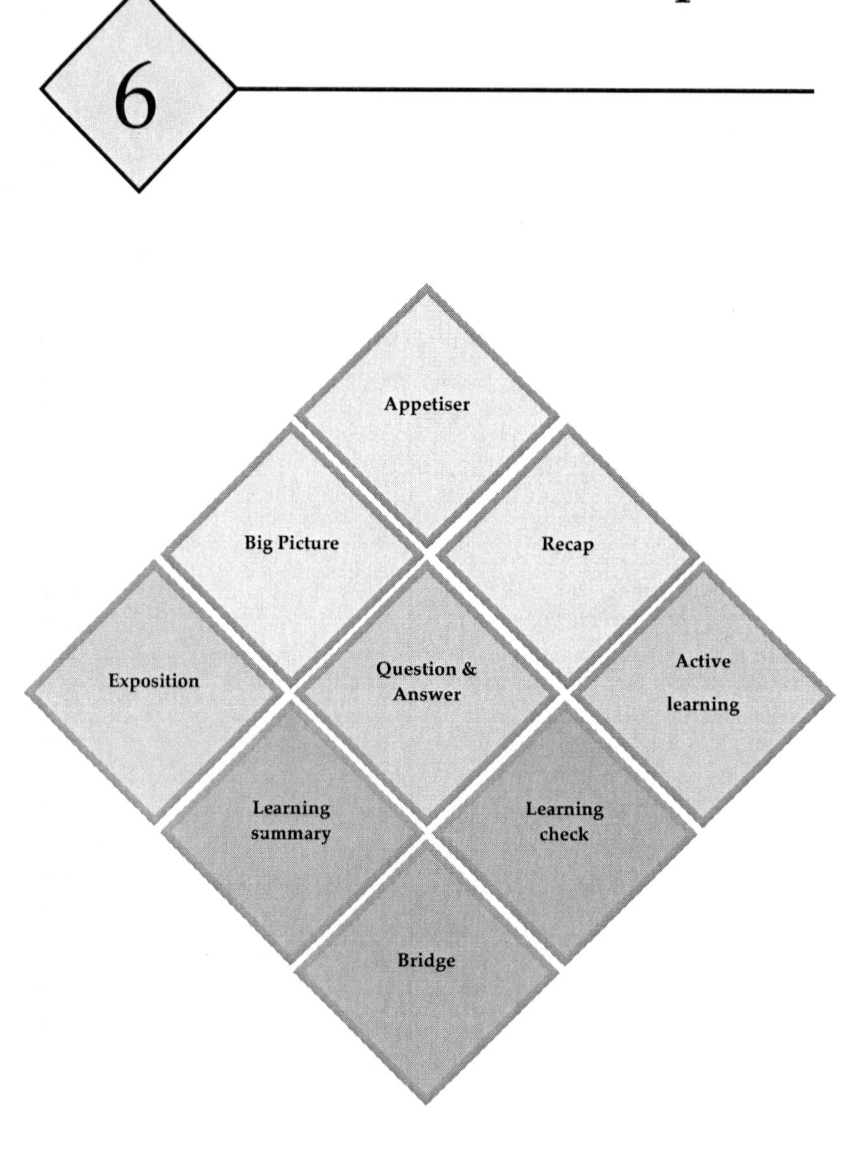

Lesson start Lesson middle  Lesson end 

The Diamond lesson plan translates the good practice guidance presented in Chapters 1-5 into practical action steps. At first glance a nine part lesson plan may seem daunting but at its core the Diamond Lesson Plan reflects the three part model detailed on most teacher training courses i.e. a successful lesson has a clear start, a clear middle and a clear end. The Diamond Lesson Plan simply stretches this model and provides three key steps as the dominant, but not the only features, of each stage of the lesson. The individual diamonds are also moveable and do not have to be introduced in the order given. Collectively they offer a template to stimulate your creativity rather than a straitjacket. For instance you might move active learning from 6th position to 1st position and perhaps as the pupils or students enter the classroom they might be directed into groups to engage in a group activity? This might be followed by the 'big picture' to explain the purpose and point of the activity and how it links to the rest of the lesson and what the students are expected to learn. Equally an appetiser might also be used at the transition points of the lesson between different episodes to energise. An effective exposition should involve regular pauses to engage the students in question and answer so that in practice the 'exposition' and 'question and answer' steps will merge into a seamless whole. The key steps specified for the end of the lesson are 'learning checks' and 'learning summary' but regular Assessment for Learning activities should be a feature of the whole lesson. The nine steps of the Diamond lesson plan are designed to promote enthusiastic and enjoyable lessons and to fully address Ofsted's 2012 criteria for 'outstanding' lessons, " *They use well-judged and often imaginative teaching strategies that, together with sharply focused and timely support and intervention, match individual needs accurately. Consequently, the development of learners' skills and understanding is exceptional. Staff generate high levels of enthusiasm for participation in, and commitment to, learning.*[1] The above criterion forms part of the 'outstanding' criteria for both Schools and Further Education 2012+.

Appetiser	Open your lesson with a bright, upbeat two to three minute activity to capture attention and enthuse, *"Innovative starter activities ensure students are quickly focused on the lesson" (Ofsted).* [2]

Big Picture	Share clear objectives with links to the last lesson, the curriculum, the exam, current affairs the real world etc, *"At the start of each lesson, the lesson objectives are explained clearly and the students are reminded of relevant previous work"* ***(Ofsted).***[3]
Recap	Check learning from the last lesson and re-teach any aspects as required. Gain responses from all and where possible move beyond basic question and answer into some active 'assessment for learning' individual or paired activity, *"Lessons often begin with individual or small group activity, followed by full group summary to recap on earlier learning and link it to the current lesson"* ***(Ofsted).***[4]
Exposition	Address the whole class to introduce new learning with a clear overview or demonstration but keeping your 'teacher talk' short, sharp, motivational and enthusiastic in tone, *"Teachers are knowledgeable and enthusiastic, and the best are inspirational, skilfully imparting their passion to students"* ***(Ofsted).***[5]
Question and answer	Engage with fast paced open and directed questions to check understanding and to promote thinking at the appropriate course level and across the ability range, *"Teachers' skilful use of questioning checks on students' understanding and requires them to justify their responses and demonstrate their grasp of topics and concepts"* ***(Ofsted).***[6]

Active learning	Direct individual, paired or group tasks to explore and consolidate the new learning and to give opportunities to practice and build functional, personal learning and thinking skills, *"A wide variety of teaching strategies are used to challenge students and encourage their participation including group and paired work, discussion and debate, role-play and student presentations"* ***(Ofsted).*** [7]
Check learning	Gain feedback from all to check and confirm the key learning points and link to success criteria, *"Learning is constantly checked and summarised well at the end of lessons"* ***(Ofsted).*** [8]
Summarise	Summarise the key points all should have recorded to avoid different versions, *"Most have good introductions followed by effective summaries at the end of lessons"(Ofsted).* [9]
Bridge	Issue a research task as a bridge to the next lesson, *"Very high quality, extra material is available for extension activities, some of which are on the college's intranet that the students access at home"* ***(Ofsted).*** [10]

The above Ofsted quotations are all from grade one 'outstanding' inspection reports and are typical of the descriptions of the most effective practice. Reflect on the quotations and consider your own practice or practice within your curriculum team against them. How far does your practice match the grade one descriptions? If you wish to explore Ofsted findings in more depth explore the Ofsted *'Identifying good practice'* publication for your curriculum area from Ofsted publications, www.ofsted.gov.uk. You should also pay regard to the Lifelong Learning (LLUK) Professional standards for learning and teaching in Further Education (as detailed in Chapter One).

Chapters 7, 8 9 and 10 will develop the Diamond Lesson Plan in-depth and provide many illustrations of the associated teaching and learning strategies. All of the strategies and examples are tried and tested but what works well for one person may not for another. Therefore test the Diamond Lesson Plan and alter the content and order of the nine steps to best suit the aims and objectives of each lesson. Effective teaching and learning should never be static or predictable.

Lesson models

The Diamond lesson plan is a nine part model but the following four part model is common in many schools and colleges:

1. *Starter,*
2. *Objectives,*
3. *Individual working and*
4. *Plenary.*

The Teachers' TV video series *'From good to Outstanding'* highlighted a six part model:

1. *Big picture introduction,*
2. *Clear learning outcomes,*
3. *Information input,*
4. *Activities to engage,*
5. *Learning application,*
6. *Plenary.*

The website Teachers' TV was closed in 2010 but all of the video material is archived and available from a number of different providers including www.teachfind.com.

Professor John Hattie (see Chapter One) in acknowledging the impact of 'direct instruction' identifies a seven stage lesson plan starting from establishing clear *'learning intentions'* and ending with promoting *'independent practice'*. All schools and colleges are free to adopt and apply the teaching strategies and models they find most effective. In his booklet, *'Essential Pieces, the Jigsaw of a Successful School'*, Professor Tim Brighouse states, *"Clearly some agreement about the planning and recording of lesson plans is necessary. Whether it should be a three, four or five part lesson will vary within and between departments, or indeed be laid down within descriptors of other possible models"*[11] The key is for teaching teams to discuss and adopt a preferred model. It is worth noting that starting a lesson with clear objectives has been the mainstay of effective lessons for many years but this should not prevent teachers from being spontaneous or from adjusting their objectives in light of student feedback or progress. Consider the Board Of Education Handbook for Teachers first published in 1904, *'Every teacher should endeavour to conceive his main purpose as clearly as possible and should constantly review his actual practice in the light of that purpose'.*[12]

Focus on learning

Regardless of your choice of lesson model ensure a full focus on learning outcomes rather than the curriculum content. It is all too easy to plan to 'cover' a topic rather than to plan for student learning. Consequently when planning a lesson ask yourself the following three questions and select the most appropriate teaching, learning and assessment activities to provide the answers.

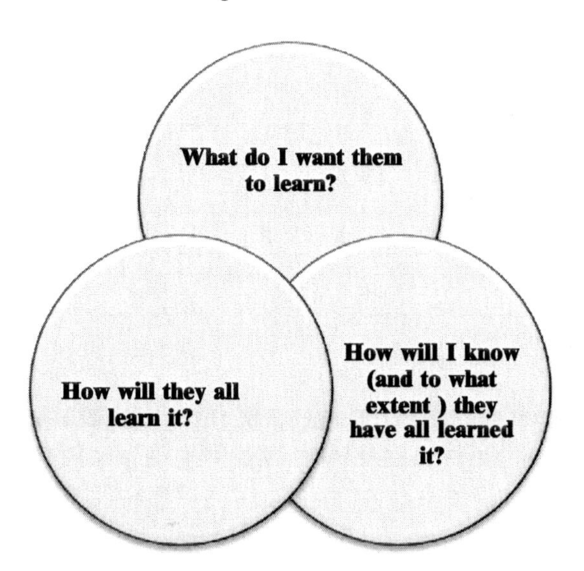

The Diamond Lesson Plan, as developed in the subsequent chapters, is designed to prompt a sharp focus on learning and assessment and offers a wealth of suggestions to help answer the above significant questions.

Lesson motivators and de-motivators

Students tend to welcome lessons that are lively and engaging rather than passive and dull. What motivates and de-motivates students? Consider the following comments made by students at Bilborough College as a part of the College's learner involvement strategy.[13] The College captured the opinions of new students on the lesson activities they liked and disliked by the simple expedient of different coloured post-it notes for motivators and de-motivators. All the comments listed are random comments by individual students. There is no horizontal link between the two columns i.e. the same student has not made both comments.

Motivators	De-motivators
Fun things. Fun people	Go through the books and notes too quickly
Competitions	Reading – too much causes me to switch off
Good activities in lesson	Student participation in lessons i.e. Group presentations
Games	Not being given satisfactory guidance
Fun	Forced group studies/work
Games (learning)	Too much copying from a text book
When they test your learning in a fun way e.g. games. It motivates you to revise and remember	copy from a textbook
interactive quizzes for students to participate	Text book lessons
Exciting exercises	Boring
Different activities	Too much writing
Doing something practical and fun	Lots of handouts, target settings
Practical lessons	A boring rubbish topic in lesson
Interactiveness	Hard tests
Active lessons	Same thing every lesson – no varied activities (boring)
Learning in a fun way e.g. doing posters and activities	Too much work

When something fun is done, but is still related to the subject	Having to work in silence – no fun – bored easily
Interesting activities	Boring lectures/presentations
Doing fun activities	Listening to a whole load of information for too long. Not being able to have a long enough break after.
Varied activities, not just copying from textbooks etc	Big group projects within lessons
Interactive lessons	When we do the same thing <u>every</u> lesson
Practical lessons, when you can do a task in groups	Repetitive lessons, difficult work, working for exams, not interested.
Practical work	No objectives at the start and poor, unorganised teaching doesn't motivate me!
Interactive lessons e.g. games, quizzes.	But, as much help as they are, time exam papers are boring
Competitive activities	Just lessons based on theory, without applications or the knowledge we have learnt
Games, quizzes	Working through worksheets and doing work out of text books
Practical so that we can help each other understand.	Doing the same thing every lesson
Physical learning	Boring lesson
Lessons that include lots of practical tasks	Boring ways of learning
Fun lessons occasionally	Long unnecessary lectures – why God Why ?
Competition	Text books
Playing games in lesson to get you more involved with groups and still helping you learn.	Things that involve loads of writing and are long and dull
Whole class taking part	Too many practise questions with no answers
Lessons that have a range of task	Too many easy practice questions
Varied activities throughout the lesson – and clear objectives	Too many dull questions

Work that has something to do with something that interests you i.e. On a computer	Too much writing!
Interactive lesson	Pointless tasks
Interactive teaching	Having a lesson where you just have to copy out of a text book
Spending a lot of time on a certain topic in class	Dictated note taking
Spending a lot of time on a certain topic in class	Dull pointless things especially first thing in the morning
Having fun whilst learning	Having to write lots of notes
Deadlines	Boring work
Having a fun lesson with variety in learning.	Lots of silly tasks
Having a different range of activities in a lesson with an occasional laugh (e.g. Psychology)	Writing off the board for the whole lesson
Active practical lessons watching things Organisation	Boredom
I'm also motivated by lessons that move at a relatively fast pace, rather than dwelling on the topic for too long, as it keeps the lessons exciting and moving forward, and it feels like more has been achieved.	Copying from a book
I also prefer a range of activities in one lesson so you feel like you have learnt a lot.	Reading and copying from a book
Chocolates	Silent bookwork
Prizes	Learning from text books
To get rewards at the end	Working from text books
Bribing with chocolate – it works!	Being in competitions
Rewards for doing something good	Working through questions on your own that I don't understand

Working in groups as you learn to co-operate and negotiate with others, being able to reflect on others views and ideas without relying on the teacher encourages independent learning.	Being in groups and being in competition with each other – especially when I don't know the group.
Group discussions (but not forcing people to volunteer answers)	Work that seems off topic or pointless - Key Skills
Interesting teaching (not just chalk and talk)	Things I don't understand so find hard to study
Teachers making you get involved – discussions	Too much work too frequently
An open, talkative atmosphere where people are regularly encouraged to contribute	Being put on the spot
I prefer sitting in open plan so discussion with the whole class are easier.	Boring lesson
Going through exam questions	Boring lessons – making pages of notes
Independent Learning (go do your own research)	Boring lessons, where it's just copying
Discussion/debates in groups/class	Too much work, causes a lot of stress
Interaction with everyone else in my lessons.	When group discussion don't happen often
Talking/discussions	Boring lessons
Discussion and in depth debates. Feeling that we're learning more than the curriculum and that this isn't GCSE all over again, getting the bare minimum of knowledge	Repetition of lessons, e.g. continuously working through a booklet which obstructs class members from expressing and sharing their views.
Working with others	Listening to teachers read aloud from textbooks, Powerpoints for long periods of time

Preparing and planning exams	I'm not motivated by lessons where we dwell on one thing for too long, as they just grow stale and boring.
Group work	No structure or not enough structure in lessons

The students' comments reveal a high degree of consensus of what they like and dislike about lessons. Clearly they like active participation in their lessons, discussions, group tasks, fun and rewards. They dislike passive lessons involving too much listening, note-taking from textbooks, basic copying tasks too much teacher talk and insufficient structure. There are a few comments expressing discomfort with participating in discussions and groups but they are the exception. Chapter One presents the views of the same group of students on the skills and attributes of effective teachers. Ofsted would appear to agree with the students because the 2012 criteria for Grade Four 'inadequate' judgements includes, *"Staff do not have sufficiently high expectations and, over time, teaching fails to excite enthuse, engage or motivate particular groups of learners, including those with learning difficulties and/or disabilities"*.[14] Teaching should clearly excite, enthuse, engage and motivate but rather than endless preparation this is largely a product of 'process' in terms of the pace and challenge presented.

Student lesson observers

In 2008-09 Northampton College[15] introduced a pilot programme of student lesson observers to provide a student perspective on what makes a successful lesson. During training for their role the students were invited to brainstorm the features of a 'good' lesson i.e. start, middle and ends of lessons on flipchart paper. Their verbatim comments are as illustrated.

Lesson start

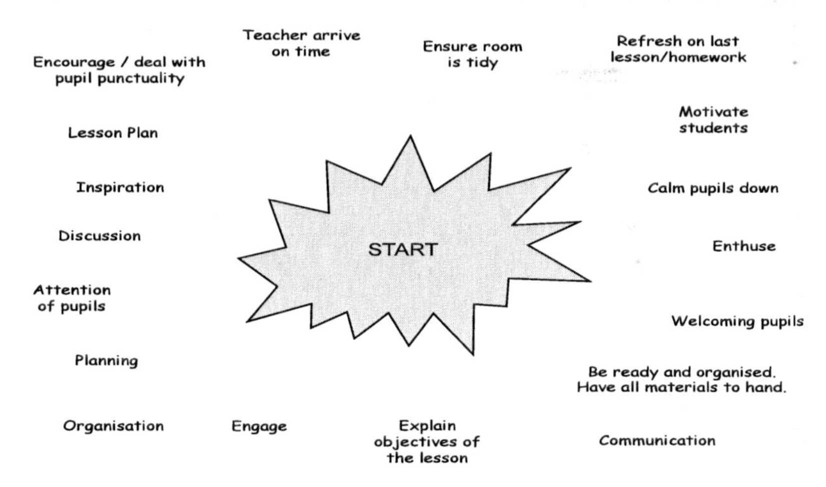

The above features of a 'good' lesson start mirror professional and Ofsted guidance and the views of teachers when they complete the same task. It demonstrates that students are very alert to good practice and have high expectations for a well organised lesson in terms of punctuality, planning, objectives, recap, motivation and the possibility of being enthused and inspired.

Lesson middle

The students' opinions of the features of the middle of a lesson also reflect established good practice as illustrated.

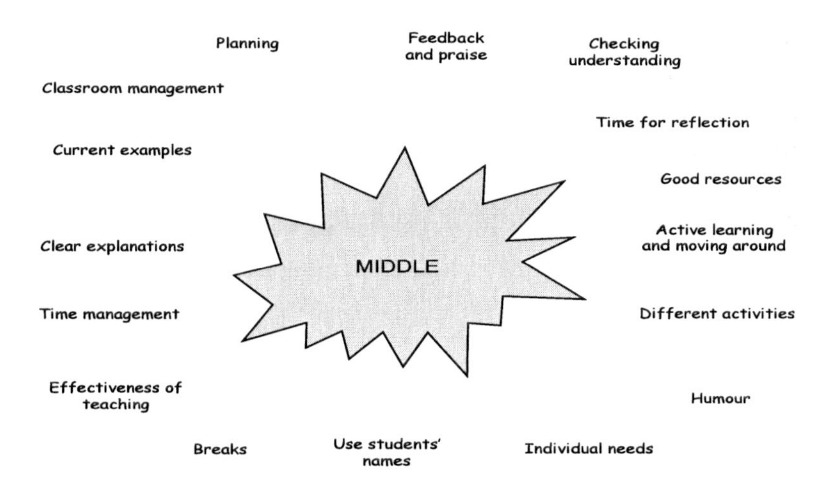

It is interesting that the students introduce humour as a feature and clearly this can be taken as shorthand for a positive rapport rather than cracking jokes. The students may not be familiar with the term 'Assessment for Learning' but note how they wish the teacher to check understanding, give time for reflection, issue feedback, offer praise and address individual needs. They also want clear explanations and active participation.

Lesson end

Finally the views of the Northampton students on the end of a lesson are as follows:

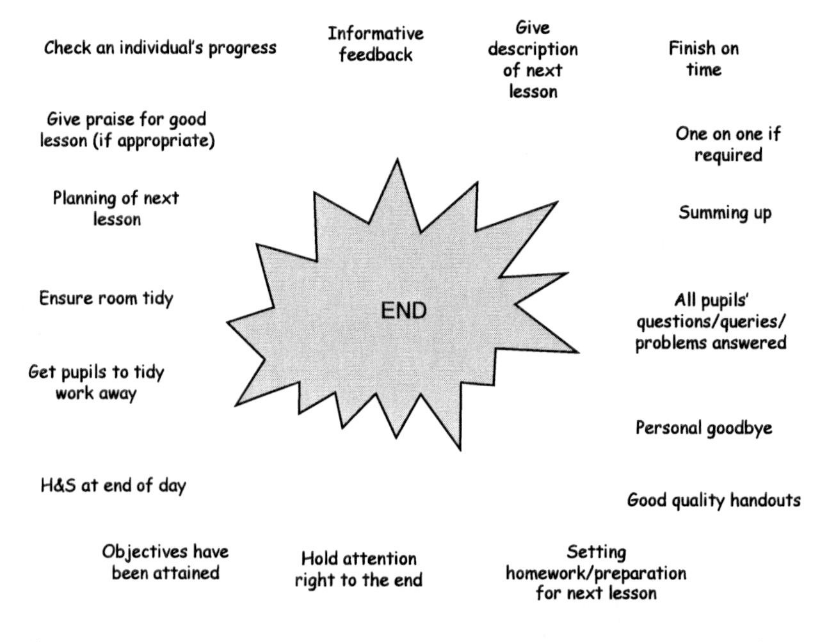

The students' comments are again quite perceptive on what constitutes good practice. They emphasise the checking and summarising of learning and on a one to one basis as required. They also want details of the next lesson, related study guidance and a 'personal goodbye'. Overall the student opinions are very sound and it is a sobering reminder that teachers are 'observed' in every lesson and that judgments are made. The students in our lessons may not articulate their views but clearly they know what makes a good lesson. Their views are important and every effort should be made to sample their opinions to inform individual lesson planning and as part of a wider quality system. Essentially the students' judgments exist and their judgments will no doubt be shared with families and friends but what are they? As a teacher I might ask what did you enjoy about today's lesson?, What did you not enjoy as much?, What would improve the lessons for you?, How do you like to learn? What sort of learning activities do you enjoy the most? Capturing student opinions is a key feature of the Ofsted 2012+ inspection framework, *"Learners' views are central to inspection. As inspectors will not have the opportunity to speak to all learners during an inspection, it is important that all learners, regardless of their mode or place of attendance, have the opportunity to express their views to inspectors about the provider.."*[23] In practice inspectors will seek to meet with groups of students and will invite students to compete the 'Learner View' questionnaire in advance of the inspection. Regardless of inspection seeking and reacting to student opinions is a high value activity because our students do hold clear views on how they like to learn and seeking their views can produce productive learning partnerships. The chapters which follow will explore how to put the Diamond lesson plan into action and hopefully deliver the learning activities that students appreciate and find enjoyable. In all cases the emphasis should be on learning. The key features in this regard are the recap activity to check learning before moving forward, question and answer strategies to uncover any misconceptions and to confirm key learning, paired and group activities to explore and deepen learning and finally, at the ends of lessons, firm checks and a summary of learning to test how far the success criteria for the lesson have been met.

Enthusiastic lesson starts

"The best lessons are well-planned and purposeful, and lead to brisk, lively and imaginative teaching that enables all learners to make good and better progress. Outstanding lessons are characterised by passionate and enthusiastic teachers who use their extensive vocational expertise to inspire a culture of learning and challenge. In these lessons, teachers' expectations of their students are high, checks on learning and understanding are frequent, questions are probing and work is appropriately challenging. As a result students learn quickly and make rapid progress".[1]

Kendal College (five overall Grade One judgments) November 2010

The start of a lesson should be positive and seek to stir interest and curiosity. Our passion and enthusiasm for our own subject or skill should be evident because it may provide the spark that lights a lifelong interest or suggests a career path. Perhaps a sport, hobby, subject or skill that you still enjoy today was kindled by an enthusiastic teacher deep in your childhood. It is difficult to always be enthusiastic and passionate because teaching is a highly demanding job but most teachers agree that the best part of their day is closing the classroom door and sharing their love of their subject or skill with others.

Sell your subject...

You are going to be the most successful hairdressers this country has ever seen...why work for someone else, you could be self-employed do you know how much Nicky Clarke charges just to shampoo and blow dry your hair? (currently £300 www.nickyclarke.com) Did Nicky Clarke know he would be a top hairdresser when he was your age? History is the most exciting subject you could ever study....To lay bricks in a straight line and to build a simple house wall or a mighty skyscraper is one of the most skilled occupations you could ever undertake.....Functional Skills are the primary reason why people will employ you and why you will succeed in life because you will be able to convert numbers into dazzling charts, wow an audience with a presentation and research and write persuasive text......look on the classroom wall at all those business leaders who have no formal qualifications but they do have high Functional Skills....Catering is having the confidence to take these simple ingredients and to transform them into a mouth-watering meal, this is not a skill – it's art and some of you could be the next Jamie Oliver or Nigella Lawson....

Every teacher should be capable of selling their own subject and their individual lessons. This is not charisma. This is your own intrinsic interest bubbling to the surface and on a regular basis renewing and reaffirming why the subject or skill is exciting and highlighting the knowledge and skills all should expect to gain. This quality was noted in an Ofsted grade one report as follows, *"A real sense of the teacher's love of the subject was conveyed to the students, who demonstrated a high degree of interest, unusual at this level, asking questions, and making spontaneous contributions".*[2] Even on a pass/fail NVQ and vocational programme it is possible to highlight and confirm commercial and even world class standards and to raise a challenge to be the best. High expectations can transform students by developing self-belief. Hattie emphasises that teachers need to enter the classroom and, *"believe that their role is that of a change agent – that all students can learn and progress, that achievement for all is changeable and not fixed..."*[3] Chapter Three has highlighted that low self-esteem and low personal confidence are significant issues for many students. Holding high expectations is the counter to turn students onto learning and to apply greater effort to succeed.

Seating layout

Ideally classrooms should be furnished with individual desks to allow for easy movement and re-arrangement to suit different learning situations. However, all too often desks are fixed or too heavy to move easily and we have to make the best of limited space and the available furniture. Lesson observers should report any limitations placed on learning by either the furniture or the classroom space and relevant managers should seek improvements. Assuming that it is possible to re-arrange furniture what are the key considerations? Move and re-arrange the desks to suit the different learning tasks:

- Straight rows theatre style to watch a DVD or a whole class presentation,
- Two facing straight rows to facilitate a debate,
- One large central block for a whole group discussion,
- Small clusters of desks for small group activity,
- A few individual spaced desks with no chairs for three or maximum of four students to stand around to brainstorm a task (we can say brainstorm).
- Two or three blocks of desks for team work.
- A single hot seat in the centre of the room preferably a swivel chair and the rest of the chairs in a circle ready to question the person in the hot seat – (teachers as well as students) on prepared topics
- A horseshoe arrangement to encourage discussion
- A circle without desks to encourage sharing of opinions

The above examples illustrate how the physical repositioning of the furniture directs attention to the task with sometimes just a single learning focus for a whole lesson. The alternative is that students will often sit beside the same person at the same desk every lesson and quickly fall into a 'comfort zone'. Sitting in the same position every lesson can also lead to the formation of sub-groups which can isolate some students and confirm adopted or 'allocated' roles within the lesson e.g. class clown, swot, trouble-maker, silent, shy etc. The Harkness method of an oval table to facilitate open discussion is a further consideration as described in Chapter Eight. This regular re-arrangement of furniture is a powerful stimulus because it raises interest levels by 'removing' each student's normal seat and by mixing up the friendship groups.

Greet and welcome

It is often not possible to be in the classroom before the students arrive but whenever possible be first into the classroom and greet and welcome the students as they enter. Offer some positive comments, ask how their day is going, what's happening in their part-time job, how pleased you are by...? A warm welcome that recognises and shows an interest in each person will quickly build a positive rapport and perhaps lift low moods and renew the learning partnership. Also scan faces for signs of any unhappiness or potential problems and provide, as necessary, a few quick encouraging words and offer to discuss any issues at the end of the lesson. The simple acknowledgement that someone is troubled is often sufficient to calm a stressful situation and to prevent the continuation of an argument or problem into your lesson. Hattie identified an effect size of 0.72 for positive 'teacher-student relationships', significantly above the 0.40 threshold for positive influences on learning, *"teachers should learn to facilitate students' development by demonstrating that they care for the learning of each student as a person..."*[4] Developing a positive rapport is a significant motivator. Avoid sharing your own frustrations or problems with the students and develop the capacity to leave personal and professional problems in the corridor or the staffroom. Aim to close your classroom door and as the legendary Van Morrison would say, *'turn it on.'* In a famous exchange during the recording of one of his live albums an audience member, shouted *'turn it on man, turn it on'* to which Van Morrison replied, *'it's turned on already'*. Make sure your students know that it is 'turned on' by adopting an upbeat presence with positive body language and an enthusiastic tone.

Start on time

Aim to start your lesson exactly on time to condition your students to arrive on time. All too often too many teachers wait for latecomers because they do not want to explain the lesson aims and objectives and then have to repeat them for the inevitable (and often the same regular) latecomers. Essentially the teacher has become conditioned, by some of the students, not to start on time and this becomes part of the class culture. Sometimes timetables do not help because one lesson may end at 11a.m. and the next starts at 11a.m. Ideally ' transfer time' should be built into the timetable but otherwise it is better for a lesson to end early than for a lesson to start late. Act on lateness by having a reputation for always starting on time and this will prompt more students to make an effort to get to your lessons on time. If lateness is a significant issue then place some A5 Late Slips by the classroom door and when a late student enters point to the late slips. The Late Slip should have space to record name, date, lesson, number of minutes late and the reason for being late. The consistent application of this approach will soon encourage most to attend on time and for those who do not you will soon have a stack of late slips to discuss with them on a one to one and/or with their personal tutor.

If there are a number of persistent offenders reinforce the importance of arriving on time by ending the lesson a few minutes early and holding the latecomers back to read and discuss their late slips. Do this every time and they will soon conclude that it is easier to arrive on time rather than always being the last into the canteen queue. It also has the advantage that those who were present on time see clear sanctions for those who do not make a similar effort. However, remember that many students will have a valid reason for being late- it is not always a discipline issue. You may end up giving sympathy for some personal emergency or problem.

Appetisers

On a regular basis reinforce the positive lesson start by entering straight into an appetiser. Perhaps this is not your preferred term and you might be more familiar with the terms *icebreaker, starter* or *awakener* activity. Another popular term in many schools and colleges is *energiser* activity. Whatever the name the purpose is to grab attention, spark questions and introduce a 'feel good' factor to immediately settle the students into the lesson. Ideally you are looking for a 3/4 minute burst of information, challenge, or fun to provide an upbeat start to the lesson. This is preferable to the negativity and delay of waiting for latecomers and displaying irritation with questions like, 'where is everybody... Has anyone seen....? As highlighted above, lessons should start on time, and by the time the appetiser is concluded hopefully the majority of the students will be in the room ready for the 'big picture' presentation of aims and objectives. The latecomers will have missed something of interest and overtime this might help to reduce lateness. The overall aim of the appetiser is to raise enthusiasm and interest for the subject by highlighting wider connections, applications, links to current affairs and in particular the promotion of independent learning. The Ofsted report, *Identifying good practice: a survey of business, administration and law in colleges, January 2008,* highlighted the impact of starter activities as follows, *"a good range of starter activities, such as quizzes, true/false questions and 'bingo' style games to test students' knowledge of definitions, provided prompt and purposeful starts to lessons".*[5] The report commented on effective starter activities as follows, *"lessons started with a few minutes on relevant current items in the news, although not necessarily linked to the rest of the lesson. Teachers and students used the BBC website and other Internet sources successfully to find relevant topics. Students clearly enjoyed applying a business concept to current issues and felt that this helped to keep the subjects 'live' and relevant".*[6] The majority of the appetisers should be curriculum linked but sometimes a quick brain teaser activity is refreshing to perk students up with a puzzle or a challenge. In May 2008 Runshaw College achieved five grade one Ofsted inspection judgements and the inspectors commented, *"Innovative starter activities ensure students are quickly focused on the lesson".*[7] A similar judgement was made in relation to lessons in Nelson and Colne College, *"Starter activities are well thought out and students quickly focus on the lessons' tasks".*[8]

Appetiser suggestions

The following suggestions can all be developed into interesting appetisers:

- **music** – capture attention with a short burst of music that is relevant to the topic or perhaps some 'brain' music to aid concentration. Select music that is associated with the topic perhaps relevant period music to accompany a novel in English Literature, atmospheric music to accompany a poem, music from the relevant region or country in Travel and Tourism, or in Languages, Beatles for 1960s Britain, Wagner for Nazi Germany, a relevant national anthem, a sporting theme tune etc. There are many legal websites for finding music to play. The major ones are itunes for purchase and download and www.spotify.com for streaming but not download. You Tube also provides music but be wary of accompanying videos because of some less than wholesome images. It is perhaps best for you to scroll and select to ensure appropriate choices. Consider the wider concept of 'brain music' or simply relaxing, soothing music to help people to relax or even to use as a timer during a paired or group task i.e. time is up when the music stops playing. Any music by Mozart or Baroque in general is reputed to stimulate the brain and to enhance concentration and learning. The website www.thetrainingshop.co.uk sells CD compilations of suitable reflective and energising music. Offer information about the music and composer to help extend general knowledge and to expose to a wider musical range. This could be extended into *music of the week* by inviting students to submit a favourite track plus why they enjoy it. This can also lead to cultural diversity in the selection of music and or types of music soul, jazz, rock, rap, garage, indie, hiphop, bangra etc. Give praise for choices of music not sarcasm if you want to build motivation, rapport and confidence over time. You should also be aware of the need to be covered by a performance rights licence because under copyright law your class is an audience. Most schools and colleges hold site licences but if in doubt confirm with the head librarian who, more often than not, will be an authority on copyright. Similar guidance should be sought before using websites to download music.

- **Image of the month or week** – Select an arresting visual of a place, event, object, person, painting etc linked to your subject. Project the image via Powerpoint, Keynote or Prezi for maximum visual impact. Multiple images for most topics can be easily sourced on Google. Remember to select 'images' as the search field on Google and to select the most appropriate image to display. The website www.flickr.com is very useful for a wide range of photographs most of which can be used for free with acknowledgement. The website www.britishpathe.com offers images of life in Britain. In addition explore:
- www.earthcam.com
- http://earth.google.co.uk
- http://worldwind.arc.nasa.gov

These sites offer arresting images of life on Earth. You might also select images to highlight cultural diversity, role models or to link into current affairs, relevant anniversaries etc. Sometimes it is as simple as displaying the photograph of a key poet, engineer, hairdresser, general, actor, sports star, scientist i.e. someone you have referred to in a lesson. It is common for students not to know what a key person they are studying actually looks like or to know any general biographical information about them. Why not introduce engineer, poet or scientist of the month or even better weekly and invite a student to research and present the person with an A4 summary handout and upload the images and handouts onto the college Virtual Learning Environment (VLE). Or overtime build a display of key people associated with your subject around the classroom. It is not necessary for you as the teacher to do all the preparation and so after a few examples seek a volunteer to research and present 'X' for the next lesson. This will ease the students into the idea of independent learning and if you provide a handout template with fixed subheadings to research and report against then it provides clear structure and will help to develop confidence and key skills. If volunteers are slow at coming forward then drop names into a hat and select a name at random. Or in this electronic age rotate the names or photographs of your students on screen and freeze at random to select a student.

- **Website of the month or week** – highlight a useful website linked to the subject area or of wider study benefit. Invite students to submit websites they would recommend to others for study help or subject information. This approach, as above, will encourage independent learning and help to build confidence and Key Skills when the students present the website. The issue of the reliability of websites can be discussed and pointers given on how to check the source of a website to ensure the use of authoritative and respected sources. We should take every opportunity to point out not just academic reliability but also the risks and safe surfing practice. Wikipedia can be recommended for a swift overview but always with the rider to question and to crosscheck the information with other sources. This is because Wikipedia is open to anyone to edit and sometimes non-experts may introduce their own prejudice or personal 'spin' to a topic. The presentation of useful websites can also be used to raise the issue of plagiarism with guidance on how to research and to use 'own words' rather than the temptation to 'cut and paste' Some students do not appreciate that they are doing anything wrong when they 'cut and paste' and need to be supported on how to quote from a source rather than copying from a source. Warn your students that Edexcel and a growing number of universities use Turnitin software from Northumbria Learning which scans over 4.5 billion web sites for text matches with students' coursework. The software is very fast and reliable.
- **Book of the month or week** – select a useful book from the library stock to highlight and encourage a general independent research and reading habit. As above invite students to be involved and to present any books or study aids they have

found personally useful. Extend this approach into looking out for new publications by looking on the shelves of a good bookshop or online. All publishers maintain online catalogues and websites like Amazon will list publications by subject or skill area. Regularly seek new publications and ask the library to stock any useful new books. Most books are also available electronically and it is often possible to download a free sample chapter. E-book readers like the Kindle, Kobo and of course the multifunction ipad are busy doing for books what itunes did for music. Ebooks now outsell printed books and they may also be read on smartphones. Visit Amazon.com or Apple ibooks to see the extent of the vast virtual libraries including literally millions of free books. Encourage a book buying habit among your students and give them regular prompts on useful books, dictionaries, study aids, revision aids etc. Maintain a high expectation that they should build their own collection of useful books rather than the low expectation that they have no money, they don't read books any more etc. Ensure that parental newsletters contain references to the purchase of useful books and study aids to raise the awareness on how parents and guardians can help support their son or daughter. Clearly sensitivity applies and for cases of genuine hardship ensure discreet access to college or school hardship funds and/or purchase of class sets of particularly useful books. In the case of electronic books a site licence can often be purchased for less than the cost of a single class set and future editions are ordinarily provided free of charge as updates.

- **Video of the month / week** – Select a subject linked video from You Tube or the Khan Academy or iplayer or source something more quirky to spark interest or perhaps find a stimulating aspect of new research on Ted.org. As always invite the students to source and present an interesting video
- **Museum/Art gallery of the month or week** – There are museums with collections linked to most subject areas and of course art galleries. Try a Google search with the name of a relevant museum or art gallery and you will probably find full access to their collections online. As before why not invite students to find and present useful museum collections as a research and presentation task. If sufficient interest is generated you might consider arranging a visit. Trips out are very

motivational and very beneficial for extending and deepening personal understanding and study.

- **Charity of the month or week** – It is possible to overlook charities but many of them fund and promote up-to-date research in the relevant field. Draw down any useful information to present to the class and note any fundraising dates or free literature or information packs for classroom displays or to support coursework etc. If there is sufficient interest then the class might mount an appropriate information display in the college or school or undertake some related fundraising.
- **Employer of the month or week** – Reference to future employment opportunities is a good motivator. Highlight the major employers linked to the relevant subject area, the sorts of jobs on offer, qualifications expected and possible future salaries. Invite students to research and present a particular employer i.e. when the company was founded, size, turnover, major markets and products. The same applies to individual entrepreneurs who have exploited an invention, discovery or personal skill to found a new business. Seek photographs and brief biographical details of suitable role models to inspire your students. Note the City and Guilds vocational rich list featured in Chapter Three. Perhaps mark the position of major employers on a map of the UK and highlight the right to settle and work across the European Union to raise personal horizons. Many large companies will also have public relations departments and may offer free information packs for useful classroom display and may also provide a speaker to visit your class. Alternatively you might be able to arrange a visit to the employer's premises to encourage and motivate your students. All of this can again make useful research tasks for your students to research and present.
- **University of the month / week** – as above but orientated towards relevant courses where university is the expected next destination for most of the students. Highlight when the university was founded, major courses, show the website, location, identify past students who have attended etc. Seek to raise ambition and promote applications to Oxford or Cambridge or a major Russell Group university.
- **Study tip of the month / week** – Some students are

disorganised in their approach to study and boys in general are reputed to be poor at maintaining their files and adopting systematic approaches to personal study and revision. Invite students to submit their study tips and how they revise and learn. Confirm good practice and encourage all to support one another and overtime aim build a learning and study culture. Girls will often enter into co-operative 'study buddy' and revision support relationships but boys less so and they perhaps need encouragement to see the benefits of co-operative study and especially in the run-up to examinations.

- **Quote of the month / week** – who said it and context – can be subject related or of wider interest. Websites like www.quotationspage.com and www.quoteworld.org should supply your needs. Adopt the same approach for the following and illustrate with any relevant photographs from Google. The approach is essentially Who, What, Where, When and How as appropriate.
- **Key statistic**
- **Key date**
- **Key discovery**
- **Key invention**
- **Key concept / subject vocabulary** plus spelling test!
- **Key event**
- **Key hypothesis**
- **Thunks** – thunks are questions without any complete or obvious answer but test the ability to think and to articulate an opinion or argument. To gain some examples go to www.thunks.co.uk. Pose a 'thunk' to your class. Interestingly our leading universities like Oxford and Cambridge and some major employers ask thunks at interview to test for not a correct answer (because there isn't one) but the ability to think on your feet. You could extend this into a three minute debate to start your lesson. Place the seating into two facing rows so that when the class enter they are immediately plunged into a debating chamber. Allocate students to each side as they enter and aim for even numbers either side. Alternatively opt for five students on each side of the argument with advance time to prepare their arguments and form the rest of the class into an audience. Overtime ensure all take a turn as a member of a debating team. Select a subject related topic that has been in the news or a

thunk. The aim is to build confidence and Key Skills overtime. Try it with some random questions like, *Could we survive without electricity? What was the world's greatest invention? Does it matter if tigers become extinct? Why is grass green? Do teenagers need more sleep than adults? Is our quality of life better than it was 200 years ago? How do we know life is not a dream? Is it important to be able to cook when you can even buy mashed potato in the supermarket? Should we protect whales? Is eating meat wrong? Should we clear up after our dogs? Should you flash your headlights to warn other drivers of a police speed trap? Is smacking children wrong? Would it matter if flies became extinct?* The ability to hold and to express opinions is an important life skill plus developing the tolerance of hearing and accepting contrary opinions. Keep a record of the outcomes of your mini debates on the classroom notice board.

- **E-skills –** The effective use of Microsoft Office™ (Word, Excel, Powerpoint and Publisher) and wider e-skills like maintaining a blog, creating a podcast, editing photographs and video from a mobile camera, searching the internet, uploading documents to the VLE, posting messages on a forum etc are important not just for study and presentations but also as future employability skills. Our students are all at different stage of IT skills development. Invite student volunteers to demonstrate various applications from how to animate a slide in Powerpoint or Keynote, import photographs, convert data into a chart, manipulate tables, design a document, use shortcuts in Word™ or Pages™ etc. This approach permits students to demonstrate their e-skills and present a 'how to...' approach of benefit to all students and perhaps even the teacher. This is an easy way to promote Functional Skills within the lesson and wider study and builds the confidence of the students involved.
- **Brain teaser challenge –** this is often regarded as no more than fun but there are academic studies highlighting that deep thinking is very beneficial in building neural connections to help link and recall information. There has been an explosion in brainteaser software and games over the past five years with many claims for high learning impact. However, to put it into perspective experts reserve the highest ratings for a daily crossword or Sudoko puzzle and to cardio-vascular exercise. Try www.brainbashers.com established by an ex-teacher for a wide range of visual, number and word puzzles. Try

www.puzzlemaker.com to compile your own word searches, crosswords etc. It is a free resource but linked to the commercial website Discovery Education.

- **Wacky fact** – Any good bookshop has lots of compendium style books, books of lists, quiz books, key fact books etc to support this and:
- **Strange but true stories**
- **Breaking records** – any relevant record from The Guinness Book of Records or wider awareness of technology or other breakthroughs in design, products, procedures, software etc.

It should be possible to have a different *appetiser* for every week of the term. One per week, at random, rather than one for every lesson might work best to ensure that it doesn't become entirely predictable. Current affairs also works well and you can quickly find what is current in your field by visiting the appropriate BBC news page e.g. http://www.bbc.co.uk/business or change the suffix to health, technology etc. Try some of the suggestions and see what your students respond to best and best suit your subject area. Many of the appetisers suggested are supported by Powerpoint or Keynote but it is also possible to have an effective and enjoyable appetiser on a handout and sitting on desktops ready to engage students as soon as they enter the room. The appetiser can be as simple as a wordsearch. Free software like *'hot potato'* will allow you to quickly generate wordsearches and other basics puzzles. *Hot Potato* is provided free of charge to educational institutions by the University of Victoria, Canada. Go to *http//hotpot.uvic.ca* to download.

Big picture introductions

Avoid a rapid reading of formal lesson objectives to your students. The formal objectives will be in your lesson plan and available for the inspector or lesson observer to scrutinise but often they will make little sense to your students. Seek instead to build and share the **'big picture'** with your students and to expand beyond a bare reading of aims and objectives. Why is the topic important? How does it link to last week? How does it link to the specification? How does it link to the world of work or university expectations? What sorts of exam questions are linked to this topic? What should they know by the end of the lesson? What are the success criteria? Hattie places 'teacher clarity' as eighth in his overall rank order of influences on learning with an effect size of 0.75 well above the 0.40 average. Clarity is defined as entering the lesson with a sharp awareness of what is to be learned, *"teachers need to know the learning intentions and success criteria of their lessons, know how well they are attaining these criteria for all students and know where to go next in the light of the gap between current students' knowledge and understanding and the success criteria".*[9] Consider a checklist of key questions that all should be able to answer by the end of the lesson (pass standard) plus some wider challenge questions for the more able. Entering a lesson with differentiated questions should promote a sharp focus on learning because the lesson should build and confirm the answers to the questions. Also highlight the range of activities that the students will be engaged in during the lesson. Apart from exploring the relevant key facts and knowledge associated with the topic what key skills will be promoted and developed by the activity? Why are these skills important for later university and/or employment? It is within this type of 'big picture' introduction that the key hallmarks of highly effective teaching can shine through i.e. enthusiasm, passion and inspiration. Can you say, '*You will all enjoy this lesson......*? If not, why not? An Ofsted grade one report commented, *"Teachers are enthusiastic, motivating, engaging and have very good subject knowledge. Lessons are well prepared, maintain a brisk pace, and provide a variety of activities".*[10]

Visual big picture

Consider supporting the 'big picture' introduction with some bright visuals to capture attention and as an aid to memory and self assessment. Try displaying your key objectives or questions within a bright, colourful chart by selecting one of the many standard organisational charts available in Microsoft Word™ and Powerpoint™. Look for Smartart on your taskbar.

Place the lesson topic into the centre circle e.g. 'Cold War' and the related objectives into the outer circles. Add circles or take away circles as required. Project the image using Powerpoint or Keynote and take the students around the circle, building the 'big picture' as you proceed. Add bright primary colours and different fonts as wished to increase the visual impact. To promote learning issue each student with a copy of the image on A4 paper or for greater visual

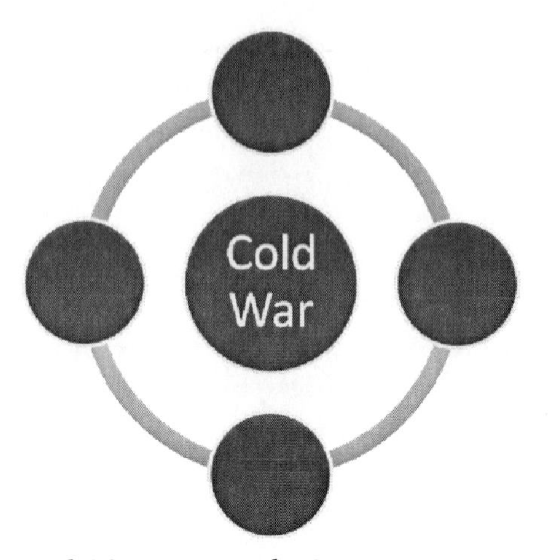

impact on coloured A3 paper. As the lesson unfolds, pause, question and invite the students to annotate the circle with key facts and information as you cover each major objective or significant question. By the end of the lesson all should have captured a neat one page summary of the key learning covered during the lesson. Overtime the students will gain a series of one page learning summaries to aid future revision. Alternatively reserve the handout to the end of the lesson and in the last ten minutes recap on learning and invite the students to take you around the circle to demonstrate their learning. All should end the lesson with a summary of key points around the circle. On the reverse of the handout you might print a self-assessment form and encourage the students to check and confirm their learning at the end of the lesson. Chapter Five illustrates a simple, to complete, self-assessment form. In the absence of Powerpoint or Keynote this diagram can be easily drawn on a whiteboard or a flipchart because essentially it is just a spider diagram. Select from a wide range of Smartart graphics.

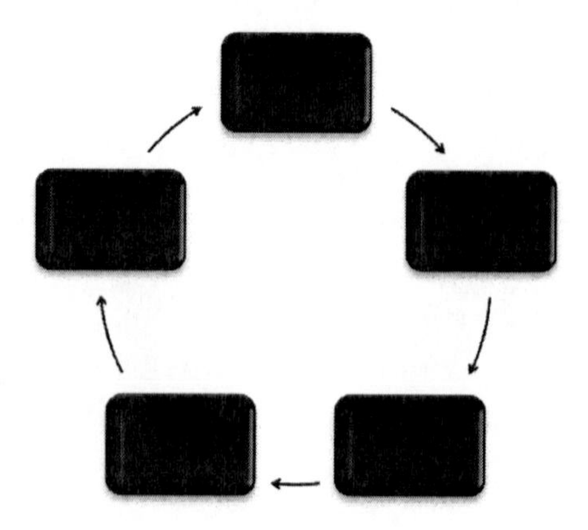

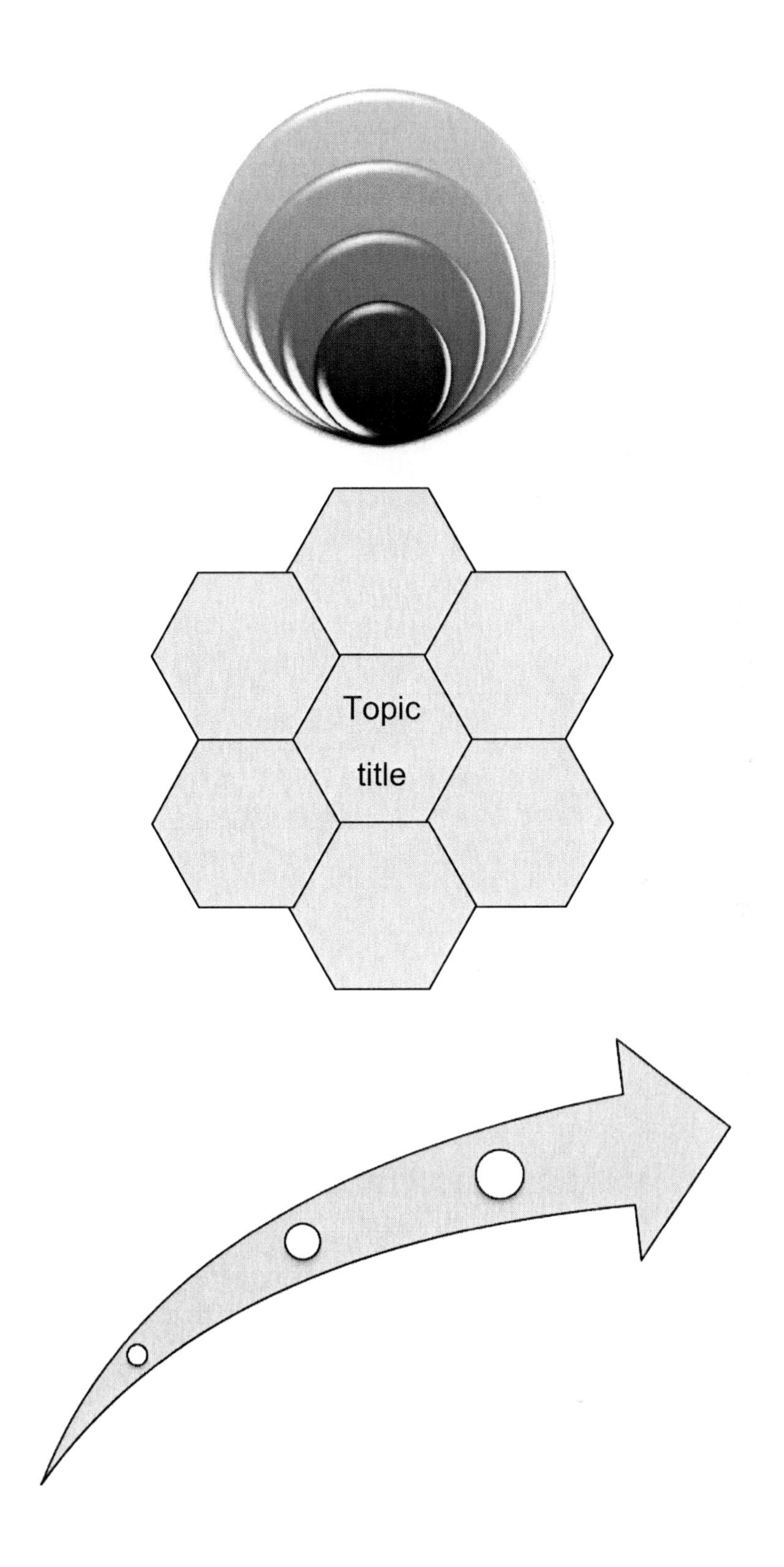
Topic
title

The examples illustrate some of the possibilities and with a bit of creativity it is easy to generate a range of visual templates for the display of aims and objectives. If presented by Powerpoint or Keynote then it is possible to extend this visual approach by attaching relevant photographs or short video clips to some or all of the individual objectives. In the Cold War template above clicking on an objective related to Stalin might display his photograph and perhaps clicking on an objective related to Churchill might produce a short audio or video podcast. Google images will provide all the images you need and Youtube.com is not just for frivolity but contains lots of short curriculum related video clips. Try a search with one of your favourite curriculum topics. You can also experiment with some IT whizz and make individual circles or hexagons 'fly in' etc. However, the basic presentation of the above visual templates requires no IT skills because they are standard charts or shapes in Word™ and Powerpoint™.

Learning recap

The Diamond lesson plan (Chapter Six) presents recap as the recommended step after the 'big picture' introduction but you may swap around as wished. However, never skip recap and leap straight into your lesson. Effective teaching leads to learning. A week is a long time for the memory. How much have your students retained and how much do they understand? Consider active recap techniques to overcome the problem of silent students and in particular avoid asking the question, *'Do you all understand'?* Most students are reluctant to admit if they do not understand and sometimes the teacher's body language and tone of voice conveys the impression that the expected answer is 'yes'. The purpose of a recap is not just to remind students of what they covered last week but how far they understand it. There is no point of moving forward to a new topic if the students are still struggling to absorb the last topic. Lesson plans are *plans* and should be adjusted if more time is needed to repeat or consolidate some key points that are still not fully understood. The Ofsted report, *'A comparison of the effectiveness of level 3 provision in 25 post-16 providers'*, highlighted as a strength, *"modifying and adapting lesson plans in the light of informal assessment of students' progress and understanding during the lesson'.*[11] Consequently follow and deepen the learning rather than rushing to cover a new topic. Our aim is not for our students to 'cover' the curriculum but to understand the curriculum.

21 active recaps

The most effective recap techniques go beyond question and answer into active learning techniques to engage **all** students so that the learning of **all** may be assessed. The aim, overtime, is to generate a learning culture whereby all feel comfortable to reveal misunderstandings or difficulties and to build a sense of personal progress for each student. The alternative is a sense of failure if students start a new topic without having fully understood the last topic. Knowing that they do not understand will eventually sap their confidence and some might indulge in playing the class clown, absenteeism or even disruptive behaviour to mask their lack of understanding. Therefore ensure a clear recap of learning and move beyond standard question and answer by experimenting with some of the following 21 active recap methods. All of these recap techniques may be employed at different points of the lesson including the end of the lesson as a final check on learning. In an Ofsted grade one report the inspectors commented, *"Informal assessment methods in class are imaginative and include quizzes and games and students assessing their own and other students' work"*.[12]

1. Space Traveller/ Earthlings

List key subject concepts, specialist vocabulary or points from previous lessons and in pairs, each person takes the role of the space traveller or earthling.

The space traveller asks:
What is meant by……?
How does X work………?
How do I …………….?

The *traveller* must play the part of being completely ignorant of all concepts and consequently the *Earthling* must provide a detailed definition/explanation. Use to assist students who were absent to pick up on what they missed. Use to test recall and understanding. Conclude by asking key questions of the whole class to confirm full understanding.

2. One Minute

Students speak for one minute on a given key topic or question. May pass – keep fast and to strict time and offer lots of encouragement. Can pre-print key topics on small cards for students to select at random.

3. Ten key questions

Issue a handout with ten key questions from last week's lesson and give only three to five minutes to answer as many out of ten as they can. Graduate the questions so that the first six are fairly straightforward but expect deeper answers for questions 7-10. Check answers with a show of hands and pick out some students to explain and say more about the answers. Encourage those who are uncertain to say so and check that they understand the explanation given by a fellow student.

Traffic lights cards

An extension of the above is to ask questions and for each one ask the students to hold up green, amber or red coloured card or Post-It notes. Green for I'm confident I know the answer, amber for I think know and red for I don't know! This ensures all participate and answer. Ask 'greens' to explain the answer to ambers and reds in small groups for an extension. Then check learning again to see if all go green.

Traffic light colours

A further variation is to issue individual sheets of coloured dots in the traffic light colours. Invite each student to stick a coloured dot against each question on their handout according to their level of understanding as highlighted above. List the same questions (by number if lengthy) on Flip-Chart paper and display on the classroom wall. Invite all to repeat their personal scores onto the Flip-Chart paper but this time using large dots for greater visual impact. This will show the consensus e.g. most of the dots against question three might be green indicating the majority are confident that they understand the answer whereas a large cluster of red dots against question five highlights misunderstandings in relation to that question to be resolved. Invite students posting green dots to confirm he answers for the benefit of all. You will discover that W.H. Smith and Staples will sell packs of small and large coloured dots.

Mini white boards

Ask multiple choice questions or questions that only demand a one word answer and invite students to write their answer on the mini white board. On the command 'show me' the students should hold up their answers for checking. Alternatively, for fun, ask them to draw an image of the answer.

4. Peer Questions

On ordinary paper or Post-It notes invite each student to note one area of personal difficulty / uncertainty / misunderstanding with their name at the bottom. Pin-up or stick up around the room and invite everyone to select one question / problem they can answer and circulate and pair up until all questions are answered. Note – repetition of the same issue or question should alert the teacher to provide more overall input on that topic.

5. Peer Sharing

In pairs, one student identifies strengths and the other weaknesses or positives/negatives or for/against etc. Swap and share notes and share with the rest of the class. Can follow up by dividing whiteboard into the related columns and draw points from each group.

6. Cartwheel notes/recap

Draw a large cartwheel shape on flipchart paper with a small centre circle and two concentric outer circles and as many spokes as there are sub topics i.e. you divide the cartwheel into segments like slices of a pie. Place the topic in the centre circle. Place key sub-headings in the inner circle and invite the students in pairs or small groups take charge of one segment and complete with as much detail as they can remember in the outer circle. It will work best if you take scissors and cut out each segment for each group to complete and then re-assemble on a noticeboard. Perhaps use different coloured pens for each segment for maximum visual impact.

7. True/False

Prepare some cards with true or false facts/information and invite students in pairs to separate into true and false piles and then explain why. You can also invite T or F responses to statements on mini white boards or T/F cards. Extend further by dividing the class into teams and seeing if they can devise T / F questions to ask of each other and see who can rack up the highest score of correct answers.

8 Identify

Place a key fact on a card, whiteboard, Powerpoint or hold up a photograph of a person, place or relevant object and ask the students to identify significance, purpose or role.

9 Concept Bingo.

Issue a handout containing a grid of nine squares. Using the whiteboard or Powerpoint display 12 key concepts or headings. Each student selects nine and copies into his or her grid. The teacher should provide the 12 definitions at random and the first learner to shout bingo i.e. correct match of definitions and concepts wins a small prize.

10. Hesitation

Divide the class into teams. Ask each team in turn to define or explain a key concept/event/discovery/person/formul a etc. The team nominates someone to answer that question. If the person hesitates then a member of another team may challenge and take over the answer. If they complete the definition/explanation they win a point for their team. Keep fast paced and aim to cover about ten key questions.

11. Knowledge tree

Place into groups of three or four with a sheet of flipchart paper and coloured pens. All are to draw a 'knowledge tree' as a summary of the topic under review. The trunk can be two vertical parallel lines and the branches can curve out of the top of the trunk to the left and right. At the end of each branch draw an oval for leaves. This is a mind mapping approach with the topic written on the trunk and individual facts written on the leaves. If the topic is major one each branch could be labelled with the title of a subtopic and more leaves could be radiated off. Place a timer on screen and give five 5-8 minutes to complete a colourful learning tree for the topic. At the end pin-up and confirm and check learning by naming students to explain different points. You might identify other key visuals to 'hang' learning points from i.e. the eight legs of a **spider**, the tentacles of an **octopus**, rays of **sunshine**, the steps of a **ladder,** the bars of a **farmer's gate**, a row of **test tubes,** a **roundabout** etc. A bright visual associated with a particular topic can significantly help memory and you might build these into your note taking. Perhaps simplest of all if you are making five key learning points is to invite all to draw around their **hand** on a sheet of paper and to write one key point per finger. You can add an extra hand to yield ten points or one hand for positive points etc and the other for negative points etc. Alternatively draw the hand in the thumb up position with the topic on the thumb and four key points on the fingers. Each student could undertake a different sub topic and then bring together for a 'thumps up' review of learning. The students might embellish their hands with rings, tattoos, veins, nail varnish for a colourful recap.

12. Guess

Issue cards to the students with key concepts, theories, names, places, people, objects etc. Each student has to enter into a description without revealing what is written on their card. The rest of the class have to guess what is being explained / described.

13. Dazzle

Place into mixed ability pairs or small groups and give each group a key question along with relevant exam board criteria for grade A or distinction standards. Add pace with a Powerpoint timer and invite each group to explain how to give a grade A or distinction level answer.

14. Truth

Place into teams of three and give each team a key concept/event/discovery/person/formula etc. One person provides the correct definition or answer, the next a near version of the truth and the third student a more fanciful version of the truth. The students have to arrive at the different versions. In turn each team comes to the front of the room to form a panel and the class question each team member and decide who is telling the truth.

15. Match

Prepare index cards with a question on one side and an answer on the reverse side. However, the questions and answers should be a mismatch. The fastest way to generate the cards is use address labels in Word and to print the questions and answers onto adhesive address labels. Ensure you identify 'question' or 'answer' as appropriate. Stick the questions and answers onto the index cards. Start by selecting a student to read out their question. Someone in the room should have the matching answer and should confirm this by reading out the answer printed on their card. The student should then turn the card over and read out their question and wait for someone in the room to identify the answer etc.

16. Line-up

Place 4-5 topic titles on A4 card and select students at random to hold up at the front of the classroom. Next issue at least one key fact card (on index cards) to the rest of the students. The students link their fact to the relevant topic and line-up behind the student holding the topic title card. Once all are lined-up each group must present their topic and link all the key facts into one fluid overview. Ask questions as they present to check for full understanding.

17. Washing line

A variation of the above is to peg the key topic card onto a washing line stretched across the classroom or simply pinned to the wall. Place related facts, events, information onto cards and invite the students to display in the correct order. This is good for chronologies, hierarchies, steps in process or procedure, calculations in a formula, rank orders, events in a plot, lines of a poem etc. The task is to place in the right order until everyone confirms that the order is correct. IKEA sell cheap washing lines on a reel with pegs attached.

18. Flip

A variation on the Bingo game. Prepare sets of nine index cards with a question on one side and the correct related facts or information or definition on the other side. Place the class into mixed ability pairs and each pair places their set of index cards face down on the tabletop. The first student asks one of the questions and their partner gives an answer. The student should turn the card over to check the answer given. If the answer is correct then this card is turned over but if incorrect it is returned to the tabletop question uppermost. The students continue to question each other until all questions are correctly answered and all cards are turned over. The first pair to turn over all the cards should win a small prize.

19. Blind date

A variation on the 'match' activity. Divide the class into two equal groups. One group sit down at their desks with a card containing topic information/facts/

definitions but not the topic title. The second group are issued with a topic title and move from desk to desk to find their matching partner. Each pair confirm the match. Alternatively simply get the students to walk around and mingle until all find their partner. Each pair should explain the match. You can make the matches relatively obscure to test knowledge/understanding.

20. Identify

In the style of the '*Have I got news for you'* quiz project a Powerpoint slide divided into four. In each quarter place a photograph, person, event, place, date, object, discovery, statistic etc and invite to make the link and guess and explain the topic. You can also insert an 'odd one out' as a variation. Can also be completed physically with four objects or facts cards in a hat which the students extract, link and explain.

21. Judgement

Type a question in large font across a sheet of A4 paper in landscape presentation. The question should invite an opinion/ judgment. Below divide the page into four squares. The first square is labelled facts, the second 'Advantages/for/strengths the third is the opposite headings i.e. Disadvantages, against, weaknesses and the final square is labelled judgement or answer. The students in pairs have to complete the boxes and in the final box enter their judgement, answer or opinion to the question.

In addition to the above suggestions the visual 'big picture' templates might be projected to support a recap and hopefully most of the students might have a copy in their files to refer to. A photocopy will be of immediate benefit to any student who was absent and missed the lesson. In association with this you might check the completion of the self-assessment grid as described above and in Chapter Five and use this as a basis for questions and answers and peer teaching and peer support. The questioning techniques described in Chapter Eight can also be successfully employed at the recap stage of the lesson.

The above lesson introduction of *appetiser, big picture* and *recap* should move at a fast pace. An Ofsted grade one inspection report commented, "*... students were given hand-held whiteboards to write their answers down during a quick-fire quiz in the style of a popular game show. Lessons proceed at a brisk pace, with students working quickly on tasks".*[13] The Ofsted Chief Inspector's report 2011 described outstanding lessons as follows, "*Outstanding teaching and learning are characterised by highly skilled and enthusiastic teachers who use their extensive expertise to inspire a culture of learning and challenge. Very effective planning leads to brisk, lively and imaginative teaching that ensures that learners' differing needs are met.*"[14] The words brisk and lively and imaginative pepper most Grade One inspection reports. Use digital timers for Powerpoint to add pace and it should be possible to complete all three steps in 20 minutes maximum. Visit *Collegenet.co.uk* to explore a range of digital timers and the free resource Triptico (www.triptico.co.uk) also offers a range of timers and other useful digital learning aids. The time devoted to the lesson start is highly beneficial because it generates enthusiasm, clarifies the learning goals, checks learning and overall raises interest and participation levels. Therefore resist the temptation to rush into a new topic and take time to raise interest levels and to check and fully develop learning. The teaching model to adopt is one step back and perhaps three steps forward every lesson to build a learning continuum. Once students feel a sense of personal progress they are more likely to enjoy the subject, undertake independent study and apply greater effort to succeed.

Active lesson development

"The large majority of lessons are lively and interesting. Teachers use very effective questioning and answering techniques to engage students and check their understanding. Teachers use ILT confidently, giving lessons a brisk pace and challenging students appropriately".[1]

Highbury College (Five overall Grade one judgments) June 2011

We learn by doing. How did you learn to:

- ride a bicycle?
- bake a cake?
- climb a tree?
- write a poem?
- write an essay?
- surf the internet?
- download music?
- build a wardrobe from a flat pack?

Learning by doing dominated the primary classroom and therefore most of us have happy memories of primary and junior school with its regular active learning strategies. However, at the secondary phase teachers, faced with lots of information to convey, often settled into the *'I talk and you listen'* model of teaching or essentially the *talking textbook!* The active learning methods and sitting in groups enjoyed in the primary sector gave way to straight rows and long presentations of information from the front. Remember the roller chalkboard? The teacher filled the board with notes as you fought to keep up and rotated it while chiding you to copy faster! Learning was reduced to listening and copying and when attention spans began to wander firm discipline was used to insist that your role in learning was to be a passive recipient of information. Questions from pupils for clarification or extension were often regarded as criticism and met with a pained expression from the teacher and the statement, *'you should know that – I covered that last week'*. Boys in particular often revolted against this type of learning experience and began to be labelled *difficult* or even *stupid*. Many by age 14 were eager to leave school or fell into regular truancy because their experience of school was largely one of personal failure and an endless flow of negatives. The well know TV presenter Michael Parkinson published his autobiography in 2008 and reflected upon his school days at Barnsley Grammar School, *" I didn't like the place. For one thing I had previously been taught by women in the main, caring and nurturing. Now I was in an all-male world, instructed by short-tempered brutes, who when all else failed, would try to beat information into you. The specialist at this form of teaching was our German master, Goodman an angry-looking man whose favourite form of instruction was to emphasise a point by drilling his knuckle into the top of a boy's head. Alternatively he would raise you to your feet by hoisting you up by your hair. If he considered a boy to be particularly stupid he would make him stand by the blackboard and belittle him by asking questions he knew he couldn't answer"*.[2] How many of us have similar negative memories of school?

Attention spans

One of the frequent criticisms of teachers attending professional development training days is how bored they become by sitting listening. One teacher who has clearly had enough is Fran Hill who wrote an article, published in the Times Educational Supplement (TES), January 2009, lambasting boring consultants, *"So, Ofsted reckons that if pupils start playing up, it's because we the teachers are boring the pants off them. Well, in that case there's only one solution: send the nation's teachers on continuing professional development days, so they can get bored out of their skulls listening to someone with presentation skills to rival those of a woodlouse"*.[3] It has to be said she does have a point because we have all endured boring presentations but not all were given by consultants. The experience, however, caused Fran Hill to reflect on her own teaching and she concluded, *" Professional development courses can also remind you just how long you can listen to someone talking monotonously before falling into your nodding dog impression. In my case , this is about 10 minutes. ...a monotone voice is as good a cure for daytime alertness as I've seen, and this is something to bear in mind on warm afternoons in stuffy classrooms...I plan my lessons now so that I never talk (or read from a book) for longer than 10 minutes at a stretch".*[4] Fran Hill has acknowledged a key issue that too many teachers (and consultants) over talk and stretch attention spans to snapping point. The much quoted formula for effective attention spans is one minute for each year up to a limit of eighteen years plus two minutes – hence 20 minutes maximum. However, we are teaching Generation Y the digital generation who have grown up with: multiple TV channels and the zapper to flick between them, Google, Facebook, Ebay, itunes, computer games, ipods, mobile phones, DVDs, digital cameras, digital video, texting, game consoles and Twitter. Generation Y is used to fast moving information and more importantly being in control of it and it is addictive. How long can you wait between hearing your mobile bleep, signalling the receipt of a text message and reading it? There is no hard science but it would appear that attention spans are dropping. In 2002 research conducted by the Massachusetts Institute of Technology (MIT) concluded, *"the addictive nature of web-browsing can leave you with the attention span of nine seconds – the same as a goldfish".*[5] Most people spend less than 60 seconds evaluating a website before moving away. Research conducted by the web watchers Tubemogul.com in 2008 highlighted that viewers of online video services like You Tube are hard to hold. 10.39% of viewers will click away after only 10 seconds, 53.56% will click away after watching for one minute and only 9.42% will watch a full five minute video. [6] However, we also know that if something really interests someone then the individual will not notice time passing. Many students will pursue particular hobbies or sports to expert level and will devote many hours to their interest. Despite the concern expressed about the decline in book reading habits J.K. Rowling still managed to snare millions of readers and sustain their concentration with books like *Harry Potter and the Order of the Phoenix* which has 766 pages and over 300,000 words. The issue of falling attention spans was raised by Julian Chapman, the President of the National Association of School Teachers and Union of Women Teachers (NASUWT) at their annual conference in April 2009. Chapman expressed the view, *"the quick-fire pace of television is reducing concentration spans in UK classrooms"* and he speculated that poor behaviour, *"was not the result of dull teaching, but pupils who expected the presentation skills of a television studio".*[7] Are some teachers boring? Where you ever bored at school? How far is boredom just a

Generation Y issue or have boring lessons always existed? In a Mori survey, commissioned by the Youth Justice Board, February 2009, 37% of the 4,750 pupils surveyed across schools in England and Wales truanted. When asked why the pupils gave the following reasons.

Mori survey of reasons for truancy in schools in England and Wales 2009	
Reason for truancy	**% response**
Found lessons boring	55
Didn't get on with the teacher	31
Had not done homework	25
Wanted to do something better	24
Found lessons badly taught	22
Found lessons difficult	17
Trying to avoid a test or exam	15
Bullied by other people at school	12
Family needed me to help out at home	10
Friends made me do it	9
I had a job and needed to work	2
Experienced racism	1
Other	11
Don't know	6

Source: Youth Justice Board, Youth Survey 2008, Young people in Mainstream Education, www.yjb.gov.uk.

The highest response (55%) is in relation to boredom and appears to indicate too many lessons with insufficient activity. However, we also know from research into poor behaviour that often pupils will say they are bored when the real issue is that they do not understand what they are being taught and are struggling to make progress. They may therefore feint disinterest and/or play truant to mask their lack of understanding. Note that many of the other significant reasons listed for truancy fall into this category i.e. issues related to not coping with the lesson or the work. A high percentage (31%) also state that they do not get on with the teacher and this may highlight problems of communication whereby explanations were not understood and in consequence the relationship becomes strained. Hattie's ground-breaking summary of educational research noted, *"about half who drop out of school claim that classes were not interesting or inviting, and two thirds claim that not one teacher was interested in their success in learning at school"*.[8] The subject of boring lessons produced some lively discussion in the educational press in January 2009. The correspondence was triggered by a statement from Ofsted that one third of lessons in schools were only satisfactory, *'those are going to be lessons where children have not been stimulated, where children were bored and where teaching was dull.'*[9] Some teachers wrote to their newspapers in defence of boredom because they believed it reflected the real world i.e. some jobs and some aspects of real life are boring and therefore boring lessons prepare young people for coping with future mundane tasks. This is a dispiriting response because if experiencing boredom was a legitimate teaching aim then it would be identified as an aim on a lesson plan but the reality is that the lessons Ofsted identified as boring and dull were not intended to be. It is doubtful if many of the teachers left the classroom congratulating themselves on having successfully bored the class. The issue has resurfaced in 2012 after the Ofsted Chief Inspector's report published in November 2011 commented, *"In the least successful lessons, teachers talk too much, suppressing learners' contributions, and deliver content that is unimaginative.... Teaching is dull and uninspiring, so learners find it hard to maintain their interest and make progress"*.[10] The answer to falling attention spans and the related issue of boredom is to keep a sharp eye on the body language of your class and to respond to it. Be aware that after only 10 minutes some might be drifting away. Scan faces for signs of frustration or uncertainty or going off task and react. After 20 minutes consider at least a pause to gain some participation if not a break into an individual, paired or group task. Therefore an effective lesson will focus on active engagement rather than too much time spent in passive listening. This is not a modern development – The Board of Education Handbook first published in 1904, includes the recommendation, *"the children themselves should take an active part in the lesson, and not merely be passive listeners.* [11] and advises that the most effective learning arises when, *"the teacher realises that his chief task is to teach the scholars to teach themselves, and adapts his methods to that end"*.[12]

Active participation

The successful development of a lesson will involve exposition or 'whole class teaching', extension into question and answer to check for levels of understanding and learning and some aspect of active learning i.e. individual, paired and/or group tasks to explore and consolidate key learning. Consider entering your classroom with the simple core model:

- Whole class engagement (exposition),
- Individual task,
- Paired task – and in a longer lesson the addition of a,
- Group task.

If you commit to this model then it should box in the tendency to over talk and will produce more interactive lessons because you will enter the classroom with a planned individual and paired task and perhaps a group task as well. The tasks will draw down resources and overall build interactive learning. In September 2008 Ofsted published a summary report of the key features of outstanding teaching and learning at Level 3 drawn from 25 colleges. Some of the features listed are relevant to the above model and to all students as follows:

- *"the use of different text books and other resources, including reference to virtual learning environments, to meet students' differing needs*
- *well-structured questioning, with open questions suitably targeted at students of different abilities*
- *students working in pairs and small groups based on ability*
- *planned independent work, including research, tailored to meet the needs of individual students*
- *the use of learning support assistants, both in lessons and for support outside the classroom*
- *a range of activities which engaged students' interest*

- *high levels of support for individual students both within and outside the classroom; teachers were generous with their time, which students valued*
- *modifying and adapting lesson plans in the light of informal assessment of students' progress and understanding during the lesson*
- *setting short and longer term learning goals for individual students".*[13]

The core of the Diamond lesson plan (Chapter Six) places an emphasis upon effective group work, questioning and the promotion of independent learning.

Exposition

In our schools and colleges exposition or 'whole class teaching' tends to be of the informal 'chalk and talk' variety or in this electronic age, 'Smartboard and talk'. Exposition has not been banned and can be highly effective. Hattie places 'direct instruction' 26th in his rank order of 138 influences on learning (see Chapter One) with an effect score of 0.59 against the 0.40 average. The secret, as detailed in relation to attention spans, is to keep it focussed, short and sharp and avoiding the temptation to over talk. Within Higher Education exposition tends to take the form of a formal lecture to introduce a major topic and as a guide to independent research and learning. A university lecture may last for at least an hour and two hours is not unusual. In Further Education we can, if wished, also deliver a lecture. However, to be successful a formal lecture must consist of more than simply extending your 'chalk and talk'. The ingredients of an effective lecture are:

- Clear points to guide the content of the lecture / exposition. If there are going to be four key points then state and list the four key points and immediately this provides a structure for the lecture.
- Up-to-date references – when students can see relevance and application it will improve motivation and interest.
- Enthusiasm and passion – when students feel that the topic means something to the presenter they will 'buy in', much more.
- Expansive body language – move and make appropriate gestures to help maintain the attention of your class / audience. Never stand rooted to the spot behind a lectern. In terms of

absorbing spoken communication our concentration and interest is sustained by a mere 7% of the actual words spoken, 38% comes from intonation and volume but 55% from the body language of the presenter. Therefore it would seem the comedian Frank Carson was right when he said, *' it's the way I tell 'em'!*

- Bright visuals – support key points with relevant visuals go for photographs, diagrams, charts, animations and short video clips for best impact. Simply do a web search linked to a key topic and you will often find a wealth of useful images.
- Avoid death by Powerpoint or Keynote – do not use a master slide which places the same logo and background colour on every slide and presents slide after slide of bullet point text. Ensure any text is large font, place text into tables instead of bullet point lists, vary background colours and layout and use regular charts, diagrams, appropriate photographs and/or integrated video clips. You Tube tends to hold short video on most topics. Never simply read aloud the text because your audience has already read it.
- Ask some questions and give thinking time before seeking answers – extend into a quick paired discussion. Even in a lecture theatre we can invite students to ponder a key question with their nearest neighbour. To punctuate further use a visual timer for Powerpoint or Keynote to add pace. Visit the Collegenet website to download a set of ten visual timers or try Triptico.co.uk
- Pause at the end of each major objective and re-state the key points all should have recorded. Ask some further questions to prompt thinking and to check for levels of understanding before moving forward into the next objective etc.
- Conclude with guidance on how the students should follow the lecture with their own independent research.

In essence a successful lecture will mimic the stepping stones of the Diamond Lesson Plan and even within a formal lecture theatre we can, as indicated above, take steps to draw the audience into participation and reflection. However, outside of the formal lecture the 'chalk and talk' style exposition, more common in our classrooms, should be followed by the application of effective question and answer techniques to probe and check learning. A presentation may be enthusiastic and motivating but what have the students learned?

Regular question and answer dialogues and assessment for learning approaches will reveal and hopefully correct any misunderstandings and also build a rapport and 'can do' culture. Essentially students who are progressing and know they are progressing will attend. This may seem simplistic but at some point many students will switch off a particular subject because they have hit a learning barrier and do not know how to get around it. Teachers must be alert to the silent students and seek to draw them in. Boys in particular are often loath to express difficulty or to request assistance. If there are learning assistants in the room they should be encouraged to assist the learning process by asking questions because they can voice difficulties or questions they have overheard or they can promote positive recognition by drawing the teacher's attention to a particular student's work or answer. By entering into a dialogue with the teacher learning assistants will encourage a wider learning culture. If you have the luxury of a learning assistant in your classroom then think *double act* rather than *magician's assistant*. Our focus should be on learning and discovering 'what is it?' some students find difficult and how can they be helped to learn?

Teaching vocabulary

All too often low reading ages compound poor literacy and the meaning of new subject specific words or academic or technical language presents a learning barrier. Do not assume that all can define and apply new vocabulary just because no one questions what a word means. Be alert to the level of language in your exposition, handouts , textbook etc because what might be a common word or phrase to you may not be to your students. This will apply even more if you have any English as an Additional Language (EAL) students in your classroom. Highlight the spelling and definitions of new key words or terms. Direct all to rule the first page in their folders to create a 'glossary of terms' page and as new words are encountered they should be added with definitions. Or issue a pre-printed pro-forma for capturing new vocabulary or an A-Z address book to record vocabulary. Marzano highlights research, *"that student achievement will increase by 33 percentile points when vocabulary instruction focuses on specific words that are important to what students are learning"*. [14] Consider issuing random spelling and definition challenges as the course progresses and use to punctuate and separate different episodes of a lesson. Simply flash up five key words on screen or invite the students to select a card at random from a set of pre-printed cards to define key words. Remember lots of praise for correct answers to encourage participation and to reinforce the correct spellings.

Question and Answer

The Diamond lesson plan displays 'question and answer' as a step after exposition but in practice, question and answer will merge with the exposition into a seamless whole. As the 'chalk and talk' or exposition progresses there might be regular pauses to pose questions and to draw the students into a dialogue. The exposition might commence with some key questions, often Socratic, (see below) to probe the extent of prior knowledge. It is rare for any topic to be totally new to everyone. In a Business Studies lesson on 'Sole Traders' opening questions might ask, what is a Sole Trader? Does anyone know a Sole Trader? Does anyone work for a Sole Trader as a part-time job? This type of preliminary questioning can raise an expectation for interaction and draw the students into participation. It also gives recognition to students who have prior knowledge and should alert the teacher to apply differentiation and to ensure that those students are stretched and extended during the lesson. Moving from what students currently know and understand about a topic is quite powerful. The Ofsted Chief Inspector's Report 2010 emphasised the importance of good questioning techniques, *"Open and challenging questions extend pupils' reasoning and vocabulary and help them to become enthusiastic and self-motivated learners, eager to contribute and share their ideas. At its very best, such teaching generates an infectious enthusiasm for learning".*[15]

However, this guidance does not appear to been sufficiently acted upon because the following year, in 2011, the Chief Inspector reported, *"Questioning is rarely sufficiently penetrating to make learners think hard enough to develop their ideas, or to research, explore or communicate their ideas independently".*[16] Question and answer appears within the Diamond lesson plan as a significant feature of the middle of the lesson but it is not fixed. Question and answer might also form the centre piece of a recap at the start of the lesson or at the end of the lesson as a final check on learning. Therefore be fluid and enter into question and answers as appropriate at each stage of the lesson and often spontaneously in response to a student enquiry.

Plan your questions

Effective question and answer is a significant skill and needs thought and planning to achieve clear learning outcomes. It is advisable to enter the lesson with a set of pre-planned key questions to ensure that all are appropriately engaged and stretched. At the lesson planning stage consider what are the basic facts and information all should know by the end of the lesson and list appropriate questions. Next consider what higher reasoning you might expect in terms of how the topic information is applied, compared, evaluated or analysed i.e. questions across the range of Bloom's cognitive taxonomy. These considerations and revisions of Bloom are explored in more depth in Chapter Two.

Bloom's cognitive taxonomy		
Hierarchy of learning	**Ability**	**Question roots**
Knowledge	To know, and be able to recall, define and describe the basic facts or theory etc.	Describe, list, identify, state, what, when, where, who, how, define.
Comprehension	To be able to interpret, summarise, illustrate and explain the facts/theory	Explain, estimate, why, in what ways.., compare, summarise, what if..
Application	To apply the knowledge in new situations and to recognise and use the knowledge to resolve or solve issues.	Illustrate, show, apply, demonstrate, predict, relate, solve.
Analysis	To break the knowledge down into associated points, reasons, sequence of events, consequences, positives, negatives etc	Classify, order, place into.. select, give reasons why..., how far.., infer, break down, differentiate, distinguish between.
Synthesis	To reason, predict speculate and project on the basis of the analysis.	Create, design, plan, what conclusions..., How might..., propose, substitute, remove..., what connections.. If ? had not happened...
Evaluation	To compare, assess and justify issues, theories, events etc. The opinion held and why.	Rank, justify, give me an argument for.., why this method..., compare, contrast, assess, defend, appraise, recommend, judge.

Marzano highlights that *"questions that require students to analyse information – frequently called higher order level questions – produce more learning than questions that simply require students to recall or recognize information – frequently referred to as lower-order questions"*.[17] Therefore ensure you pose sufficient questions at the higher end of Bloom's taxonomy because as Marzano adds, *"unfortunately most of the questions teachers ask are lower order in nature."* [18] This point was reinforced by Hattie's research which concluded, *' 60 percent of teachers' questions required factual recall, 20 percent were procedural and only 20 percent required thought by the students'*[19] The Ofsted Chief Inspector's Report 2011 for the Schools sector also highlighted this issue of too many lower order questions contributing to low inspection grades, *"In the weaker lessons observed, a tendency to ask closed questions means that pupils give simply factual low-level responses. In these cases the teachers themselves elaborate on a pupil's initial response rather than probing them to explore the ideas more deeply, and debate or share views. Teachers' questions can often be focused on low-level cognitive activity and not sufficiently on extending or reinforcing pupils' understanding"*.[20] To guard against asking too many lower-order questions enter your classroom with three levels of questions that mirror the relevant exam board expectations for pass, merit and distinction or grades D/E, C, and A/B at A-Level. Start by asking questions that will check and confirm the knowledge of the subject and basic factual understanding e.g. *what is a Sole Trader?* Ask for examples and check for awareness of how the facts apply, *How do Sole Traders operate?* Finally invite comparisons, opinions, and judgements e.g. *what are the advantages and disadvantage of Sole Traders compared to other forms of business organisation?* In essence first establish and confirm the core facts (closed questions) before extending thinking into application and analysis etc. (open questions). Ofsted inspectors regularly comment on the effectiveness of question and answer techniques as illustrated by this example from a grade one report for an Engineering lesson, *"Skilful questioning by teachers encourages contributions from students, both to recap on their previous learning and to stimulate thought on current tasks"*.[21] Teachers also need to listen well and to *hear* the answers and interpret what the answers mean in terms of levels of understanding and to address any misunderstandings. Hattie highlighted this as a hallmark of the most effective teachers, *"know where to go next in the light of the gap between current students' knowledge and understanding and the success criteria"*.[20] At all times the key is the success criteria:

what are the students expected to know? How far do they know it? Why are some struggling? How can the block to learning be overcome? The development of a learning dialogue that involves Socratic questioning techniques may assist with this process to deepen responses.

Socratic questioning

Socrates the Greek philosopher (470 B.C. – 399 B.C.) famously engaged his students, including Plato and Aristotle, in a question and answer dialogue that probed how opinions were formed and supported by evidence. Socrates applied six forms of questions to test propositions:

1. Questions for clarification	Why do you think that? What do you mean by? Could you explain what you mean?
2. Questions that probe assumptions	Can you give me an example of that? What do others think? Why do you assume that?
3. Questions that probe reasons and evidence	What is your evidence? Why do you think this is true? How do we know this?
4. Questions about viewpoints and perspectives	What would be the alternative? What are the strengths and weaknesses? Are you saying..?
5. Questions that probe implications and consequences	How could we test this? What would happen if...? Why is this important?
6. Questions about questions	Is this the right question to ask? What am I trying to say? How could I re-phrase this question?

Socratic questioning is very powerful because it drives reflection, *How do I know that? Why do I think that? Can I justify that statement?* Socratic questioning can promote objective reasoning by ensuring, as far as possible, that decisions and conclusions are underpinned by evidence rather than emotional attachment or even guesswork. Questions of the above type can significantly deepen learning and fully engage students because they are drawn into questioning their own assumptions, possible prejudices and ultimately why they hold a particular opinion. At its most basic the questioner is assuming complete ignorance of the issue and driving deeper and deeper responses. Providing sufficient thinking time, as described in Chapter Five, is also a key consideration because all too often teachers intervene too early and answer their own questions. In the Ofsted report, *'Identifying good practice: a survey of Post-16 science in colleges and schools'*, the practice of giving thinking time was favourably recorded, *"teachers in the outstanding schools and colleges were alert to the performance of individuals in their classes. They asked direct probing questions and left time for the students to think before answering"*.[23] In all cases also be aware of your body language – smile, nod, grin, thumb up, use your hands and gestures to encourage more detail or longer responses via informal recognition.

21 question strategies

Ideally all students should be drawn into question and answers sessions but many are reluctant to get involved for fear of being wrong. A range of active questioning techniques can assist passive students to become engaged. They also offer the teacher *real time* feedback in terms of what the students know and understand so that misunderstandings can be corrected. In addition many of the questioning techniques highlighted below are designed to invite the students to pose the questions and this will help to significantly deepen learning. Experiment with the following selection of 21 active questioning strategies and adopt or adapt as appropriate.

1 Stand up	Invite the class to stand-up and each person can only sit down after they have answered a question correctly. Clearly you can direct basic factual questions and more demanding questions to different students as appropriate.
2 Step forward	Invite the class to line-up along one wall of the classroom and for each correct answer each individual can advance one step towards the facing wall. The first student to touch the facing wall can win a small prize.

3 One minute	Place the class into pairs and give one minute to consider an answer to a key question or concept. Use a countdown timer to add pace. Gain answers and comment **from each pair** before confirming the answer(s) and build full understanding of the issue or concept. Discuss any wrong answers and why and how the wrong conclusion was reached.
4 Bronze, Silver and Gold	Place the class into pairs or small groups and have questions pre-prepared on small colour coded cards. Bronze questions are worth one point, Silver two points and Gold questions three points. Each team selects which level of question to answer. Set a time limit or a points total and the team with the most points at the end of the time limit or first to hit the points total wins. For correct Gold answers perhaps offers a Gold coin as a reward available from any supermarket or for a real treat large gold coins available from Starbucks. For a special quiz attach ribbons to the gold coins and present to the winning team.
5 Mini White boards	Issue mini whiteboards and invite each individual to write their answer on their whiteboard. Keep fast paced. This is good for questions that demand a one word answer or for multiple choice questions whereby they only have to indicate answer A, B, C etc. Throw in for fun a question where they have to draw the answer i.e. an object, person, place. Remember when scanning the answers not to immediately state which answer is correct. Question students who are holding-up the incorrect response. You should probe to see how their thinking diverged from the correct answer before confirming the correct answer.
6 Traffic Lights	Issue the students with coloured card in the traffic light colours and enter into fast paced question and answer. A student who is confident of the answer holds up green, a student who is unsure on some aspects holds up yellow/amber and a student who is totally stuck holds up red. Check the green answers by asking three or more students holding green for consistency and accuracy before confirming the answer is correct. Alternatively invite 'greens' to explain the answer to 'amber' and 'reds'. This can also work well in pairs or threes.
7 Thumb Up	Invite the students to raise their thumb if they confident they know the answer to a question. Thumb sideways if they have a few uncertainties and thumb down if they are stuck. Select students with their thumbs up to provide the answer but also select students with their thumbs sideways or down to explain their uncertainties or aspects they find difficult.

8 Electronic voting	Invest in an electronic voting system like Quizdom www.quizdom.co.uk whereby each student holds an electronic remote and responds to multiple choice questions by pressing the appropriate button. The software permits answers to be displayed on screen in a variety of ways and the teacher can printout each student's score.
9 Graffiti wall	Write the topic at the top of a sheet of flipchart paper and invite all to write at least one question each about the topic, plus any appropriate drawings/graffiti they wish to add. Once complete ask the questions and supplement with some of your own to test understanding. The process of thinking and writing the questions is quite valuable and often reflects an uncertainty held by the student.
10 Deep thought	With a suitable burst of fanfare music announce the 'Deep Thought' question named after the famous computer on the *Hitchhikers Guide to the Galaxy* that was asked, *'what is the answer to the ultimate question of life, the universe and everything?* After seven and a half million years of deliberation, Deep Thought famously answered 42! Ask a 'deep thought' question relevant to your subject that is a matter of debate or opinion rather than a straightforward question. The aim is to promote ' *deep thought'* and to encourage the students to form and justifying opinions. Note the 'Thunk' concept in the recap section of Chapter Seven which adopts a similar approach. Give your students thinking time to consider their *'deep thought'* in pairs or small groups using a Powerpoint or Keynote timer and then check all answers and promote a discussion. You can play the relevant clip of the TV series (lasts for 2.40 minutes) by going to You Tube www.youtube.com and selecting the video clip, *'the answer to life, universe and everything'*.
11 Post-It	In a variation of the above invite all to write a question on a Post-It note and stick to a sheet of flipchart paper. Use a standard colour for the questions. Next ask each student to select a question they can answer and to write their answer on a post-it note but adopt a different standard colour for the answers. Finish by placing the Post-It notes into two columns with questions and answers matched up. Confirm all answers. As a variation place the class into two teams and ask each team to write questions on a specified topic. Post the questions on a sheet of flipchart paper and each team should answer the questions set by the other team. Set a time limit with a Powerpoint or Keynote timer to give a competitive edge; check the answers and declare a winning team.

12 Four corners	Label the four corners of your classroom A, B, C and D. Set-up some questions with multiple choice answers A,B,C,D on a handout or projected on screen. Ask the first question and invite the students to stand in the corner that matches their chosen answer. After a while you may get a herd instinct whereby they all decide who is most likely to get it right and select the same corner. To check this tendency ensure you follow-up by selecting students to explain why their answer is correct and do select students who you suspect are just following the crowd.
13 Hotseat	Invite a student to take the 'hotseat' at the front of the class and to answer questions on a specified topic. This could be pre-prepared with a week's warning and particularly useful at revision time with different students covering a range of key topics. The teacher might also take a regular turn in the hotseat because the learning is also related to thinking of questions to ask. Ensure all students ask at least one question each. To add further interest conduct in a 'Mastermind TV quiz' format and download the Mastermind theme music to play.
14 Frequently Asked Questions (FAQ)	On your Visual Learning Environment (VLE) have a link to FAQ for each major topic. When each major topic is concluded invite two students to write and post a summary list of FAQ linked to the topic. Display the completed FAQ in the lesson and in Wikipedia mode invite any corrections or extensions to the questions and answers.
15 Quiz formats	Any quiz formats work well with *Blockbusters* and *Who wants to be a millionaire* perennial favourites. Many enterprising teachers and organisations have placed free templates to support both quizzes on the internet. Simply Google 'who wants to be a millionaire template' or 'Blockbusters template' and you will be spoilt for choice. Some templates come complete with the music and recreate the whole atmosphere of the TV quiz. .For, *Who wants to be a millionaire* devise fifteen questions ranging across Bloom's taxonomy with four possible answers to each question. Divide the class into teams and after the first ten (knowledge based) questions ask each team to nominate one person to answer the remaining five (analytical/evaluative) questions. They may of course use their three lifelines ask/phone a friend (on this occasion they may use their mobiles) ask the whole class/team or go for 50/50.

16 Connections	Connections is a questioning technique taken from the writings of Rudyard Kipling, ***I keep six honest serving men. They taught me all I knew. Their names are What and Why and When and How and Where and Who.*** Display the six question roots on the board and apply to a topic to test and check understanding. You could experiment with a stimuli like the photograph of a key person, place, event, discovery etc and the class in pairs have to race to be the first to answer all six questions. A similar approach to this is referred to in Chapter Eleven for checking learning at the ends of lessons but here the How is missed out to make it the Five Ws question.
17 Dictaglos	Draw into a Socratic dialogue by building up on screen a series of linked photographs, quotations, data etc.. The links should not immediately be apparent but picture by picture question the students about what they see and draw information from them. As the sequence continues the additional images should confirm or reject their thinking. The images could be names, facts, statistics as well as photographs but what is the link? Ultimately with the final photograph or image all should realise the link and confirm the relevant learning.
18 Snowball	Write around 10-12 single questions on individual sheets of A5 – one question per page. Crumble all the sheets together into a 'snowball'. Throw the snowball to a student who unwraps the outer page and has to answer the question. He or she then throws the snowball to another student and so on. You may place a sweet in the last sheet. For variation divide into two teams and throw the snowball between the teams. You may also have two colours of paper to identify challenge and pass level questions. If anyone is uncertain on an answer remember to open the question to other team members or the wider class.
19 Catch	In a variation of the above buy a soft rugby or football from a toy shop and throw it into the air. Whoever catches it answers a question and they then throw it for someone else to catch and so on.
20 Nominate	In a further variation to the above approaches randomly select a student to answer a question. When they have answered invite them to ask a question and to nominate who should answer it. Let this roll forward and perhaps give the students three minutes advance warning to think of questions they might ask so that hesitation is reduced and the questions move quickly around the classroom. The process of thinking of questions is quite powerful and tests subject knowledge as well as the giving of answers.

21 Relay	Divide the class into two teams and line-up at one end of the classroom. Place a set of question cards for each team at the other end of the classroom. The first person for each team runs to the questions and must give a correct answer before they can sprint back. If incorrect they must return and another team member sprints forward to answer. The first team to answer all of their question cards wins.

Some of the strategies suggested for 'Recap' in Chapter Seven, like the traffic light method, can also be used at this stage of the lesson and vice versa. Remember to ensure that each technique does not just become 'entertainment' but invite the students to explain their answers, prompt to expand and encourage other students to add information. A key consideration for question and answer strategies is to consider a *'no hands up'* policy i.e. you control and decide who will answer the question. This approach keeps all students on their toes because they do not know if you will suddenly turn to them and ask them a question. If someone appears very uncertain in the spotlight then reduce the 'glare' by inviting another student to help out or by inviting them to 'phone a friend'. If the answer is a partial rather than a full answer then invite others to add what they know and build a deeper answer. This approach is important to guard against the more able students in your lesson from spontaneously answering all of your questions. If you do not check this tendency then the less confident students will hold back and the more able might be placed into the spotlight too often and attract teasing or even bullying from their classmates. Overtime you can ensure that all are drawn in and the students will realise that they are expected to answer and participate. However, fast paced, spontaneous, first to answer *'popcorn'* style question and answer sessions are also engaging but in this case use factually based questions that all should be able to answer. Many of the technique lend themselves to paired working and this is often very beneficial because it can help to build confidence. The fact that your partner shares your answer removes a lot of the hesitation and uncertainty. Ask a key question and give thinking time in pairs to arrive at an answer. Give only one minute or less. Have a clock in the room with a large second hand so they can see the time or use a cooking timer with the alarm set or sound an air-horn or place an electronic countdown timer on Power Point or Keynote. Gain answers from four or five pairs around the room and introduce some of the Socratic questioning methods to probe the answer given by each pair before confirming the correct responses. Remember that all must be helped to have the confidence to be wrong.

Random student selection

Add a sense of fun by using a variety of ways to randomly select students to answer questions. You might consider:

- This question is for anyone with blonde hair
- This question is for anyone wearing glasses

Once the relevant sub-group identify themselves then select one person to answer and invite the others to confirm that the answer is correct or to add to it. You can increase the impact of this by asking all the relevant students to stand. Once you are satisfied with the answer(s) they can sit down. You can then extend this approach to all manner of personal identifiers, colour of shoes, trousers, shirts etc and to introduce a sense of fun isolate an individual by naming something specific that only that person is wearing etc. A further variation is to draw a room plan and allocate a letter to each row of tables or individual tables i.e. Row A, Row B or Table A, Table B and so on. Then count off the students in each row or seated around each table i.e. one, two, three. When you then enter into question and answer mode simply at random shout out question for Student B2, or Question for E4 etc. A favourite random technique recommended by Dylan Wiliam is to write each student's name onto a lolly pop stick and stand them all in a cup. Then during the lesson select a student to answer a question by selecting a lolly pop stick at random. Each lolly pop stick could be set to one side to ensure all students are asked a question over the course of the lesson or return them to the cup to keep them all on their toes or they may sit back having answered 'their' question. It is also possible to place photographs of your students onto a Powerpoint or Keynote and to spin the photos and freeze frame to select a student. Triptico.co.uk also offers some further random name generators.

Recognition

All students take a risk in answering a question because they fear the embarrassment of being wrong. Remember that some students are so lacking in confidence that they will look down to avoid your eye or give silly answers to avoid revealing that they do not know. Aim to create a learning culture where it is safe and OK to be wrong. Acknowledge that some questions are difficult. Emphasise that they are learning new information and so they should expect to get some answers wrong. In other words make it easy for your students to say, *"I don't understand..."* Encourage all to ask when they are uncertain. Take on the blame for speaking too quickly or for not explaining it well enough – never imply they should know this or that it is easy. Overall, try and give positives to all. Ignore any minor silly behaviour and give praise to those participating to reinforce the behaviour you want. Marzano recommends the term 'recognition' rather than praise because of the dangers associated with empty praise, *"praise given for accomplishing easy tasks can undermine achievement. Students commonly perceived it as undeserved; further praise for accomplishing easy tasks might actually lower their perception of their ability"*.[24] Therefore attach the praise to the answer and explain why it was a good response. Recognising contributions in a positive way will encourage further participation whereas the embarrassment of getting it wrong may cause students to clam up. Here are 21 ways to say well done.

1. I'm impressed,
2. That's good
3. Excellent answer
4. You've got it
5. It doesn't get better than this
6. Good example
7. Spot on
8. Perfect
9. Nice one
10. That's a gold medal response
11. Brilliant answer
12. That's a good comprehensive answer
13. You know your stuff
14. I'm delighted by that answer
15. You are on top of this
16. Couldn't be better

17. That's a grade A answer
18. I like that
19. Much better
20. Terrific response
21. That's really sharp and clear

However, as indicated, praise appropriate answers rather than every single utterance or in practice it will become patronising and ineffective.

Building discussion the Harkness method

To move beyond question and answer to deepen discussion perhaps experiment with the Harkness seminar style investigation of a key topic.

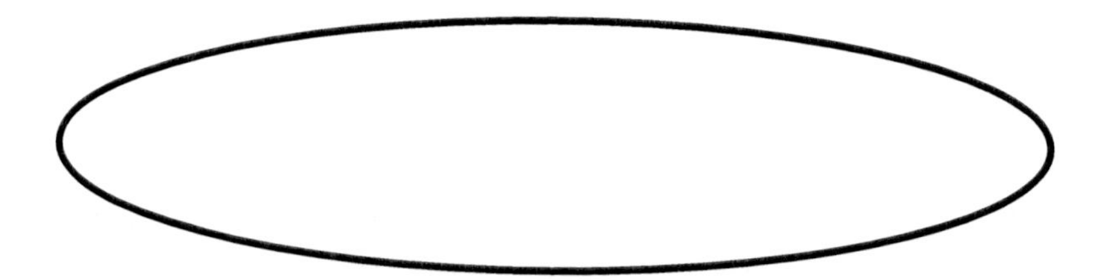

The above diagram of an **oval table** illustrates the Harkness method of promoting student discussion. Edward Harkness (1874-1940) was an American heir to an oil fortune who administered a family foundation devoted to promoting education. His original and surviving concept was to seat no more than twelve students around an oval table and to adopt a seminar style of learning whereby the teacher chaired a discussion to interrogate and discuss key concepts. The oval table is reputed to promote effective discussion because the physical proximity engages all and literally removes the 'back seat' of the traditional classroom rows. Negative or passive behaviour is also reduced because the teacher is not the focal point. The discussion and learning is centre stage with a focus on exploring, discussing, questioning and evaluating key concepts rather than listening to a teacher at the front of the room. This in turn raises the responsibility of all (rather than just the teacher) to enter the classroom having researched the topic. Facts are absorbed outside the classroom and the lesson time is devoted to discussing the facts, raising and answering questions and arriving at conclusions. The Harkness method was first adopted in 1931 by the Philips Exeter Academy in New Hampshire and is now practised in many American and English schools – although largely in the independent sector. The reality in most colleges is that we do not have classes of only twelve students nor Principals who will readily buy and install oval tables in all of our classrooms. Therefore a pragmatic solution and a fast way to experiment with the Harkness method is to re-arrange your classroom desks to form a rectangle and to implement the spirit of Harkness if not the physical oval reality?

Around the table

How do we learn around the table? Consider the following approaches;

- ✓ Expect advance reading / research – How do you support independent learning?
- ✓ Introduce Socratic questioning – establish the facts and extend into evaluation
- ✓ Give thinking time – on average teachers pause 0.9 seconds before intervening
- ✓ Engage all – invite and support all to share an opinion or raise a question
- ✓ Reciprocal teaching – a student leads a learning summary and questions
- ✓ Summarise and check key learning at the end of each session – check recording.
- ✓ Stretch all – suggest extension activities to extend learning.

Clearly you need to consider the level and ability of students if this is to work well. Some will need much more structure to guide advance research than others and in-class support with clear step by step prompts to advance and build the discussion. Successful whole class presentations, questions and answers to check understanding and wider discussion should establish a clear learning platform of shared information ready for exploration in group discussions and co-operative research.

Developing learning

"..organising students in cooperative learning groups has a powerful effect on learning, regardless of whether groups compete with one another."[1]

Robert J Marzano

The core of our lessons should focus upon developing learning and this means giving space and time for student to reflect upon new learning via individual, paired and / or group tasks. Few people immediately understand a new concept and need to time to reflect upon it, to question it, to discuss it with others and to seek clarification of some of the points made. Simply spending most lesson time imparting information may 'cover the curriculum' but what do your students know and understand? The regular use of individual, paired and group learning tasks will develop and deepen learning by giving time for reflection and opportunities to develop Functional and employability skills. Open-up space in your lessons by applying the Flipped Learning' model as detailed in Bradley Lightbody's book, *The i-Learning Revolution: A new pedagogy.* Set your students key questions to answer in advance of each lesson and expect them to find the answers from resources placed on the VLE and from their own webquests and design individual, paired and group tasks to explore and confirm the answers.

Individual working

All individuals welcome the opportunity to work alone and this is important to ensure that all apply themselves to the key topics and to test their own understanding and knowledge. Some effective methods of promoting individual working are:

- Worksheets to accompany watching a DVD

- Note-taking from a chapter of a textbook
- Completing gapped handouts
- Completing a test
- Completing assignments / projects
- Answering questionnaires
- Answering written questions
- Practising / demonstrating a practical skill
- Internet / library research
- Interviewing someone
- Giving a presentation
- Hotseat activity – individually answering questions on a prepared topic
- Creating a poster / display summary of key learning
- Creating a spider diagram summary of learning
- Answering past exam questions
- ICT application – wordprocessing, spreadsheet, database, desk top publishing, digital video,
- Creating a Powerpoint, Keynote or Prezi presentation
- Brainstorming
- Mindmapping
- Creating a timeline
- Creating a photo slideshow
- Recording own opinion / suggestions / answers by using post-it notes or traffic light coloured dots
- Worksheets / templates to rank and sort information
- Keeping a journal or learning diary – or online blog
- Creating a podcast
- Creating a video podcast
- Writing to a time limit
- Tabulating information
- Displaying statistics in a chart

The reading tasks, in particular, can be the basis of reciprocal teaching i.e. invite a student to summarise, explain or lead discussion on the text or task. Marzano identified four interlinked steps for successful reciprocal teaching, summarising, questioning, clarifying and predicting.[5] The lead student summarises the theory, concept or simply the key points in the text/video/data etc and asks the other students some key questions. The act of summarising and questioning will deepen and extend understanding and lead to key points being highlighted for closer clarification or explanation. Finally all should be asked to predict outcomes, results, consequences etc. as appropriate. Reciprocal teaching is ninth in Hattie's top ten of influences on learning (see Chapter one) but he emphasizes the need for teachers to first model and demonstrate how to structure the dialogue for best outcomes. Initial close teacher support should be gradually withdrawn as the students become more comfortable and confident in taking the lead. This strategy may also be linked to the Harkness method described in Chapter Eight with a student arriving prepared to take the lead on a particular topic.

Paired working

Paired working is very effective because it permits individuals to compare their thinking with someone else and if in mixed ability pairs of even greater benefit. However, you may also pair by ability with appropriately differentiated tasks. The paired discussion provides reassurance and perhaps valuable correction and 'rehearsal' of answers within the shelter of the paired discussion before answers and ideas are shared with the full class. Overtime paired work will build confidence and boost participation in wider class discussions. Most students will sit with their immediate friends in the classroom and this can be the basis of paired work i.e. working with your immediate neighbour to complete a task. This is quick to arrange with no need for movement or re-arrangement of seating. However, wider working/bonding within a class is also important to help break down any gender, ethnic and ability divides. Random paired working can be achieved by asking the students to turn their chairs around and to work with the person in the row behind. Clearly this technique relates to a classroom set out in rows and can also work well in a lecture theatre. Within a horseshoe setting you might invite those on the left hand side to take their chairs and to sit and face the person on the right hand side of the classroom. To make it more interactive generate random pairs by dropping labels into a hat and asking each student to select a label. You might consider natural pairs, *Fish and Chips, Cup and Saucer, Salt and Pepper, Tom and Jerry, Fruit and Nut, Sugar and Spice, Becks and Posh, Ant and Dec, Mork and Mindy, Gavin and Stacey* etc. With imagination you can generate some curriculum linked pairs like *split* and *ends* for hairdressing. In Travel and Tourism perhaps select the names of major rivers with the matching cities or small photographs of landmarks with locations etc. In English, go for characters like *Romeo and Juliet, Cathy and Heathcliffe* or names of poets and opening lines from their poems etc. In Maths, try a formula and an answer. Within Engineering perhaps select famous bridges and locations. Finally, in Catering try matching-up celebrity chefs with the names of their restaurants or a list of ingredients and a dish etc. Each student simply selects a label and by comparing labels they match-up and find their partner and as they move into pairs we tease out a bit of wider knowledge. Fastest of all, with least preparation, is a pack of snap cards. All of the suggestions made above for individual working can equally be completed as paired activities. The strength of pair working is the involvement in discussion about key issues/topics which may reveal misunderstandings and will help to build confidence overtime by arriving at shared opinions and agreed answers.

Group learning

Our aim, as teachers, is not only to equip students to pass exams or practical tests but, as far as possible, to develop the higher order thinking and reasoning skills that characterise Distinction level or Grade A answers and now A* answers at A-Level. Beyond satisfying exam requirements our students will also need the skills to interact in a diverse society and possess the Functional and personal skills for effective performance in the world of work. A Business Studies student might be able to recite all the key facts about limited companies but how often in their future employment will they be asked to recite them? Indeed will anyone ever ask, 'tell all you know about limited companies? It is more likely that they will be asked at a junior level to work well in a team, to tolerate and respect other opinions, to be well acquainted with Microsoft Office applications, to demonstrate sensitivity and awareness of different cultures and religions, to manage their time well, to work to deadlines, to spell and write clearly, to handle numbers and statistics and to be well organised. At a more senior level of employment, it will be common to be asked to lead a team, chair a meeting, précis a complex report, articulate and sustain own opinion, wordprocess a crisp clear report, analyse a spreadsheet, research a topic, give a 'persuasive' presentation, design sharp, visual Powerpoint slides etc. A narrow range of teaching methods directed at cognitive learning might result in the student passing his or her examinations but lacking those wider social and employability skills.

Functional and employability skills will not be developed while sitting and listening to a teacher but they will be developed once students are set individual tasks or placed into pairs or groups and asked to research and present information in different forms. The Ofsted 2012 criteria for Further Education specifies a focus on the development of personal, social and employability skills:

> ***"Learners develop personal, social and employability skills***
>
> *To make this judgement, inspectors will consider:*
>
> - *the development of English, mathematics and functional skills required to complete learners' programmes and progress*
> - *the achievement of additional qualifications and/or experience gained in the workplace*
> - *broader skills relevant to learners' progression and career aims, such as communication, teamwork, leadership, taking responsibility, reflective thinking, problem solving, independent enquiry and employability".* [2]

In terms of grading judgments the accompanying criteria for Grade One, 'Outstanding' states: *"They apply skills and background knowledge to great effect, including: personal, social, English, mathematics and functional skills, and practical vocational skills that will prepare them exceptionally well for the next stage in their education, training or employment".* [3] The same focus on skills development is repeated in similar words in the Ofsted 2012 criteria for Schools, *"They develop and apply a wide range of skills to great effect, including reading, writing, communication and mathematical skills across the curriculum that will ensure they are exceptionally well prepared for the next stage in their education, training or employment".* [4] How will the students in your lessons develop those skills and abilities over time? A large part of the answer rests with regular paired, group and independent learning tasks because once students are engaged in researching and presenting information their skills will be developed and enhanced. The wider significance of employability skills is detailed in Chapter Two.

Random group memberships

Most people are territorial by nature and drop into 'comfort zones'. Perhaps you have a favourite part of the supermarket car park where you always like to park? Even if your favourite row is full you may be prepared to wait for a space to come free rather than try another section of the car park that you rarely, if ever, visit? Comfort zones also apply to the classroom and after only a few lessons most students will adopt a favourite chair and sit in the same chair alongside the same friend every lesson, every week. This is detrimental to effective participation in learning and wider social interaction because our students are all different in terms of:

- high school attended
- family background
- neighbourhood background
- levels of achievement / ability
- levels of participation in sports and social clubs
- social class
- religion
- gender
- ethnicity

It not unusual to look around a classroom and to see students of different genders, ethnicity, ability etc. seated together and as the lesson unfolds mounting evidence of limited sharing and co-operation between the different sub groups. Indeed, sometimes, there might be evidence of rivalry and antagonism between the different sub groups and worse still evidence of one or two isolated students seated alone and rarely participating in the lesson. Our aim as teachers, from the first lesson forward, is to engage and enthuse all students to bond as one group on a common learning journey. Our subtext is to build mutual trust, co-operation and friendships across the different subgroups and hopefully to help build a more tolerant wider society. The key strategy is to regularly place the students into random pairs, as discussed above, and groups so that they all work with each other and especially within the first month at college or joining a new class. If you leave the students in the same seats then after only two to three weeks you may discover that it is already too late and that some of the students will resist moving and working with someone beyond their immediate friendship group. Marzano has also highlighted that the most effective learning takes place in mixed ability groups. Grouping by ability has some benefits but should be used sparingly in comparison to mixed ability. Two of the most effective learning strategies we can employ are peer learning and peer teaching but they work best when all the students are comfortable working with each other and preferably in mixed ability groupings. However also ensure some challenge tasks for the more able. The optimum group size for maximising participation is three students because above that number there is greater likelihood of 'passengers' taking a backseat.

Top ten random selections

The most commonly used strategy of random group selection is numbers i.e. for three groups count 1,2,3 around the class and all the students allocated number 1 form a group etc. This is very quick and involves no resource requirements. However, it is possible to be much more imaginative – remember Lifelong Learning criteria refers to, *'innovative ways to enthuse and motivate'*. Experiment with the following top ten strategies for random group selections and adopt your own favourites.

Strategy	Method
1. Birth date	Invite all to line-up in order of birth dates from January to December and then sub divide into the number of groups required e.g. January to March is Group A.
2. Alphabetical	In a variation of the above divide into groups by the alphabetical order in your register.
3. Colours	Allocate a red table, green table etc. Use coloured A5 paper mounted on a vertical place stands (available from stationery shops) to identify each table. Next buy Starburst or similar wrapped sweets with appropriately coloured wrappers. Drop the right number of sweets into a large envelope (if you want six students on the red table include six red sweets etc) and invite each student to select a sweet – a red sweet move to the red table etc. When the students are all working you might casually drop one more sweet each onto their tabletops. However, ensure one sweet per table is a unique colour e.g. only one purple sweet per table. When it is time for feedback

	ask, 'who ate the purple sweet'? This will produce some fun when they all realise it is linked to feedback. However, in a further twist just invite the student identified to act as human billboard and to come to the front of the room and hold up the flipchart paper. The rest of the group should be directed to deliver the feedback. This is a useful strategy to build confidence because your purpose is to accustom the students to standing in the spotlight at the front of the class. This is a first step to giving a presentation because as they do not have to speak they will relax and some will start to spontaneously add comments and before they realise it they are speaking in front of the whole class. **Coloured dots** – For a faster and less elaborate approach buy a booklet of coloured dots from a stationer's shop. Stick a coloured dot in the corner of each student's handout. When you are ready to move into groups then it is simply a question of drawing attention to the dot and asking all those with a blue dot in the top corner of their handout to move to the blue table etc. You can also use this method to 'invisibly' move students into mixed ability groups by controlling who receives each colour or to place all your most able students into a single group for a more challenging task. Like the extra sweet method described above, you can also put an extra coloured dot e.g. a green dot on the appropriate number of handouts. When it is time for feedback ask students with a green dot in the bottom corner of their handout to be the human billboard. Overtime attach different tasks and roles to the extra dot so that it doesn't become too predictable. For a less resource intensive version, avoiding the need for sweets or dots, simply use coloured flipchart markers to place a coloured dot in the corner of each handout.
4. Restaurant	Place the chairs and tables into the number of required groups. Stand a restaurant menu on each

	group table e.g. Italian, Chinese, Indian, Mexican. Next time you are in a restaurant ask the waiter if you could take a menu and build up a collection. You might also reflect the popular choices of the age-group e.g. Nandos, Chiquito's, Frankie and Bennys, Pizza Express. To divide the students write typical food choices on labels and drop into a hat e.g pizza, Chicken Chow Mein, Onion bajai, Chilli con carne. Ensure you reflect ethnic diversity as appropriate and select some more unusual choices. The students should select a meal at random and move to their associated 'restaurant' table. As a variation you might risk a free choice of the meal options from a mock menu. However, be prepared to be directive and if too many are choosing the 'Italian restaurant' table intercept a few and tell them the restaurant is full ...you've not booked ... and redirect into the Indian restaurant next door to get even numbers. On a special occasion you might source paper tablecloths and put Italian breadsticks, Popadoms, Prawn crackers etc on the relevant table tops. Once in their groups pass round a mock menu i.e a list of pizzas for the Italian table but if five people in a group then only five pizza choices and each person has to select a pizza. Then attach a role to the pizza choice. Whoever selected Pepperoni will be the presenter etc.
5. Star signs	Print the star signs and titles onto A5 or A4 paper and place the different combinations of star signs on the identified group tables. The students should move to the relevant table.
6. Curriculum categories	Divide into groups with labels linked to your curriculum i.e. In Motor Vehicle for three groups you might name name Honda, BMW and Ford or in Catering Jamie Oliver, Nigella Lawson and Ainsley Harriot, or three poets or novelists in Literature, three Prime-Ministers in History, three resorts in Travel and Tourism, three scientists in science etc.

	Perhaps have their photographs on card or projected on screen Tease out some information about each person or category. Wherever possible consider equality and diversity in the range of people selected. Gain a random split by placing the names/categories in an envelope. All dip in and select a name and if Honda go to the Honda table etc. Alternatively use the method described for the restaurant above and on a slip of paper invite the students to tick the car they would buy and then move into the relevant group. Note you could also carry this forward from a 'bridge' task' (see Chapter Nine) i.e. at the end of the previous lesson invite the students to select and complete a two page handout on Honda, BMW, and Ford. Create a standard layout for the handout with a title page with a photograph and on the reverse standard sub headings to capture some basic information about the person, place, event, product, car etc. Use the completed handouts as 'place cards' for the different groups. Do not signal this purpose in advance for maximum impact when you create the groups.
7. **Jigsaw**	**Word jigsaw** - Decide random categories as above or perhaps the group task will dictate the labels e.g in a lesson on business organisations we might want a group to report on partnerships, another on sole traders and a final group on limited companies. Wordprocess and print out Partnerships, Sole Traders and Limited Companies in large font on card i.e a long strip. If you want four students in each group then cut each word label into four and jumble all the pieces of card in an envelope. Invite all the students to select a piece and to form three groups. Do not intervene unless you have to but hopefully the penny will soon drop and the students will compare cards and find who has the matching pieces to spell each word. Once each word is assembled the relevant students form that group.

	Picture jigsaw - a variation on the word jigsaw is to print an A4 sized photograph of the person, place, product, event etc and again cut into four or five pieces. Drop the pieces into an envelope and all the students select a piece and match to re-form the photograph.
8. Wacky fact	Put a random question on the board with multiple choice answers to choose from. If you want four groups then four possible answers labelled A , B, C and D. The random 'wacky fact' questions can be anything e.g What is the population of Tokyo, the world's largest city (answer 34.9 million), How high in metre is the average Oak tree? (answer 24 metres), Dermaptera is the scientific name for what? (answer earwigs), Which is the world's largest island? (answer Greenland), What is the average depth of the Pacific Ocean? (answer 4,300 metres), How deep is the deepest part of the Pacific Ocean, the Marianas Trench? (answer 11,040 metres), How many miles is it from John O'Groats to Lands End? (870), What was the hottest temperature ever recorded ? (answer 136.4F in El Azizia, Libya), What is the coldest temperature on record? (answer minus 127F in Vostok, Antarctica), Which is the smallest planet? (answer Mercury). Buy a 'facts' book from a good bookshop or the Guinness Book of Records and you will have a never ending supply of questions. You might also be able to come up with curriculum linked questions. Perhaps in Catering – how old is Gordon Ramsey? How long is a standard length of spaghetti? In Motor Vehicle – how many seconds for an airbag to inflate? How many miles to the gallon will you get out of a Hummer? In Land-based what is the average weight of a cow? Use your imagination for some ridiculous facts and keep the possible answers grouped tight to ensure that you get guesses across all the possible answers. If you do classic multiple choice with one outlandish

	possible answer then you will end up with no students in that group. Once all have selected an answer then reveal the correct answer and all move into their groups i.e group A, group B… If there are too many students in a particular group then simply direct some of them to move to even up the group sizes.
9. Random categories	This is a variation on the curriculum categories and any random category will suffice. Print small cards with shapes e.g for four groups perhaps a diamond, circle, hexagon and triangle. Drop the relevant number of shapes into a large envelope and invite all to select one. The individual students then move to the relevant table with the matching place label. The labels might be different fruits (why not actual fruits) or any random category. **Playing Cards** - adopt a similar approach to the above with playing cards. Diamond team, Hearts team etc. If there are five people in a group then drop five Diamond cards into a box and then you might go for random roles within the group by attaching a role to the Jack of Hearts, the Ace of hearts, the King of hearts etc. The student selecting Jack of Hearts might be the presenter, the Ace of Hearts the Scribe etc. For added impact you can buy packs of giant playing cards from outlets like www.thetrainingshop.co.uk A further variation is **dominoes.** The above company also sells giant, soft dominoes. Issue a domino to each student and they have to match-up around the room. Then simply decide the cut-off point for each group. They also sell a wide range of other learning games and aids. Or go to a toy shop and buy sets of random small toys e.g. cars, figures, animals and place an appropriate mix into a box. In many cases you can achieve a curriculum link.

10. Musical selection	A variation of the classical game – play a track of music and make all circulate around the room in a large circle or figure of eight around the four groups of tables (if four groups). When the music stops all should touch the nearest table. Select one student to sit down and resume the music. Continue until you allocate each student to a group. Note the comments about musical selection within 'Appetisers' in Chapter Six and invite students to select a track or invite to name the composer or artist etc.

Once we have divided the class into random or planned friendship groups the next significant issue is individual performance within the groups. Many teachers are wary of group working because of unsatisfactory learning outcomes i.e. some group members become 'passengers' and sit back and contribute little while others may fear the prospect of writing on the flipchart paper or the worst fear of all giving an oral presentation to the whole class or a wider audience. Forget phobias about snakes, spiders or flying – public speaking is perhaps the most commonly held and greatest fear.

Group roles

Part of the answer is to introduce more structure and to allocate roles within the group. Students are often uncomfortable in groups because they are uncertain of their role and how to best to interact with other group members. Social embarrassment of what to say and do inhibits some from full participation. We can help to overcome the barriers to participation by allocating clear roles to the group members i.e. once they have a clear job to perform they will have a sense of purpose. Not all students are confident presenters but remember that is only one skill area. Can we praise some students for their abilities with number, writing, internet research, designing Powerpoint or Keynote slides etc. By allocating roles within the group we can differentiate and play to the strengths of each student. However, ensure that overtime the roles are rotated and that appropriate teaching and support models and helps to develop the skill set related to each role. Make reference to programmes like ***The Apprentice*** to help your students to realise the importance of developing skills as well as knowledge. Many of our leading entrepreneurs have no formal qualifications but they do have high key skills and an ability to lead and inspire others. The following group roles might be considered and allocated:

- **Leader** – co-ordinates the discussion / task and ensures all have a say and complete the set task within the time limit.
- **Recorder** – records the key points made and any decisions arrived at and prompts as appropriate.
- **Visualiser(s)** – produce any specified visual outcomes for the discussion i.e. spider diagrams, posters, Powerpoint, display.
- **Statisticians** – produce any tables, charts, diagrams required.
- **Researcher(s)** – find out additional information as required from textbooks, video, library, newspapers, internet etc
- **Interviewers** – plan questions and conduct any necessary interviews / surveys of opinion etc
- **Writer(s)** – draw together all the information from the different sources and produce an overview summary findings
- **Presenter(s)** – deliver the oral overview presentation of all findings / outcomes.

In a grade one report for Engineering Ofsted noted, *'Effective use is made of group work. In some groups, students are given the role of team leader for a particular project. This increases their confidence and sense of responsibility'.* [5] Prepare a 'job card' for each role on A5 card and laminate them to make them durable for regular issue. Provide an upbeat description of the role and its importance and bullet point the particular skills they should aim to practise and how these might contribute to their formal key skills portfolio. Offer the students a choice of role and highlight the importance of each person's role – all roles are essential to the successful completion of the task – this mimics future employment demands and team working. There is also a teaching role here to help the students build and develop the relevant skills and also peer teaching because all students will have different strengths and weaknesses across these skill areas. Engineer the mix of skills within each group and overtime the students will learn from each other and offer each other direct support on how to write a report, give a presentation, produce a chart, design Powerpoint slides etc. Design the group task so that there are sub tasks to 'feed' the roles identified. Ensure the tasks have the right degree of challenge for the individual and the course level. Invent more roles as appropriate or for a straightforward group task simply appoint a group leader. More often than not start a group task in the lesson but expect it to be finished outside of the classroom. This will build independent learning and effective learning co-operation outside of the classroom. In this way large parts of the curriculum can be explored to a greater depth than class time permits and will result in much deeper and more meaningful learning. Clearly many students will let their groups down and not complete their specified task. This should be taken as a symptom of a lack of confidence and uncertainty in how to proceed and should be tackled in a one to one discussion in 'doctor / patient' mode i.e. express your concern, enquire what they are finding difficult, invite them to identify the learning or motivational block, offer any appropriate guidance, offer to arrange additional support, express your full confidence in them and reset the task. You can fit these one to one discussions in while everyone else is working. How many repeats of this sort of 'supportive' discussion will the student 'endure' before they conclude that it is easier to complete the task rather than have a repeat of your one to one concern and exploration of how best to help them. This is a much better strategy than entering into discipline or sanctions because you are focussing on the completion of the learning task rather their behaviour. Most research into behaviour management tends to highlight that many young people will indulge in disruptive or poor behaviour to mask their inability to complete a task. Therefore your discussion may reveal a genuine support need or a significant personal issue – non completion is not always just a lack of effort and a discipline issue. You might invite another class member who has done something similar to provide the support. For students who are not making sufficient effort then peer pressure will eventually start to impact because they will feel the disappointment of their fellow group members for leaving a gap in their overall report or presentation. In an Ofsted grade one inspection report the benefits of observed groupwork were highlighted, *"Some good use of group and presentational formats coupled with skilful questioning elicits from learners sustained enthusiasm, concentration and excellent progress. In one observed lesson, a group of sport learners delivered presentations on the planning and risk assessment for a residential excursion to the Lake District. Group work was energetic, well planned and focused. The presentations were delivered with skill and confidence, and all were comprehensive and well researched.*

Learners demonstrated very good organisation and oral skills".[6] Consequently, consider introducing more group work into your lessons but taking care to add the structure of clear roles and tasks.

21 active group tasks

The following selection of 21 group tasks is the tip of a large iceberg but enough to convey the flavour. In all cases the strategies involve minimal preparation but will enhance your lessons by placing students at the centre of learning and avoiding the trap of teacher dominance. They will also provide your students with opportunities to practise and develop their Functional and employability skills. All of the strategies are accompanied by a related graphic organiser template to provide structure to the group task and to prompt a 'clear' outcome from the group discussion. This approach helps all. The less able students gain support in terms of the outcomes expected and the more able students gain a prompt to in-depth analysis and evaluation of the issues. All too often students are presented with a blank sheet of flipchart paper to record their discussion but this can be too open ended for many whereas the graphic organiser provides clarity on what to record. The process of discussion and recording will help all to move beyond the capture of basic facts into higher order thinking and reasoning skills and to arrive at opinions they can justify and defend. Within this approach differentiation will naturally occur because the tasks will present opportunities for extension into deeper research or presentation to a high professional standard. Everyone benefits and all will be prompted to move beyond bare factual reporting into the higher reaches of Bloom's taxonomy. Marzano has highlighted that activities to explore 'similarities and differences' prompts reflection and deeper learning and it works equally well in terms of direct teacher presentation or active exploration by the students. The impact is enhanced with graphic representations, *"one of the more powerful findings within this general category of instructional strategies is that graphic and symbolic representations of similarities and differences enhance students understanding of content".*[7] The following graphic organisers will support the exploration of similarities and differences via a range of classifying, ordering, categorising and comparing tasks.

Visual learning

Hattie refers to graphic organisers and Marzano to 'nonlinguistic representations' but perhaps visual learning is more descriptive. The intention is to give tasks a clear structure with explicit learning outcomes and an aid to memory through the use of bright, eye-catching templates. Marzano notes that teachers primarily operate in a linguistic mode but that images combined with words promote 'dual coding' and that research indicates, *"when teachers help students in this kind of work, however, the effects on achievement are strong. It has even been shown that explicitly engaging students in the creation of non-linguistic representation stimulates and increases activity in the brain".*[8] The following templates, wherever possible, draw upon standard 'Shapes' and 'Smartart'™ available in Microsoft Word™ and PowerPoint™ 2007+. You can adopt and adapt the relevant templates, print onto A4 paper and with a photocopier expand onto A3 paper to offer more space. Many of the basic shapes can also be drawn onto flipchart paper relatively easily and when finished you gain instant classroom display. Please adopt and adapt as wished and arrive at activities that best match your lesson aims. An Ofsted grade one inspection report included the following observation, *" the use of thoughtfully designed templates helps students to record their findings in a structured way and encourages them to make differentiated responses to the graded tasks".* [9]

21 visual learning group tasks

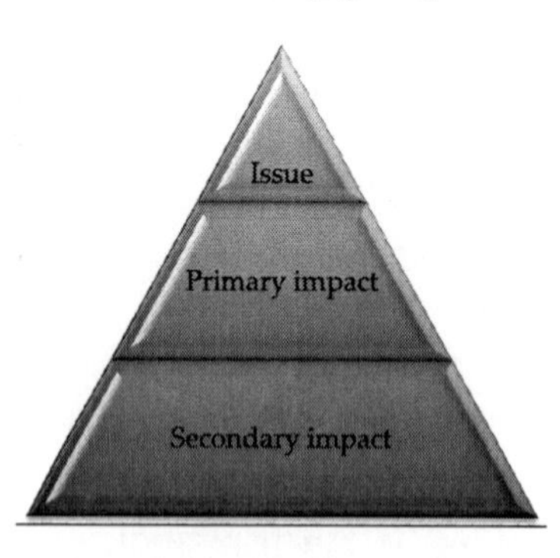

1. Impact pyramid

Issue your class with a case study of a new theory, new product in the market, new development, new road, new airport, new law, outbreak of food and mouth disease, rise in unemployment, increase in population, increase in global temperature, discovery of a major new oil field etc. We can also introduce the 'What if' question in terms of what if this change occurred? There are changes and developments within all subject areas and we can encourage higher order thinking by inviting completion of the Impact pyramid. Reproduce on flipchart paper for instant classroom display.

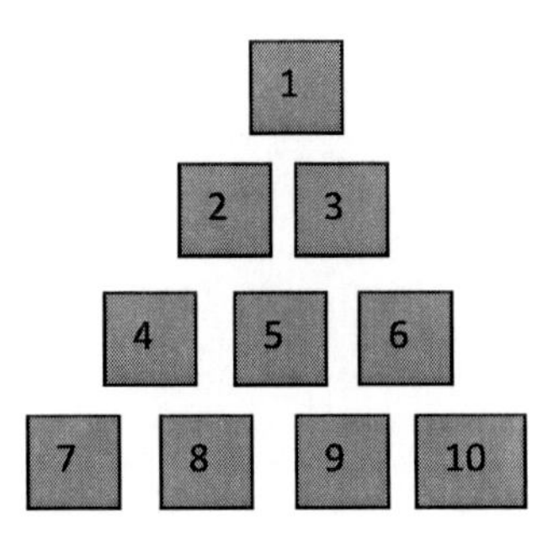

2. Rank order pyramid

Can you identify a top set of reasons, theories, explanations, factors etc and invite the students to place into a rank order of importance, difficulty, logic, relevance, impact, change i.e whatever is most applicable to the issue under discussion. The pyramid can be placed on a handout for individual or paired discussion and completion followed by a class consensus on flipchart paper. Alternatively the pyramid can be constructed from individual Post-it notes with one issue per Post-it. For greater impact prepare a set of the ten points/issues in giant font on individual A4 coloured paper/card. Invite the class to stick on the wall in their preferred order. If you have a Smart board then duplicate as text boxes on screen and invite the students to re-arrange into their agreed rank order. For a fun task (but still curriculum linked) dip into one of the many top ten list books on the market and invite student opinions on the top ten holiday destinations, best selling cars, best-selling albums, most popular Prime-Ministers, fastest sprinters, most popular vegetables by sales, highest selling laptops etc.

Concept	Definition

3. Match

Issue a worksheet with two columns of key concepts and definitions and list as many as you wish. Mismatch the order of the concepts and the definitions and invite the students in pairs or small groups to correctly match-up by drawing lines between. Alternatively print onto card and cut out to make a set of cards for the students to sort into matches on their desk top. In Maths it can be questions and answers etc. Attach a timer to add pace. This can also be placed onto a Smartboard™ for students to drag and drop.

4. Poster

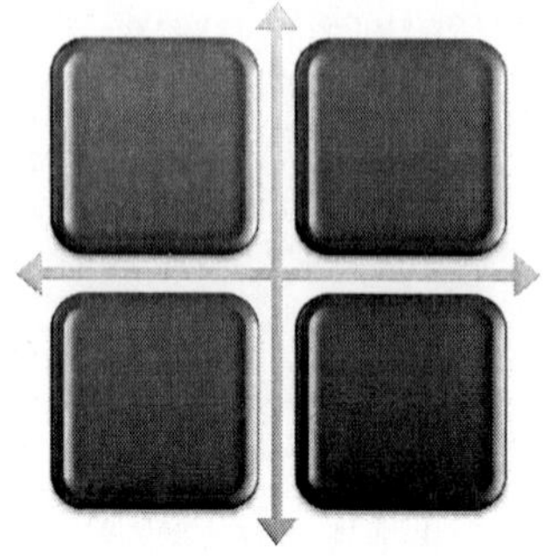

Invite students to research a topic in more depth by creating a poster composed of at least four sections. The title goes across the top. The first square should be an image that illustrates the topic theme e.g. a person, place or object. The second square a text box with some descriptive overview text. The third square some relevant data or statistics linked to the topic and presented as a chart or a table. The fourth square recommend key websites, books or periodicals for further information on the topic. Perhaps in groups of four one student can take charge of a section each and overtime all rotate to develop and refine the different skill sets. You might also generate an electronic copy and place onto your VLE with relevant parts clickable to further information, short video clips, web sites etc.

5. Similarities and differences

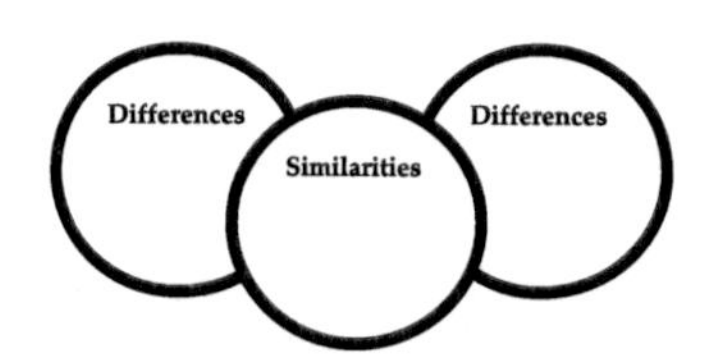

Discuss and compare and contrast two theories, developments, products, leaders, events etc. List similarities in the centre circle and significant differences in the outer circles e.g. comparison of two cars in motor vehicle, two computers, two holiday destinations, two leaders, two economic policies, two pathogens etc. Marzano identifies this as one of the most significant activities for promoting evaluation.

6. Problems and solutions

Problem/Issue	Solution/Strategy
1.	
2.	
3.	
4.	

Drop topic headings into the left hand column and alongside invite groups to discuss and arrive at the recommended solution or strategy. This grid has four rows for four groups. Adjust according to the number of problems or issues for discussion. Each group are given time for discussion and to arrive at their conclusion. They might complete some brainstorming on a flipchart and present their thoughts. The teacher can help to guide their conclusions and after some discussion confirm what all should record in the solution/strategy column. The table illustrated might be on A4 paper so that all of the students end the lesson with a record of the recommended solution or strategy. The topics do not have to be separate topics but might be sub topics related to an over arching lesson theme.

7. Tri-angular connections

Place the title of a topic, issue, event, person, place etc into the centre triangle. Place a mix of three related facts, formula, statistics, quotations, people, objects etc into the outer triangles. Print on card and cut out. Devise at least three sets and jumble all the pieces into an envelope. Issue an envelope to each pair or small group and invite to sort. Add a timer for pace and perhaps a small prize for first to finish and then invite connections and explanations to confirm key learning.

8. Blue Sky thinking

Place the topic into the large cloud and radiating outwards identify key sub topics and sub, sub topics. This is essentially a brainstorming task along the lines of tell me all you know about...? The first set of sub topics might be placed into different colours and a smaller set of clouds linked to each sub topic. Extend as far as possible across the page as a summary of a key topic or issue i.e. lots of linked facts and information. You might also place the large cloud in the centre of the page and below the sub topics as falling raindrops if preferred. A whole class presentation of topic information in this format can make an attractive wall display. Alternatively have you noticed the giant starburst post –it notes you can buy from stationers' shops? Use a giant one for the main topic heading and then different coloured standard (or more fancy shaped) post-it notes for the sub topics radiating outwards. This can be mounted on a sheet of flipchart paper in the landscape presentation and placed on the classroom wall.

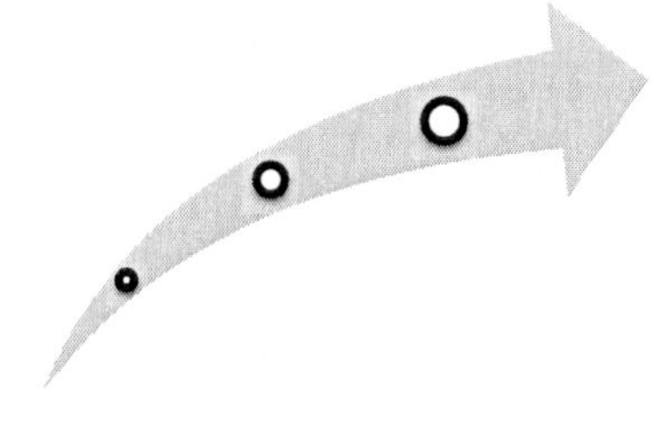

9. Advance

The diagram provides for three major points but you could insert more. Start at the base with an event, person, discovery, invention etc. You could place a relevant photograph at the base to illustrate the topic. Place labels along the arrow in terms of key development steps, influence, impact, significance or perhaps how a small insignificant event, discovery, observation rises to produce a key theoretical, scientific, engineering advance etc. You also do not need just to attach a label it could be an A4 page summary of the relevant development step. Does anyone remember the TV series Connections with Raymond Burke?

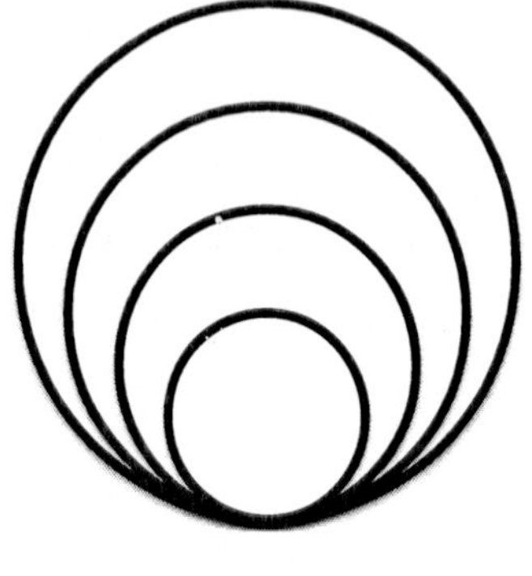

10. Ripples

A variation on the above. Insert a key event, person, object in the base circle and identify the major outward ripples. Ideally you are charting the spread of a new idea, theory, discovery. Perhaps the spread of a epidemic, rises in global temperature, growth in retail sales, growth of the European Union member states with, in all cases, related descriptive detail etc.

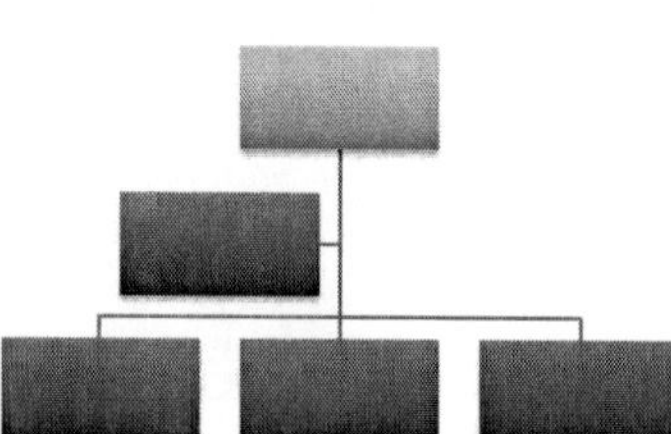

11. Hierarchy

There is a wide choice of hierarchal charts in Word and you can select the one that best suits your purpose. Perhaps in Health Care we chart the structure of the Health Service from Secretary of State down to individual health trusts, or the police force, or typical business organisation or in Land-based flora and fauna groupings/ families etc. In each appropriate description and explanation. It might also reflect a sequence of linked consequences. Perhaps the first box has the title a rise in global temperatures by 2 degrees. What are the key consequences and then for each major consequence the linked issues etc.

12. Links

This is a variation on the hierarchal chart above. Place the topic in the first bar and below the linked concepts or related sub topics. You might also use a topic label to create a title bar and use post-it notes to build up the hierarchy. Students might also simply draw this structure onto flipchart paper.

13. Jigsaw

This image is found within the clipart choices in Word. Print the topic title across the top of the page and expand the image to fill one side of A4 to create a title page. Select four relevant sub headings and word process the sub headings into the jigsaw pieces. On the reverse of the page divide the page into four squares. Have at least 3 or 4 students per group to investigate a single sub-topic and arrive at a sharp summary to fill the square. Once the groups have completed their research reform the groups to draw together one person from each original research group. Each person in turn briefs the rest on their group's research. Once all complete, tutor to check and confirm learning. Alternatively each group presents their research and everyone completes the relevant section and build up the full picture of the event, concept, theory, development etc.

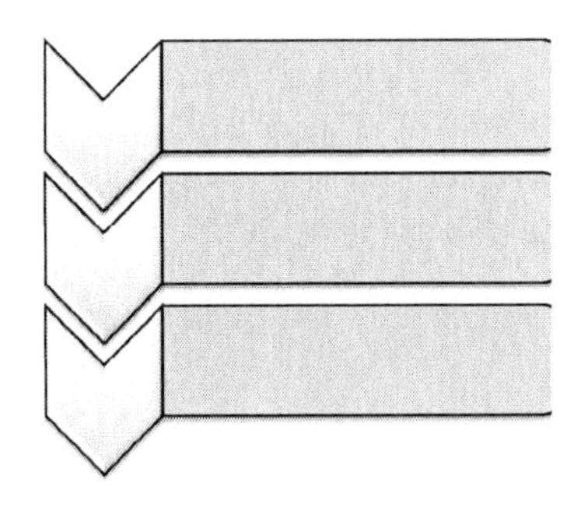

14. Process

Invite the groups to confirm the best / correct order for a sequence of steps e.g instructions for operating a machine, preparing a meal, completing a task, a chronology of developments, events, a sequence of consequences – A leads to B and B leads to C etc.

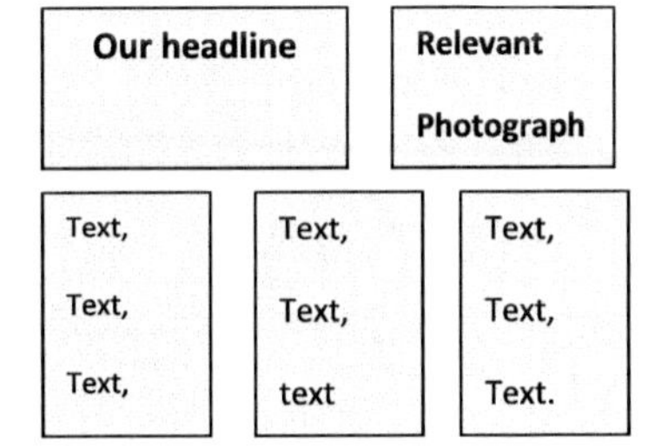

15. Front page

Invite the students in pairs or small groups to write up a key topic, theory, development, event, discovery etc as though they were reporting the news at the time. This will encourage concise writing and creativity in the reporting style adopted. You might also invite to write an obituary for a famous individual, artist, scientist, engineer etc. Each group can choose a different, standard newsletter template from Word or better still if you have Microsoft Publisher with its many more design options. All the templates can be customised and are ready to type into. The completed newspaper front pages will instant bright classroom display. To increase the challenge invite the students to write in the style of relevant vocational journals or relevant magazines like New Scientist, The Economist, Time Magazine, New Statesman. They could include relevant photographs and statistics etc.

16. Biography

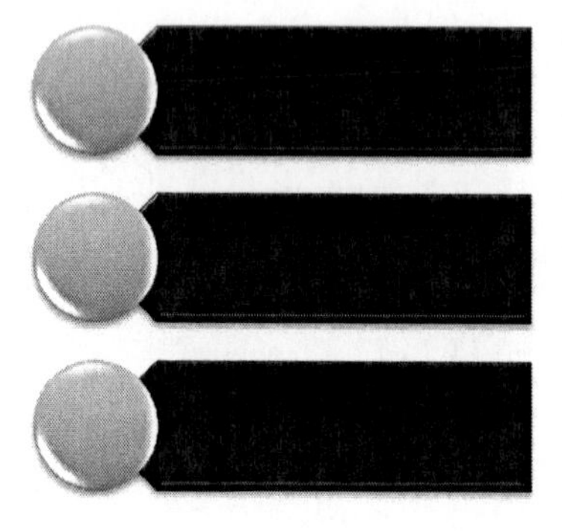

Once opened in Word, as an A4 document the circle contains a prompt for inserting a photograph. Select a list of key people linked to your subject for study e.g key scientist, poet, writer, artist, engineer, hairdresser, sports star. Drop in their photograph and complete the text box with a short sharp summary of the individual's importance, contribution, theories etc. The groups could research an individual each and provide feedback. The feedback could be a Powerpoint or other presentation but ultimately reduced to a short, sharp summary to be recorded by all into the textbox. Clearly the textbox will expand and so you can decide in designing the worksheet whether to have two or three mini biographies to a side of A4 or perhaps print onto A3 paper to give more space. Alternatively just place one row across the top of an A4 page with the photograph in the circle and the name of the person in the text box as a title bar. Below decide a series of standard sub headings to report against e.g. place of birth, education, career highlights etc. Instead of biographies the same approach might be taken with events, objects, places etc. All should produce a standard one page biography etc and makes instant classroom display.

17. Funnel

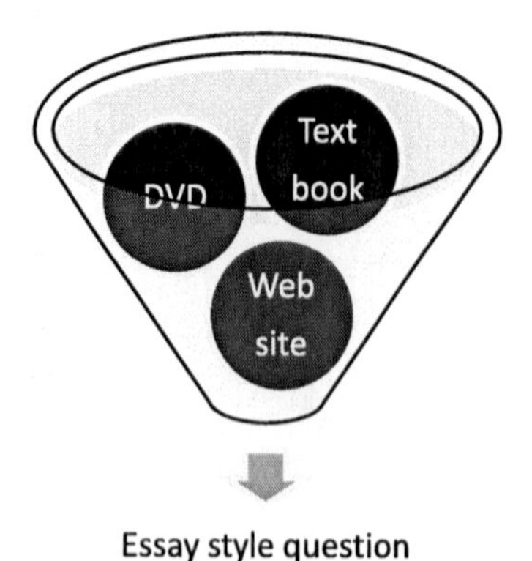

Print a topic title and the funnel diagram at the top half of an A4 page and place a text box in the bottom half of the page. At the top of the text box print an essay style question to answer or a past exam question. To support the answer identify a DVD, library textbook, periodical article or reference book and a web site as information sources. You might also substitute or add relevant data for analysis or other information sources e.g field trip, experiment etc Rotate the groups around each resource and provide prompt questions against each resource to guide thinking. Invite all to write a short, sharp answer to the question and if need be spill over onto the back of the handout. However, best to specify a word total as a test of ability to develop sharp, concise writing.

18. SWOT analysis

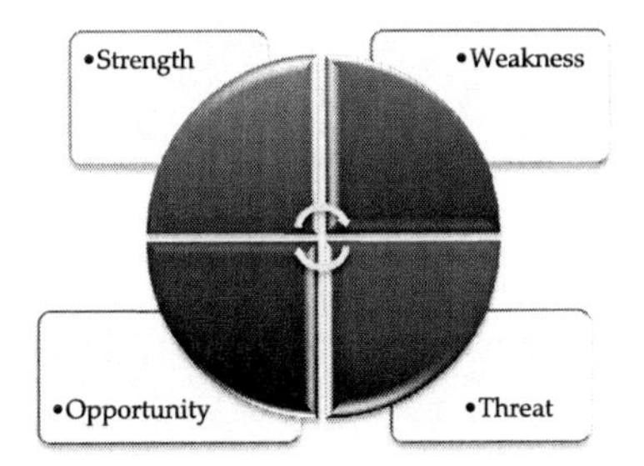

Swot encourages analysis by looking at an issue from the different viewpoints. Key bullet points can be placed into the relevant segment of the circle. On the reverse divide the A4 page into four quarters to capture more depth of comment. The students could be divided into four groups to take charge of one aspect each and then draw together. A case study often supports this activity well.

19. Debate

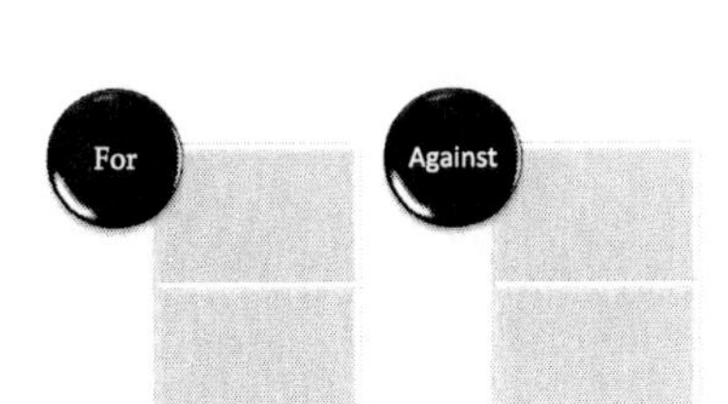

Set a key question for debate and invite all to review and investigate both sides of the argument by creating two vertical columns of key debating points. Draw lots to divide into 'for' and 'against' teams of no more five students per team. The rest of the class should form the audience. Issue the audience with a blank copy of the A4 handout and as the teams present the audience members should list the key arguments presented and consider questions they would like to ask. After both presentations and an opportunity to ask questions the audience should place their vote on slip of paper and post into a ballot box for counting. The teacher should announce the winning team.

20. Judgment

Question	Personal opinion
For/Positives	**Against/Negatives**
Group consensus	**Answer**

This table is designed to support a step by step discussion to arrive at a group consensus. To use the table write the issue for debate and judgement into the first box. Next give five minutes of individual thinking time and invite the students to enter their personal opinion into the second box. Next enter into a group discussion to share individual opinions and to confirm the key points to enter into the 'for' and 'against' boxes. When all points are exhausted the group should draw together into an overview group consensus statement. Finally enter a succinct final answer to the original question.

Essay question		
Introduction 100 words		
Key points – one paragraph per point		
Para 1.	**Para 2**	**Para 3**
Para 4	**Para 5**	**Para 6**
Conclusion 200 words		
Finished essay 800-1000 words		

21. Academic skeleton essays

Invite students to write skeleton essays as an individual or paired task in the lesson and as wished complete the whole essay outside of the classroom. This will quickly lift the performance of marginal students and especially if placed into mixed ability pairs. First enter the essay question and underline the key 'instruction' words. Discuss and confirm the instruction words with the class i.e what is the question asking? Next all write an introduction of a maximum of 100 words or essentially three sentences. Then enter one key point per paragraph box – your significant arguments, reasons etc. Space is provided for six points but there may be more or fewer. Finally write your conclusion in a maximum of 200 words. If the students are directed to write only the introduction and conclusion in full several exam questions can be covered within one lesson. Different pairs can tackle different questions and present their skeleton answers to the class. Or select one skeleton answer and invite the students in groups to write up one key paragraph each. Overall essay when fully written 800-1000 words.

Microsoft Publisher™ or similar desktop publishing software offers lots of colourful templates to support many of the above presentation options. Commercial software is also available to develop and support mind mapping techniques. Consider www.inspiration.com or www.mindgenius.com. Take a look and gain inspiration for how your students could develop and apply resources of this type. However, for all group tasks ensure you issue a precise brief and where possible specify job roles as indicated earlier so that each group member has no doubt what is expected of them. Over time regular active learning methods of this type will involve the students directly in their own learning, embed Functional skills and raise their personal confidence and self-esteem. In addition to the above 21 suggestions consider the following wider methods of presentation to increase the active learning impact and use of IT resources:

- **Powerpoint, Keynote or Prezi**- but model the structure expected i.e. title page like this...
- **Flipchart** – design colourful spider diagrams or mindmaps
- **Posters** – condense a whole key topic onto one side of flipchart paper

- **Pyramid ranking** – use Post-it notes or A4 pages on the wall for each point
- **Washing Line** – stretch across the room to display students' work.
- **VLE pages** – develop links to resources and guidance for key topics.
- **Blog** – invite students to maintain an online journal of their placement etc
- **Podcast** – record a discussion/roleplay or directions on how to do something.
- **TV News** – shoot video of a mock news bulletin on a key topic
- **Advert** – design an advert story board to 'sell' a new theory, product etc
- **Cartoon strip** – as above but present as a cartoon strip storyboard
- **Radio broadcast** – as above record a radio style news programme
- **Video / photographs** – use mobiles to capture trips out, fieldwork etc
- **Display** – mount a display on a notice board or for a parents night etc

Many of the above wider methods of presentation emphasise the use of ILT and the extension into resources held on a Virtual Learning Environment (VLE). This is an essential aspect of learning development for students for 21st Century living and working. The following extract from an Ofsted good practice survey published in January, 2008 illustrates the scale of ILT developments in some of our colleges, *"The business and economics department in a sixth form college used a fully interactive site of e-based learning resources. This included online text books, links to websites, student 'test yourself' questions with instant feedback, quizzes and a particularly innovative chat room known as 'ask the teacher'. The latter provided useful extra support for students. They emailed their homework to the teacher and received prompt, informative and detailed feedback. The site contained a log of students' marks for their written work to enable them and their teacher to monitor their performance closely. Teachers had used the site to set extension work and stimulate topical debates. Students were very positive about the resource. One commented, 'Without the online discussions I had with the teacher and other students in my class, I do not think I would have been successful in my university interview.' The site was used well in lessons and by students for independent study, particularly for revision".* [10] Remember that many of the group tasks can be started in lesson time and carried forward to be completed outside of the lesson. Triggering and sustaining independent learning, responsibility, team working, time management etc will all flow from this. Finally keep your eye on time and keep the lesson moving along *–a brisk pace.* In a one hour lesson you will perhaps only have time for the completion of an individual or paired task but lessons lasting one and a half hours or longer will open up the necessary time for the group tasks. Ultimately regular active participation in lessons will build interest and prompt independent learning outside of the classroom.

Effective lesson summation

"A crisp end to the lesson summarising what has been learned and avoiding, 'tailing off".[1]

(Ofsted, criterion for good or better lessons)

Often the first clue that a teacher receives that the end of the lesson has arrived is the sound of chairs being pushed back and files being packed away. If control is not immediately asserted then some students will be out of their chairs and walking towards the classroom door before the teacher can even say, '*see you next week*'. It is a natural tendency to be tired towards the end of any lesson or any presentation (no matter how engaging) and so care must be taken to manage the lesson end and to paraphrase T.S Eliot to end the lesson with a bang rather than a whimper. Aim to end exactly on time and to close the lesson with a final check on learning, a summary of learning and a 'bridge' to the next lesson. All of this should be kept brief and sharp because we appreciate that the students are tired and that their minds are already fixed on the next lesson, getting into the canteen queue or checking their mobile etc. As the Ofsted criterion states our purpose is a crisp end. Definitions of crisp may vary but essentially crisp means short and to the point and so our summation will target 10 minutes. Consequently keep your eye on the clock and warn the students that the end of the lesson is approaching. Take control or else the students will. Some may pack away regardless but insist that they stop before continuing with your summation. In the case of significant defiance dismiss the class early and speak to the relevant student(s) about their behaviour. Be firm and consistent in controlling any restless behaviour at the ends of lessons with any new class. It is important to establish your authority that the lesson will end on time and under your direction.

Learning check

Return to the key objectives or questions stated at the start of the lesson and enter into a final check on learning. Learning should have been checked at regular intervals during the lesson and therefore at the end of the lesson the aim is to quickly assess overall levels of confidence. If you used a visual template to display your objectives or questions, as recommended in Chapter Seven, then re-project it to capture attention. Otherwise return to your objectives / questions, however, you introduced them. Effective teaching produces learning and after a re-confirmation of the key learning points the important step is to check how far everyone has understood and matched the success criteria. You will need to be upbeat and fast because remember that all are tired and ready for the end of the lesson. Consequently consider one of the following active checks on learning to end the class with full engagement and a positive endpoint. Many of these techniques encourage meta-cognition i.e. encouraging the students to be more self aware about the progress they are making and to question what they are finding difficult and to actively seek improvement guidance.

Checking learning

1. Visual template	Invite the students to work around the key objectives displayed on a visual template as described in Chapter Seven to confirm key learning. This can be accomplished in a fast dialogue to question, check and confirm the key points to record.
2. Self-assessment	Use the self-assessment table described in Chapter Four for all to identify; I understand... I have a few questions about... I need further help with...
3. Summary	Invite all to write a paragraph summary of key learning and to ask any questions that the activity provokes. Or alternatively to write three bullet points on what they have learned and to compare with their neighbour.

4. Twitter	As above but tap into the 'Twitter' culture by asking all to write a learning summary of no more than 140 characters. This is approximately two average sentences or if you want to stretch it a bit set a limit of three short sentences. Display the most succinct and imaginative summaries. This is perhaps the modern day equivalent of writing a Haiku that many of us Generation X types will remember writing.
5. Post-It!	Place a sheet of flipchart paper on the classroom wall have two different colours of post-it notes available. On one colour direct the students to write one key thing 'I've learned in today's lesson' and on the other to note one key thing 'I'm still uncertain about'. Clearly they can write more than one thing in each case but all should write at least one point each. All can post their notes as they leave the room and this should form the basis of the recap in the next lesson.
6. Big question	Highlight a related exam question that the students should now be able to answer or devise an appropriate question and invite all to apply their learning to provide a clear answer. This might be best in pairs or small groups. You can leave when you can answer this question...
7. Poster summary	Issue sheets of A3 paper for an individual task or flipchart paper for a group task and invite to write the topic in the centre of the paper and devise a visual mind map or spider diagram summary of the key learning.
8. You missed...	Ask all to imagine one or more students have missed the lesson and to write a summary list of the key learning points they have missed. Clearly if someone is absent then at the start of the next lesson hand them a photocopy of one of the summaries and ask the relevant student

	to explain their summary.
9. Quick-fire questions & answers	Enter into a quick-fire round of questions and answers first confirming basic key facts and forward into more application or evaluation based questions. You may use any of the 21 questioning strategies described in Chapter Eight.
10. The W question	This may not fit the context of every lesson but wherever possible place the key name, place, event, discovery etc under discussion in the lesson at the top of board and below pose the following five questions: Who...? What...? Where...? When...? Why...? The class can leave once they have provided the answers. This is a variation on the 'Connections' questioning technique listed in Chapter Eight and has its origins in the same saying by Rudyard Kipling.
11. Five in a row	The class have to answer five questions in a row before they can leave. If they give a wrong answer you return to question one. This captures attention because the class can leave the lesson early if they correctly answer the first set of five questions. However, you can have some fun with this by asking four straightforward factual questions and then asking a challenging question for Question Five. This should produce a sense of fun (or rebellion) but once they've had enough ease the challenge to allow them to escape.

12. Odd one out	Put four facts, concepts, photographs, quotations, statistics etc drawn from the lesson material on the board but include an odd one or something entirely incorrect. Ask the class to identify the odd one out and to explain the other three.
13. Feedback	This is useful method in particular for study centres and studios. Place a postbox by the door and invite all to post an index card with any aspect they found difficult and would welcome more help with. Refer to the cards during the recap section of the next lesson and re-teach any aspects as appropriate.
14. Splat	Write some key concepts, facts, names events, theories etc as relevant to the lesson content onto the board. Divide the class into two teams and describe a concept, person etc. The first person to recognise the answer runs from their seat to the board to 'splat' the answer i.e. they put their hand over it. The teacher can then remove this answer from the board and so on until the board is clear and you have a winning team. As a variation invite each team to nominate who is going to 'splat' and /or give the 'splatters' a board pen to draw a circle around the answer on the board or to place a cross through it. You might also try putting 'splat template' into Google and selecting some good shareware.

Learning summary

What has everyone recorded? You may get a shock if you collect in student files and take a look at their notes and what they have all have recorded in relation to a major topic. Remember those micro sleeps and lapses in concentration described in Chapter Five? There can be many versions of what you said! Therefore throughout the lesson it is important to direct note-taking and to regularly check the notes that everyone is recording as the lesson unfolds. Marzano presents *'summarising and note-taking'* as one of his central tenets of effective practice because both are high level skills in terms of listening, evaluating information followed by discarding information and selecting key points to record. All students will arrive at different conclusions of what to discard and what to record and therefore there is a need to steer note-taking. Teachers should model note-taking in different forms and offer clear 'frames' to capture key information. Some students fool themselves that they do not need to take notes because they believe that they will be able to remember but this is never the case. Detailed note-taking helps students to sift and think about what they are learning and may prompt questions for clarification which will either correct misimpressions or deepen learning. Therefore confirm what you have covered and the key notes all should have recorded and seek an agreed summary of learning. At regular intervals, and perhaps as a recap activity, invite students to refer to their notes on a key topic to support a review of learning.

Bridge

Our lessons should be part of a learning continuum rather than isolated events and the key to securing this is to extend learning between lessons. Marzano specifies *'homework and practice'* as one of his nine steps of effective practice as outlined in Chapter One. One of the key purposes identified is, *"to prepare students for new content or have them elaborate on content that has been introduced"*. [2] Teachers prepare for lessons and so should our students. Teaching and learning are two sides of the same coin and students need to meet us at least half way but most will need a push and encouragement to extend their learning. This is the purpose of the *bridge* i.e. a bridge to the next lesson. The intention is not to set 'homework' because of its negative connotations as a chore but to offer 'extended learning' or 'independent learning' tasks designed to explore topics to a deeper level. All will benefit. The less able students will be more likely to secure a pass after some additional research and the more able a Distinction or a Grade A or Grade A*. The bridge task also facilitates 'Flipped Learning' if this is a strategy you are pursuing. Simply set two or three key questions to be answered during the next lesson and direct the students to relevant supporting resources on your VLE to find the answers. Otherwise the *bridge* tasks recommended below will assist all students to extend their learning and to become independent learners. The tasks are primarily research based because the marking load for most teachers is already too high and therefore the tasks do not involve marking. In many schools the policy is to set extended learning (homework) tasks at the start of the lesson because there is concern that students do not listen carefully enough at the ends of lessons. If this is your school policy or personal preference then move '*bridge*' to the start of your lesson and set the extended learning task after the objectives or recap. As highlighted in Chapter Six the order of the steps within the Diamond Lesson Plan may be adjusted as wished. Consider the following *bridge* tasks to extend learning and to promote independent learning:

Independent learning tasks

1. Biography	Devise a standard A4 template with space for a photograph and a series of standard subheadings to trap key information about the individual e.g. early life, education, employment, contribution. Go for a standard one page layout to keep it short and sharp with standard sub-headings to prevent a simple print-off or cut and paste from the internet. The aim is to prompt some investigation, reading and summarisation of the individual's career and importance. You might offer a choice of individuals to research because students often like to exercise choice and the outcome is instant classroom display.
2. Fact sheets	As above but in relation to key places, events, discoveries, equipment, objects, concepts – whatever fits your topic area. In Land-Based it might be plants or animals, in Travel and Tourism a holiday resort and in Science a discovery etc.
3. Web Guide	Identify useful websites to support the topic or subject. Invite evaluation and recommendations and prompt a few students to present useful websites to the rest of the class. Extend into a collation of recommended websites on

	the College VLE or as a short Web guide to…?
4. Read	Specify a reading and note-taking task from a recommended textbook held in the library collection to encourage the students to explore the library collection. While they are there they might take other books off the shelves. Keep the task brief i.e. to read a specified chapter rather than a whole book. Issue a question to explore and to find an answer from the specified chapter or to arrive at an opinion.
5. Watch	As above but a recommendation to watch a specified DVD within the library collection. If the DVD is held by you or your Programme Area then the library staff will probably agree to holding it for a week and issuing it over the counter for viewing within the library. The same might apply to the reading task if the recommended book is not held by the library. Issue a worksheet with four or five key questions to answer while watching the DVD. Watch might also apply to an up and coming TV programme or to find and recommend a good video sourced from You Tube to recommend to others or part of the Khan Academy collection www.khanacademy.org. Build any useful ones identified into future lessons.
6. Chart it	Most subjects have some key statistics in tables. Invite the students to convert into a Pie or other chart in a standard A4 presentation format of your devising with space for some summary evaluation.
7. Map it	Invite the students to find some examples of whatever is under discussion or study and map it. This often a more appealing task for many

	students because is largely spatial and visual with minimal writing. Health and Care students might map the local health service in their area, Catering students might map the origins of all the vegetables in their local supermarket, travel and tourism students might collect in brochures on a particular destination and map the resorts with arrows and resort descriptions, History students might map a battlefield, Business students might map all the fast food outlets in their local area and identify the scale of competition etc.
8. Photograph it	Most students have mobile phones and most mobile phones have a built in camera and often video. Ask the students to photograph relevant examples of …?
9. Opinions	To follow-up a class discussion/debate ask the students to find the opinions of 5 other people in relation to the issue e.g immediate friends and family. How far is there a consensus on the issue? Has their personal opinion been affected?
10. Find	Invite all to find examples of objects under discussion and to bring them into the next lesson, brochures, adverts, products, artefacts etc.
11. A-Z	Challenge your students to find a subject related word for each letter of the alphabet. The most words should win a small prize. Mount as a list on the classroom wall and tease out definitions, descriptions, explanations etc.
12. Issues	Invite the students to visit the website of a subject related government department, charity, museum to identify current research or policy

	issues.
13. Jobs	Invite the students to find examples of subject related jobs in specialist periodicals, websites or relevant supplements in the national press. Collate and display key examples. Invite the students to write in response to one of the adverts and to request the post description and person specification. The description of the person might reinforce the need for good Functional skills as well as exam passes. The application forms might support a later mock job application and interview activity.
14. Fundraise / promote	Encourage involvement with any official charitable fund raising day that is linked to your subject area or national commemoration event. The relevant dates should be entered into your course Year Planner and a campaign agreed and implemented. Sometimes, as adults, we can have a jaundiced view of some events or groan that a certain day has come around again but for your students it may be only their first or second exposure and their involvement can be very stimulating, and significantly raise their horizons and awareness of wider issues.
15. Chronology	List the key dates in someone's career, the steps to a discovery or invention, the development of a process or procedure, the evolution of a new organisation or a new development. A simple table to capture the key date or key step down the left hand column with the appropriate event or development down the right hand column. Top with a bright title sheet for instant classroom display.

The outcomes of the above independent learning tasks can be carried forward into the next lesson as instant 'Appetisers' at the start of the lesson with some students presenting their research or integrated into the recap session or into group tasks as background information. Note that many of the group tasks started within a lesson (as described in Chapter Nine) might also be extended into *bridge* tasks to complete and to prepare for any related group presentations. Do not be too concerned by students who do not complete independent learning tasks. Some are quite immature in their attitudes to study and will take more time to respond but eventually more and more will conform as you repeat this approach lesson after lesson. Remember to issue lots of praise to the students who do complete the tasks and speak to those who do not on a one to one basis in the doctor / patient mode as described in Chapter Nine. Seek to motivate by asking if they were uncertain what to do or how to do it and offer more help. This is preferable to expressing disapproval because our aim is to build a rapport and an interest in personal research. Overtime your repeated encouragement and display of faith in their ability might trigger greater effort. However, do not become too dispirited if some students never respond because often it will betray very low self-esteem that the student is unable to overcome. Time and patience are the tools but if you suspect deep seated personal problems then encourage more one to one time with the relevant personal tutor or even referral to a professional counselling service. As teachers we must always be on alert for personal difficulties or circumstances that are a barrier to learning as described in Chapter Three.

Thank you

Your lesson will have started with a warm greeting and welcome and so as the students leave the room offer an equally warm thank you for their participation. We all thrive on positives and building a positive rapport is one of the most significant steps we can take to encourage and sustain learning.

11 Independent learning

"so often students become passive recipients of teachers' lessons ....the aim is to make students active in the learning process...until the students reach the stage where they become their own teachers, they can seek out optimal ways to learn new material and ideas, they can seek resources to help them in this learning, and when they can set appropriate and more challenging goals."[1]

(Professor John Hattie 2009)

The holy grail of all teaching and learning is to develop independent learning or more fully to promote meta-cognition i.e. assisting students to hold clear personal goals, to be self aware of their progress towards those goals and promoting their confidence to seek and act on feedback. The target is mastery of subject or skill by sheer din of systematic learning process and effort. Hattie's conclusion is not new. Consider the following quotation from the Board of Education, Handbook for Teachers first published 1904, *"instruction will only have its full effect when the teacher realises that his chief task is to teach the scholars to teach themselves, and to adapt his methods steadily to that end"*.[2] At the highest levels, of ability independent learners will not only outpace their less determined classmates but often their teacher in terms of their depth of reading and research or perfection of vocational skills. The Nobel laureates Sir John Cockcroft (Physics 1951) and Sir Geoffrey Wilkinson (Chemistry 1973) were both taught by the same science teacher in Tormorden High School. This is the hallmark of the most successful and satisfying teaching when students are inspired to delve into the subject or skills with a hunger to know more and to advance to the next level i.e. the mastery of the standards relevant to each level whether level 1,2,3 or 4 and on vocational pass / fail course not only targeting commercial standards but world class standards. The latter point is significant because it easy to regard vocational pass/fail criteria as a terminal point but as the Ofsted Chief Inspector has noted, *"The best providers of work-based learning routinely take learners on apprenticeship programmes well beyond the specification of the qualification, providing them with a wide range of highly professional employment skills".*[3] A popular column in the Times Educational Supplement (TES) relates the recollections of highly successful people about the teachers who inspired them. In most cases they identify teachers who gave them the gifts of self belief, self worth and self awareness. Professor Hattie noted the importance of this positive rapport, *" it is sobering to realise that these teachers will be remembered...because they cared about teaching the students their passion for their subject, gave students confidence in themselves as learners and as people, treated the students as a person , and instilled a love of learning of their subject(s)."* [4]

Ofsted criteria

The Ofsted Common Inspection Framework (CIF), 2001-2008, set criteria for the development of independent learning skills and an expectation of working beyond the specification:

> *"Good teaching enables learners to make the most of their potential and advance their knowledge, understanding and skills well beyond those they had when they started their course. Inspectors will assess, through observation and discussion with learners, the extent to which learners (irrespective of their age, gender, race, ethnicity, learning difficulty or disability):*
>
> - *acquire knowledge and skills, develop ideas and increase their understanding*
> - *become confident in what they are doing*
> - *understand how well they are progressing and what they need to do to improve*
> - *work productively and make effective use of their time*
> - *are interested in their work and able to sustain their concentration think and learn for themselves*
> - *make use of the resources available to them, for example in libraries and ICT centres and other learning technologies*
> - *show determination to complete assignments on time and see problems through to resolution*
> - *are prepared to seek help and act on advice they receive."*[5]

It should not be assumed that such criteria no longer applies because the qualities and aptitudes listed are at the core of effective learning. The 2012 inspection framework for Further Education is more succinct and directs inspectors to judge, " *the extent to which teaching, training and coaching encourages and develops independent learning*" [6] and this is extended to state, *the promotion and development of independent learning skills, for example, through the use of a range of technologies, including a virtual learning environment*". [7] The Ofsted 2012 criteria for schools also touches upon the importance of promoting independent learning, "*the extent to which teachers enable pupils to develop the skills to learn for themselves, where appropriate, including setting appropriate homework to develop their understanding*".[8] Clearly students who apply the above criteria will make faster progress and achieve higher learning outcomes than students who do not. However, how far do your students walk into your classroom with those skills or share this expectation of their role in learning? Assuming many do not, how do you and your course team raise and support this expectation of independent learning at interview, induction, tutorial, assessment, in newsletters, on the Virtual Learning Environment (VLE) and within day to day lessons? The *bridge* step at the end of the Diamond Lesson Plan, as described in Chapter Ten, is one way to raise a clear expectation of independent learning between lessons. In addition how do you teach independent learning skills to those who lack them and motivate all to learn to the best of their abilities

Lifelong learning

The Lifelong Learning professional standards have governed the award of FE teaching qualifications since September 2007 and in relation to independent learning there are two specific criteria: " *Use a range of effective and appropriate teaching and learning techniques to engage and motivate learners and encourage independence*" and "*Implement learning activities which develop the skills and approaches of all learners and promote learner autonomy*".[9] The successful development of independent learning is a key hallmark of 'outstanding' lessons i.e. evidence that the students are motivated to apply themselves outside of the classroom and are successful students relevant to the course level. There is evidence of the regular application of this criteria from published Ofsted inspection reports, In a college awarded five overall grade one judgements the inspectors noted, *"Lessons are well paced and with a strong focus on student participation and independent learning".*[10] In a further college that also achieved the accolade of five overall Ofsted grade one awards the inspectors commented,*"the college has pushed the boundaries in developing innovative and creative practice in lessons which supports highly effective learning and the development of students' independence and responsibility for their work"*[11] Ofsted will equally be critical if there is limited evidence of planning to build and reinforce independent learning skills. In a survey report of Level 3 provision across 25 Sixth Forms, published in September 2008, the inspectors recorded, *"In six of the nine school sixth forms visited, the opportunities for students to develop independent learning skills were limited. In one school this meant that the knowledge of potentially high-attaining students was not fully extended".*[12] In applying this Ofsted and Lifelong Learning criteria we need to respond to the individual because as noted in Chapter Three each individual is different in terms of their motivation and capacity for learning as shaped by community, home, peer and personal influences. Our task, relevant to the course standard, is to personalise the learning experience and to help each individual to achieve their full potential or as defined in the Vision 2020 report, *"personalising learning and teaching means taking a highly structured and responsive approach to each child's and young person's learning, in order that all are able to progress, achieve and participate".*[13]

Learning skills pyramid

The pathway to personalisation starts with recognising the learning and support needs of three broad ability groups who largely populate our classrooms, **independent, dependent** and **directed** learners. Each group presents different learning and support needs and once satisfied we can identify the learning needs of each individual and begin to personalise our support. Broad classifications are useful tools to steer the development of teaching and learning strategies but ultimately the individual is our primary focus.

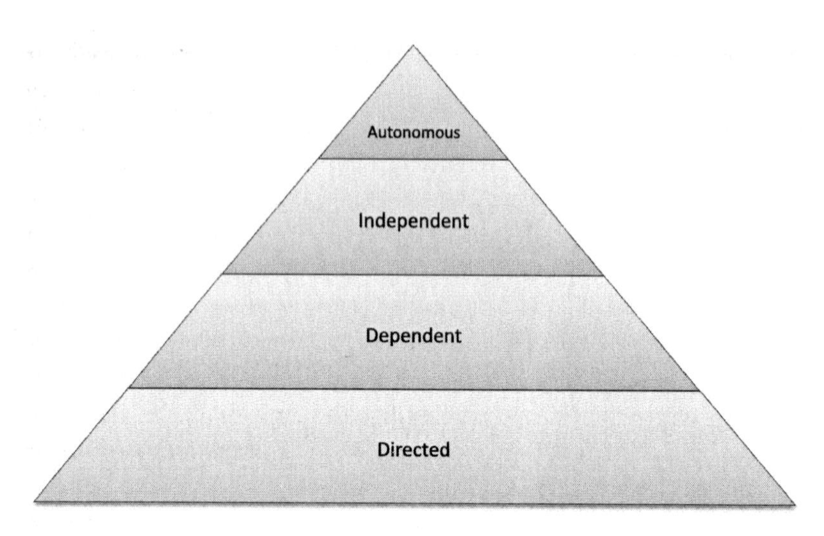

Learning autonomy is the ultimate outcome of successful independent learning when students not only set their own learning and achievement goals but have acquired the skills to enable them to do so.

Independent learners

Independent learners will often have enjoyed high achievement at High School and may have been identified as 'gifted and talented'. Alternatively they may be adults who have returned to study to pursue a particular qualification or simply for their own interest. They will tend to be highly motivated and often possess good study, social and learning skills. Outside the classroom they will make effective use of library, study centre and internet resources and/or by dint of effort read and work ahead and explore the course specification to a depth beyond what can be covered in the classroom. In the classroom they will participate to a high level and regularly ask as well as answer questions and share aspects of their personal research. The ninth principle of the Assessment Reform Group ten principles for Assessment for Learning (see Chapter Five) highlights the skill of independent learners as follows, *"Independent learners have the ability to seek out and gain new skills, new knowledge and new understandings'. They are able to engage in self-reflection and to identify the next steps in their learning. Teachers should equip learners with the desire and the capacity to take charge of their learning through developing the skills of self-assessment"*.[14] All of this extra depth will more often than not produce high grades at GCSE and later A-Level or equivalent vocational qualifications. In the Ofsted publication, *'Why Colleges Succeed,'* published in November 2004, the skills and attributes of highly successful students were summarised as follows: *"Learning is exceptional. Students are highly motivated, are intrinsically interested in learning new information and are enthusiastic about extending their understanding. They quickly develop good study habits, including independent research skills, and work hard to improve their knowledge. Much collaborative work in lessons is outstanding, with students co-operating most effectively on tasks set by the teacher. Teachers in these colleges work hard to inculcate a spirit of enquiry in their learners, encouraging them to think things out rather than always be told, to challenge received wisdom and to develop the right language to articulate their views: Students learn how to be critical and analytical as well as gaining good subject knowledge. Students are given confidence in their growing autonomy as learners. They aspire to achieve beyond their previous expectations or predictions, and have both the curiosity to ask questions and the maturity to admit difficulties. Discussion is a frequently used teaching strategy for checking learning as well as for ensuring that students can express themselves lucidly and persuasively and that they can reach conclusions, however tentatively at first, for themselves: Teachers encourage students to contribute fully to class discussions, and students are able to speak confidently and knowledgeably about their subjects. Many students ask, as well as answer, pertinent questions... Some teachers display very good listening skills and are adept at helping students to focus on key points. In an excellent lesson, students challenged the teacher, who enjoyed the lively debate that ensued and used it to steer learning and broaden the students' knowledge. Indeed, the development of articulate, self-confident students is a common characteristic of many of these colleges: Students are expected to articulate answers to questions in some depth, and are generally discouraged from monosyllabic responses. Students are confident and fluent in their oral work".*[15] The above description identifies a very high skill set and students who are self-directing. At its base lies a sustained feedback dialogue between teachers and students which drives interest, effort and significant achievement. Self-belief is high. It is easy to assume that independent learners of this type do not need our help. However, without additional challenges there is a danger of 'coasting' and even boredom if they find the pace and content of their studies too pedestrian. Independent learners also need to have their learning extended so that they might fulfill their full potential and raise their horizons towards universities and careers, including self employment, they may not have considered. In 2008, 733,000 students in our High Schools were identified as *'gifted and talented'*. The gifted aspect is gifted in terms of high academic progress and talented relates to a talent for sports, music, arts etc. The hallmarks of gifted and talented students in our schools are reported as:[16]

- Good readers
- Articulate
- Give quick verbal responses
- Generally knowledgeable
- Learn quickly
- Be interested in 'older' age-group topics
- Communicate well with adults
- Problem-solve unusually
- Be self taught in many of their interests
- Have a good memory
- Excel at art, music or sport
- Have strong views
- Have a lively and original imagination/ sense of humour.
- Be very sensitive and aware
- Be arrogant and socially inept
- Be easily bored by routine
- Not necessarily well behaved or well liked.

The overall challenge for teachers working with independent learners is to help them to achieve their full potential and to become autonomous learners. How far is 'gifted and talented' status picked-up by colleges as a part of initial assessment procedures and how far does this status translate into appropriate targets in Individual Learning Plans ? The key learning strategies in this regard relate to extended learning tasks, challenge tasks, entry into relevant regional, national or international competitions, peer teaching, mentoring, organizing exhibitions, displays, events and membership of relevant school or college committees. Independent learners will also make natural recruits for participation in learner involvement strategies. The Vision 2020 report made the following suggestions in relation to strengthening the 'student voice':

- *"using pupils as learning resources for one another, helping their peers to learn and develop, within the classroom and beyond*

- *inviting pupils to work with teachers in curriculum teams to review schemes of work and develop plans for improving learning and teaching*
- *asking pupils to provide feedback on particular lessons, either through general surveys or by training them as observers of lessons*
- *conducting regular surveys on the quality of the school experience and how it could be improved, sharing the results with all pupils*
- *involving pupils in the selection process for new members of staff".*[17]

All the above measures are powerful drivers of student autonomy and learning partnerships and need not be restricted to independent learners only.

Dependent learners

Dependent learners tend to form the majority of the students in our classrooms. Most will have left high school with average achievement i.e. four or five GCSEs at grades A*-C and will often enter Level Three programmes with the minimum entry standards. In the classroom they will be co-operative and will complete all necessary tasks but they will tend to be passive learners who will rarely participate or volunteer information. This under-participation will often signal a lack of confidence in speaking up and many will display underdeveloped study, social and learning skills which limit their ability to be effective participants. However, this is where personalisation is important because there are always exceptions. Many very able young people, who will go on to achieve high academic success, can be passive and remain aloof from debate or alternatively, as the above list of hallmarks for gifted and talented students indicates, some very able young people may be judged, *arrogant and socially inept*. The key concern with dependent learners is their dependence because outside of the classroom they will rarely undertake additional study beyond completing homework or necessary preparation for an examination. In 2008 Ofsted noted this over reliance on the teacher in its criteria for satisfactory lessons, *"teachers take steps to encourage them to work effectively on their own but a few learners too dependent on the teacher"*. [18] Dependent learners may lack the motivation and/or the study skills to undertake deeper independent study and may be poor at time management. Consequently, they are largely dependent on what is covered and issued in the classroom each week. In addition many will hold a part-time job and will often put more hours into their job than into their studies. Whereas their job may be beneficial in helping to develop wider skills and confidence it can also be a significant distraction. Online distractions also exist. 83% of British young people aged 18-24 maintain personal pages on a social networking site like Facebook. Research published by Aryn Karpinski of Ohio State University in 2009 has indicated that 68% of student Facebook users *"had a significantly lower grade point average"*[19] because of the regular distraction of updating and maintaining their social network. Dependent learners are often uncertain about their future career path and whether or not to progress to university. They will probably pass the course but not with high grades. In 2007 the Department for Education and Skills (DfES) dubbed these learners as *' invisible'*. In a related article, in the Times Educational Supplement (TES), entitled '**Stuck in the middle**' the following concerns were raised, *"Who are the most overlooked pupils in schools? Is it the white working class boys, the gifted girls or perhaps those who barely speak any English? Surprisingly perhaps, it is none of these. The ones most likely to slip through the net are the silent majority of 'average' pupils according to heads and teachers. They work quietly and conscientiously, get their homework in on time and are barely noticeable in class. By definition they become invisible"*.[20] The expansion of Higher Education is drawing heavily upon this pool of students and whereas many will gain entry into Higher Education there is a danger that their weak independent learning skills will cause them to struggle and many may drop out. In response it is becoming common for universities to offer learning support services to improve literacy and numeracy and to coach research and writing skills because of an over reliance on 'cut and paste' from the internet and in the worst cases detecting and countering plagiarism. To lift the performance of dependent learners we first need to address their motivation in terms of careers and future prospects. The word 'future' is quite scary at age 14-16 and often many cannot see beyond their local community and do not have the confidence to set a challenging goal because they instinctively believe it is out of reach. At induction and first tutorials it is a vital task to draw a line between past underachievement and to offer a ladder of future opportunity that is both challenging but obtainable with sufficient effort. Next to offer clear guidance on what to learn, to set clear targets which are regularly reviewed and followed-up with useful feedback on how to improve. Hattie noted, " *passive learners preferred teachers who were organized, had clarity of structure, and could specify clear learning objectives, whereas active learners preferred teachers who promoted interaction in class, used a variety of teacher approaches, and displayed high levels of enthusiasm*". [21] A higher level of structure is the key requirement for building the skills of dependent learners but there is also a need to check and address the amount of effort and time they put into study. Young people in a full-time job will work for a minimum of 37 hours to earn their wage packet but often full-time course hours are as low as 16-17 hours in the classroom. What happens to the other hours? Some may be spent in a part-time job but even with 10-12 hours part-time working most dependent learners will still be operating below the time commitment of a standard 38-40 hour working week. Too many dependent learners share a limited view of the job of a student – they attend the lessons and make assumptions that this is all they need to do. However, they might also not know what to do. Whereas independent learners will naturally visit the library, search the internet, watch relevant TV programmes, read relevant newspapers and journals and/or visit relevant museums etc most dependent learners will not. Dependent learners need more structured support with clear references on how to follow-up their lessons – note the *Learning Portal* suggested in Chapter Two and the 'bridge' suggestions at the end of Chapter Ten. Beyond motivation and knowing what to do the difficulty may be as simple as a lack of organisational, study and/or time management skills. Essentially course teams and individual teachers need to provide much more structured support to assist dependent learners to learn.

Directed learners

The most challenging students to teach are 'directed learners' because more often than not they will need explicit directions and direct support to complete a task, hence directed learners. Most will have underachieved at GCSE or even have absented themselves from school and many may come from dysfunctional or unsupportive homes. Many will exhibit low self esteem and a lack of appropriate social, study, organisational and learning skills. In the classroom they will often be easily distracted, go off task or even indulge in disruptive behaviour. They will often attend lessons ill-equipped for study lacking the textbook, pens, paper, files etc and at the end of the lesson they may submit incomplete work or work below pass standards. Outside the classroom they will rarely undertake any independent study and may need support and even pressure to submit homework. They will often have no career plans and may struggle to meet the minimum course standards and will be in danger of failing. Overall these students tend to have negative memories of classrooms and learning. Managing their behaviour and helping them to adopt more positive attitudes and to identify future goals is a significant challenge. Ofsted in the publication, 'Why Colleges Fail' published in November 2004 commented on the challenges as follows: *"Many young people arrive in GFE colleges with little enthusiasm for what they are doing, with poor basic skills and negative memories of 11 years of compulsory schooling which have equipped them poorly for independent learning. Where colleges have not understood the need to enthuse and reinvigorate these young people and where staff have few strategies for dealing with the range of learning and behavioural shortcomings presented by at least some of this cohort, they struggle to teach them successfully".*[22] Teachers often believe that it is impossible to get a Grade One judgment from Ofsted inspectors if they are observed with a class of 'directed learners' who may display inappropriate or challenging behaviour. However, as the passage above indicates it is a question of applying the appropriate strategies to deal with the range of learning and behavioural shortcomings presented. The teaching and learning strategies required will very different to the strategies and teaching skills required in an AS classroom composed of largely independent learners. The 2008 Ofsted Inspectors' Handbook offered the guidance, *'inspectors will be aware of contextual factors, which might contribute to only modest progress, even when the teaching is very good'.*[23] The grade one judgement can be earned in any teaching situation but what are the appropriate strategies? How far has your course team arrived at a consensus on how to motivate, support, develop, correct and improve the behaviour, as necessary of typical directed learners? The key is consistent team rather than individual actions as highlighted by Sir Alan Steer in 2009, *"The importance of schools establishing baseline consistency in their learning and teaching practice cannot be exaggerated. Where there is such consistency teachers become mutually supportive with their individual efforts being strengthened by the work of their colleagues".*[24] Consistency will yield the most positive results in relation to clear, negotiated and displayed learner contracts, clear short-term learning goals, how to maintain a file and other key study skill requirements, attachment of learning support assistants, mentors, parental involvement, bite size learning tasks, active rather than passive learning tasks, modelling and scaffolding of requirements, regular praise and rewards, clear assessment for learning feedback and well understood and firm sanctions for any disruptive behaviour. The Ofsted Chief Inspector's Report 2008 contained the following example of a strategy to assist low achieving pupils to organise their time, *"Pupils sometimes fail to meet their targets because they do not understand how to do so and have not been involved in setting the targets initially. The survey of provision for white boys from low-income backgrounds found that using diaries for subjects helped them to improve their work. The diaries included advice on how to approach key topics and how to extend ideas further; tips on how to construct essays; and simple explanations of the technical terms used in particular subjects. They also included guidance on how pupils could identify their progress against the National Curriculum level descriptors for the subject, and what they needed to do to meet their personal targets. The pupils filled in the subject diaries and reviewed them every fortnight or three weeks with their tutors. They, in turn, passed on relevant information to the subject teachers. In the best examples, parents also contributed to these diary reviews".* [25] Clearly this is a very practical way to help less organised students to engage with their learning. What are your team strategies to lift the performance of directed learners? The final Steer Report in Behaviour Management, published 15th April, 2009 notes, *"For children with behaviour problems or other learning needs it is particularly important that their classroom experience is rigorous, but personalised. Much poor behaviour has its origins in the inability of the child to access learning, rather than as a result of an unchangeable character defect".* [26] The latter point is a crucial point because the challenge is to identify and respond to the individual blocks to learning. Chapter Three provides a deeper analysis of the issues involved and in particular highlights that the key starting point relates to strategies to enthuse and introduce self belief and personal confidence. If this is successful then the behaviour issues will sharply diminish and attention can shift to improving study skills and from this platform to build achievement.

Generic study skills

Independent learners often possess superior study and organisational skills in comparison to dependent and directed learners. How far do you check and coach generic study skills to ensure all can make suitable progress?

note-taking skills?
file management skills?
basic Word functions?
basic Excel functions?
basic Power point functions?
researching on the internet?
researching in the library?
using statistics?
basic writing skills?
basic reading skills?
basic written presentation skills?
oral presentation skills?
revision, memory and learning skills?

What steps do you take in the induction course or first lessons to discuss and identify how far all students possess the above skills? How do you translate this into a higher level of functions/ expectations for independent learners? Without the above skill set most students will struggle to make progress. A student who is struggling with basic study skills in week one will still be struggling in week six without appropriate intervention and support. Address effective personalisation by introducing a 'learning dialogue,' around this skill set i.e. who is good at what and begin a process of peer support and peer co-operation to develop and improve generic study skills. Perhaps you could develop a study skills questionnaire to check for different levels of generic study skills by extending the following approach:

Study Skills Questionnaire			
Study skill	**Easy**	**OK**	**Difficult**
I can take notes from a presentation and capture all the main points			
I can take notes from a textbook and summarise what I've read			
I can use the internet to research			
I can wordprocess			
I use the library to research my subjects			
I can give a clear presentation			
etc			

What is your definition of the study skills and wider skills required for the successful completion of your course and preparation for related employment and/or progression to university? How do you develop those skills in tutorials, by learning support staff, library and study centre staff and teaching staff? How do you check for progress and acquisition of these skills? Kingsbridge Community College in Devon adopted this approach, in conjunction with its sixth form students, by *"formulating a comprehensive list of actions students could take to improve their learning...each target is followed by a series of specific actions to help students achieve the targets...but just as important as the document itself, has been the effect that the process of discussing and writing has had on almost everything surrounding sixth-form learning"*.[27] Addressing how to learn is very empowering and prompts consideration of how best to help students to learn effectively. You might open a drop-in study skills / basic English /Number/ ICT workshop at set times to support any students with their study skills. You might place self-directed study packages to complete within the Library resource centre or on the Virtual Learning Environment (VLE) to build these skills. Microsoft ™ offers free self tuition packages for most of its popular functions but how about more basic things like how to use the apostrophe for students who keep getting it wrong or how to apply the Harvard Referencing system within a formal assignment etc. A simple one side of A4 guide to using the apostrophe etc available on the VLE may make the difference. You might develop short podcasts and video podcasts for students to download on key Microsoft applications. Invite some of your skilled independent learners (or IT students) to create the podcasts and give them appropriate recognition. Offer more advanced functions/skills for more able students. Why not make available and encourage short touch typing programs to eliminate two finger typing and especially among computing students. It takes only 20 minutes to learn the *qwerty* keyboard! In terms of Assessment for Learning this approach permits a teacher to specify the completion of one of the support packages as a Personal Action Step to Success (PASS) action (see Chapter Five). Individual learning support and action lies at the heart of assessment for learning and effective personalisation. This personalised approach also addresses the common complaint from students that they have covered all of these basic study skills topics at school. Do not leave this study support to be covered by a Personal Tutor because the relevant study support may be delivered too late for individual students already struggling within the first month. In addition the guidance will lack subject content and relevance – build how to complete the assignment etc into your own teaching. Model how it should be completed and set minimum expectations and leave open ended to motivate the independent learners. Once Personal Tutors are freed from delivering a standard study skills programme they can use the time for more one to one personalised support.

Subject specific study skills

All subjects will involve preferred methods of working and presentation of information. Students engaged in Science, Humanities, Engineering, Catering, ICT, Maths, Media etc will encounter different demands in how files should be kept, how information should be recorded and presented. A common complaint, made by students, is the absence of a standard approach between staff to the layout of an essay or a laboratory report etc. Specialist staff teams need to agree their standards and to issue and reinforce common standards. The development of standard templates for essay writing, assignment layouts, business reports, drawings, tables, laboratory reports etc gives weaker students the support and confidence they need. Place the agreed learning templates onto the VLE for ease of access. This is also a good staff development activity because it encourages 'team talk' about the standards expected and ensures a consistent approach. The relevant study skills and how to complete a given task or assignment should be explicitly modelled in each lesson. It is important for all staff to teach appropriate 'how to study' techniques or preferred presentation methods etc as each topic unfolds. There should also be regular checks that learners are maintaining their files appropriately and know how to record and present information to the standards expected. Praise accuracy and coach those who need support on a one to one during group work sessions or reserve five minutes at the end of a lesson to coach a small group. If this becomes a wider issue build a short instruction session into your lesson plan. Once or twice a term reserve some teaching time for one to one appointments (around formal assessment times) to check progress and to motivate all to reach higher standards.

Effort

Ultimately, the promotion of independent learning is all about effort and how far we can motivate each individual to apply effort to succeed. Marzano indicates, "*Not all students realize the importance of believing in effort…In fact, studies have demonstrated that some students are not aware of the fact that the effort they put into a task has a direct effect on their success relative to the task…The implication here is that teachers should explain and exemplify the 'effort belief' to students*".[28] Personalisation is the answer i.e. working with each student to identify their personal barriers to effective study. What is holding each student back and what actions are they going to take to improve and if they are not taking actions to improve what are the appropriate interventions?

Teaching and Learning policy

"In order to ensure consistent high standards in the classroom and to support pupils and teachers, all schools should be required to produce a written policy identifying their key learning and teaching aims, strategies and practices. The production of this policy should engage all staff and it should be regularly reviewed".[1]

Recommendation 6 of Sir Alan Steer's Learning Behaviour report, 15th April 2009

On 15th April, 2009, Sir Alan Steer, Principal of Seven Kings High School, London, published his final report on behaviour management entitled, *Learning behaviour: Lessons learned* in his role as the Government's 'Behaviour Tsar'. His report made 47 recommendations and all 47 were accepted by the then Secretary of State for Children, Schools and Families, Ed Balls. Recommendation Six as quoted above relates to the writing of a teaching and learning policy. Although the report and its recommendations relate to the Secondary sector the benefits of a teaching and learning policy are applicable to the whole 14-19 sector. The writing of a teaching and learning policy can be a unifying and motivating experience for a course or subject team because it presents an opportunity to pool experiences and better still to disseminate practical 'how to...' examples. This practical approach is the key to a successful policy rather than broad statements of aspirations or intentions. Sir Alan Steer appended the teaching and learning policy for his own school as an exemplar and it illustrates how helpful and supportive a teaching and learning policy can be e.g. it lists 50 examples of starter activities to encourage positive lesson starts. The dissemination of practical suggestions to improve teaching and learning was commented upon in the Ofsted report, *'Twelve outstanding secondary schools'* as a hallmark of highly successful schools, *"An accompanying appendix of good practice provides a rich array of ideas, but the main purpose of the policy is to set down very clear expectations about what will happen in every classroom"*.[2] Most staff have good ideas for engaging learning activities and the key is to provide 'swapshop' opportunities to explore tried and tested methods for inclusion within an overall teaching and learning policy and ideally to disseminate relevant examples and materials on a Virtual Learning Environment (VLE) for universal access. Ofsted highlighted team working as a feature of outstanding schools, *"Time is ring-fenced for staff to work in teams: engaging in productive discussion about pedagogy, planning lessons that inspire students to become independent and effective learners, and being reflective rather than simply dealing with administration"*.[3] Team working can also expand into consortiums of like-minded colleges or schools. A highly professional example of this in action is provided by the S7 consortium of high achieving sixth form colleges in Surrey www.s7colleges.com. The S7 website is a hub for collaborative practice and includes S7 Talk which is an acronym for Teaching and Learning Kit – a set of resources for all to share. S7 pool their best practice and resources to the benefit of all and plan a collaborative programme of staff development opportunities.

Learning and teaching strategy format

Schools and colleges should consider generic teaching and learning policies that specify core aspects of good practice but also permit individual Programme Areas and Departments to extend the generic policy to reflect the challenges of teaching within different curriculum areas or particular student groups. The evidence of effective practice from lesson observations and wider research can guide the writing of a generic policy but 'ownership' is important and significant benefits arise when course teams build their own consensus of agreed good practice i.e. the requirements for successful teaching and learning will differ from a Motor Vehicle Workshop to an AS History classroom. Each teaching team should be encouraged to confirm and 'publish' a teaching and learning policy. The policy might have some of the following features:

Title page

Design a bright title page with a relevant photograph – preferably taken by students of an event, educational visit, awards evening, exam success, exhibition, drama etc. The photograph is shorthand for the excitement and outcomes of successful teaching and learning within the relevant curriculum area.

Foreword

Include a foreword by the Principal or the relevant Programme Manager highlighting the mission, culture and values of the school, college or individual programme or curriculum area. In the case of an individual department or programme area also list the staff team who have contributed to the policy.

Index page

List the contents of the teaching and learning policy. The headings might include:

- Socio-economic profile – an overview of the area / or typical student intake in terms of behavior, skills and entry qualifications.
- Initial assessment procedures
- Induction course arrangements
- Scheme of Work and lesson plan exemplar guidance
- Resources
- VLE development
- Good classroom practice
- Assessment methods and feedback
- Marking policy and criteria
- Behaviour code
- Functional and basic skills strategies

Decide the most appropriate key headings and devote a staff development day to writing a Teaching and Learning policy as a statement of the whole team and/or school, college as appropriate. Sub groups can be invited to undertake a heading each and to draft the relevant section for discussion and agreement. Once agreed each section can be collated to form a short booklet. After appropriate editing the Teaching and Learning policy should be adopted and updated, revised and/or extended on an annual basis. The intention is a short, sharp document and this can be achieved by referencing any detail or associated policies to supporting documents. Ideally the

Teaching and Learning Policy should be an electronic document and the above headings can be clickable straight to the relevant page or to recommended websites or short podcasts etc to illustrate the content.

Focus on IMPACT

What will make the difference? The teaching and learning policy should steer staff energy and attention into developing strategies that will have the greatest impact on learning. Impact is a useful and memorable acronym that embraces six key aspects of effective practice. Consider developing team answers to the following six 'impact' questions:

The related 'impact' questions for course teams to answer are:

- How do you inspire, motivate and raise the personal horizons of all of your students?

- How do you set and monitor the achievement of significant personal learning targets by all of your students?
- How do you share the major curriculum goals and drive independent learning with all of your students?
- How do you show all students how to improve their work and offer real time (in-lesson) improvement guidance?
- How do you develop personal learning, Functional and employability skills for successful study and later university and/or employment?
- What are the most effective teaching and learning strategies for your students and how are they disseminated?

Pose these questions on a staff development day and seek and capture clear answers and set your Teaching and Learning policy.

The *impact* questions draw together much of the evidence in this book and the answers will collectively drive outstanding teaching and learning by empowering staff teams to confirm and 'publish' their own outstanding practice strategies. No single teacher can possess all of the answers or have the time and energy to investigate every aspect of effective practice but overtime a team can. Answers to the above questions should also involve your students and a questionnaire or focus groups to discuss effective teaching and learning can be very beneficial as part of your learner involvement strategy. The Ofsted document, Why Colleges Succeed' highlighted the importance of good teamwork as follows, *"Central to the good curriculum management encountered in these colleges [outstanding colleges] is effective teamwork where teaching staff meet regularly and good practice is disseminated as necessary: Teamwork is often outstanding with much effective co-ordination of good practice"*.[4] The evidence presented in Chapter Once highlights that outstanding teaching and learning arises from what *'some'* teachers do but with a well-developed teaching and learning policy *'some'* can become *'all'*. Ultimately the answer to outstanding teaching and learning is team co-operative practice.

References

Chapter One

1. Wragg Ted, Guardian website, 31st October 2000, http://education.guardian.co.uk/specialreports/teachingawards2000/story
2. Google search www.google.com July 2012.
3. Hay McBer, Research into Teacher Effectiveness: A model of teacher effectiveness, DfES June 2000, page 8.
4. Hay McBer, Research into Teacher Effectiveness: A model of teacher effectiveness, DfES June 2000, page 36.
5. Ofsted, Handbook for the inspection of Further Education and Skills, 2012, Pg. 44.
6. Abid
7. Ofsted, Handbook for the inspection of Further Education and Skills, 2012, Pg. 49
8. Ofsted, The evaluation schedule for the inspection of maintained schools and academies, April 2012, Pg. 12.
9. Ofsted, Handbook for the inspection of Further Education and Skills, 2012, Pg. 53
10. McKinsey and Company, How the World's best-performing school systems come out on top, September 2007, Pg.20.
11. Abid, Pg. 31.
12. Abid, Pg. 38.
13. McKinsey, How the world's best performing school systems came out on top, 2007, Pg. 15.
14. Hanushek, Eric A, Teacher Quality, Hoover Press, 2002, Pg. 3.
15. Wiliams, Professor Dylan, Invest in teachers to raise achievement, Institute of Education, press release, www.ioe.ac.uk /news press release 2nd April 2009.
16. Teaching and Learning Research Programme, www.tlrp.org/themes/themes/tenprinciples.html 19th February 2008.
17. BBC, What makes a good teacher, 28th January 2008 http://news.bbc.co.uk/2/hi/uk_news/education/7209096.stm
18. McKinsey, How the world's most improved school systems keep getting better, 2010, Pg. 112.
19. Hattie, Professor John, Visible Learning: A synthesis of over 800 meta-analyses relating to achievement, Routledge, 2009, Appendix B.
20. Abid, pg. 126.
21. Abid.
22. Lifelong Learning UK, New Overarching professional standards for teachers, tutors and trainers in the lifelong learning sector, 2007, www.lluk.org but note legacy site on www.lsis.org.uk
23. Institute for Learning, Guidelines for Continuous Professional Development, Feb 2008, www.ifl.ac.uk, Pg.4.
24. Abid.

25. Tomlinson Mike, 14-19 Curriculum and Qualifications Reform, DfES, October 2004, Pg. 96, Para 258.
26. Teaching and Learning Research Programme, www.tlrp.org/themes/themes/tenprinciples.html 19th February 2008, Ninth principle.
27. BBC, What makes a good teacher, 28th January 2008. http://news.bbc.co.uk/2/hi/uk_news/education/7209096.stm
28. Ofsted, Handbook for the inspection of further education and skills from September 2009, July 2009, www.ofsted.gov.uk, Pg. 58
29. Ofsted, Handbook for Inspecting Colleges, September 2008, www.ofsted.gov.uk/publications, Pg.82.
30. Abid, Pg. 86.
31. Abid, Pg. 84
32. Ofsted, Handbook for the inspection of Further Education and Skills, 2012, Pg. 49.
33. Hattie, Professor John, Visible Learning: A synthesis of over 800 meta-analyses relating to achievement, Routledge, 2009, Pg. 114.
34 Ofsted, Handbook for the inspection of further education and skills from September 2009, July 2009, www.ofsted.gov.uk, Pg. 52
35. Ofsted, Handbook for the inspection of Further Education and Skills, 2012, Pg. 49
36. Abid Pg. 46
37. Board of Education, Handbook of suggestions for teachers, 1927, Pg. 13
38. Ofsted, Handbook for the inspection of Further Education and Skills, 2012, Pg. 46
39. Hay McBer, Research into Teacher Effectiveness: A model of teacher effectiveness, DfES June 2000, pg. 17.
40. Teach First, Lessons from the Front: 1000 new teachers speak up, February 2008. www.teachfirst.org.uk
41. Hattie, Professor John, Visible Learning: A synthesis of over 800 meta-analyses relating to achievement, Routledge, 2009, Pg. 35
42. Ofsted, Handbook for the inspection of Further Education and Skills, 2012, Pg. 44.
43. Canfield Jack and Hansen Mark Victor, Chicken Soup for the Soul, Random House, 2000, Pg. 21.
44. Pearson Teaching Awards, www.teachingawards.com, July 2012.
45. Ofsted, Handbook for the inspection of Further Education and Skills, 2012, Pg. 44
46. Ofsted, Inspection reports, Kendal College, January 2011, Pg. 10, Para. 20.
47. Ofsted, Handbook for the inspection of Further Education and Skills, 2012, Pg. 44
48. Ofsted, The evaluation schedule for the inspection of maintained schools and academies, April 2012, Pg. 11.
49. Pearson Teaching Awards, www.teachingawards.com, July 2012
50. Ofsted, Twelve outstanding schools, excelling against the odds, www.ofsted.gov.uk, 2009, Para 61.
51. Ofsted, Why colleges succeed, www.ofsted.gov.uk/publications, November, 2004
52. Ofsted, Report of the Chief Inspector, November 2011 , Pg. 97, Para 261.
53. Ofsted, Handbook for the inspection of Further Education and Skills, 2012, Pg. 49
54. Ofsted, The evaluation schedule for the inspection of maintained schools and academies, April 2012, Pg. 12.
55. Lifelong Learning UK, New Overarching professional standards for teachers, tutors and trainers in the lifelong learning sector, 2007, www.lluk.org Domain C legacy site within www.lsis.org.uk
56. Tomlinson Mike, 14-19 Curriculum and Qualifications Reform, DfES, October 2004, Pg. 96, Para 257
57. Hattie, Professor John, Visible Learning: A synthesis of over 800 meta analyses relating to achievement, Routledge, 2009, Pg. 23.
58. Lifelong Learning UK, New Overarching professional standards for teachers, tutors and trainers in the lifelong learning sector, 2007, www.lluk.org, Domains B and C but now legacy site within www.lsis.org.uk

59. Ofsted, Handbook for the inspection of Further Education and Skills, 2012, Pg.44-51
60. Department of Education, Teachers Standards, 2012, www.education.gov.uk
61. Hattie, Professor John, Visible Learning: A synthesis of over 800 meta-analyses relating to achievement, Routledge, 2009, Pg. 240.
62. Mitchell Geoff, Headteacher, Tadcaster Grammar School, North Yorkshire.
63. Brighouse Tim Professor, Essential pieces: the jigsaw of a successful school, Research Machines, 2006, Pg. 33.
64 Balls, Ed, Secretary of State for Education, What makes an outstanding teacher, The Guardian, 21st October 2008, http://www.guardian.co.uk/education
65. Fento, Standards for teaching and supporting learning in further Education in England and Wales, 1999, LLUK archive, www.lluk.org legacy site within www.lsis.org.uk
66. Teacher of the Year Awards, www.teachingawards.com
67. Unesco, What makes a good teacher, 1996, www.unicef.org/teachers/teacher/teacher.htm
68. Jussab Farina, What makes a good teacher, UK Centre for Legal Education, www.ukcle.ac.uk/lili/2005/jussab.html
69. Abid
70. Varnava Tracey, What is excellence in Law teaching, UK Centre for Legal Education, 2008, www.ukcle.ac.uk
71. Fento, What makes a good teacher? Learners and Teachers give their verdict, 30th November , 2001, LLUK archive, www.lluk.org legacy site within **www.lsis.org.uk**
72. Bilborough Sixth Form College, Nottingham, www.bilborough.ac.uk
73. Hay McBer, Research into Teacher Effectiveness: A model of teacher effectiveness, DfES June 2000, pg. 3.
74. Hattie, Professor John, Visible Learning: A synthesis of over 800 meta-analyses relating to achievement, Routledge, 2009, Pg. 250.
75. Department of Education, Teachers' Standards, 2012, www.education.gov.uk Pg. 7
76. Ofsted, Handbook for the inspection of Further Education and Skills, 2012, Pg.44.

Chapter Two

1. Ofsted, Handbook for the inspection of Further Education and Skills, 2012, www.ofsted.gov.uk, Pg 37
2. Abid, Pg 44.
3. Abid, Pg. 54
4. Ofsted, Twelve outstanding schools, excelling against the odds, www.ofsted.gov.uk, 2009, para 60.
5. Department of Education, Teachers' Standards, 2012, www.education.gov.uk Pg. 6
6. Ofsted, The evaluation schedule for the inspection of maintained schools and academies, April 2012, Pg 12
7. Lifelong Learning UK, New Overarching professional standards for teachers, tutors and trainers in the lifelong learning sector, 2007, www.lluk.org
8. Ofsted, Handbook for the inspection of Further Education and Skills, 2012, www.ofsted.gov.uk, Pg 44
9. Abid, Pg.45
10. DCSF, 14-19 briefing, Make change happen notebook, college version, 2009, Pg. 1
11. DfES, White Paper, 14-19 Education and Skills, February 2005, Para 4.6
12. DfES, Leitch Review of skills, Prosperity for all in the global economy – world class skills, final report, December 2006, Pg. 6
13. Gilbert Christine, 2020 Vision: report of the teaching and learning in 2020 review group, December 2006, Pg. 10.

14. CBI, Learning to grow: what employers need from education and skills, June 2012, www.cbi.org.uk, Pg. 32
15 Ofsted, Handbook for the inspection of Further Education and Skills, 2012, www.ofsted.gov.uk, Pg 40
16. Abid, Pg.44
17. Ofsted, The evaluation schedule for the inspection of maintained schools and academies, April 2012, Pg 11
18. Ofsted, Handbook for the inspection of Further Education and Skills, 2012, www.ofsted.gov.uk, Pg 40 & 45
19. Ofsted, Handbook for Inspecting Colleges, September 2008, Para 247.
20. Ofsted, Why Colleges Succeed, www.ofsted.gov.uk, November 2004, Para. 44.
21. Ofsted, Identifying good practice: a survey of Post 16 science in colleges and schools, www.ofsted.gov.uk, January 2008, Para. 20.
22. Ofsted, Identifying good practice: a survey of business, administration and law in colleges, January 2008, Para 26.
23. Ofsted, Oldham Sixth Form College, Inspection report, January 2008, Para 17.
24. Ofsted, Kendal College, Inspection report, 2010, Pg.
25. Ofsted, A comparison of the effectiveness of Level 3 provision in 25 Post 16 providers, September 2008, Para. 19.
26. Ofsted, The evaluation schedule for the inspection of maintained schools and academies, April 2012, Pg 11
27. Hattie, Visible Learning, A synthesis of over 800 meta-analyses relating to achievement, Routledge, 2009, Pg. 186.
28. Coffield Frank, Should we be using learning styles? What research has to say to practice, Learning and Skills Research Centre, 2004, Pg. 56.
29. Coffield Frank, Just suppose teaching and learning became the first priority, Learning and skills network, May 2008, Pg 32.
30. Marzano Robert J et al, Classroom instruction that works, ASCD, 2001, Pg. 94
31. Hattie, Visible Learning, A synthesis of over 800 meta-analyses relating to achievement, Routledge, 2009, Pg. 239.
32. Ofsted, Handbook for Inspecting Colleges, www.ofsted.gov.uk, September 2008, Para 276.
33. Ofsted, Twelve outstanding schools, excelling against the odds, www.ofsted.gov.uk, 2009, Para 111.
34. Ofsted, Handbook for the inspection of Further Education and Skills, 2012, www.ofsted.gov.uk, Pg 46.
35. Hattie, Visible Learning, A synthesis of over 800 meta-analyses relating to achievement, Routledge, 2009, Pg. 43.
36. Ofsted, Handbook for the inspection of further education and skills from September 2009, July 2009, www.ofsted.gov.uk, Pg 177
37. Abid, Pg. 1
38. Ofsted, Handbook for the inspection of Further Education and Skills, 2012, www.ofsted.gov.uk, Pg 45.

Chapter Three

1. Lifelong Learning UK, New Overarching professional standards for teachers, tutors and trainers in the lifelong learning sector, 2007, www.lluk.org/standards/standards_index.html, Domain C.
2. Ofsted, Handbook for the inspection of Further Education and Skills, 2012, Pg. 44
3. Ofsted, The evaluation schedule for the inspection of maintained schools and academies, April 2012, Pg. 11.
4. Ofsted, Handbook for the inspection of Further Education and Skills, 2012, Pg. 53
5. LSC, 'Getting that dream career is easy' July, 2008, www.lsc.gov.uk

6. LSC, The jobs you love to love' May 2008, www.lsc.gov.uk
7. The Times, 3rd April, 2009, Pg. 9.
8. NASUWT, One more broken window: the impact of physical environment on schools, 2008, Para 2.38.
9. Abid, Para 2.12
10. Financial Times, Poor pupils in North face worst prospects, 26th April, 2011, www.ft.com
11. Church Urban fund, Poverty in England, May 2012, www.cuf.org.uk
12. Institute of Education, University of London, Effective provision of Pre-School, 13. Primary and Secondary Education, July 2008, www.ioe.ac.uk, Pg. 45, Paras 72-77.
13. Institute of Education, University of London, Huge gap in reading scores between bright children in top and bottom social groups, 29th June 2012, www.ioe.ac.uk / newsevents/64722.html
14. Goodman Alissa and Gregg Paul (Editors), Poor children's educational attainment: how important are attitudes and behaviours? Joseph Rowntree Foundation, March 2010, Pg. 26.
15. Obama Barack President, Back to School Event, 8th September, 2009, Pg. 3, www.bbc.co.uk/education.
16. Ofsted, Twelve outstanding secondary schools: excelling against the odds, 2009, Paras 5 and 32.
17. Ofsted, Access and Achievement in Urban Education, 1993, Paras 72-77.
18. Ofsted, Annual report of the Chief Inspector for Schools, November 2011,Pg. 52, Para 101.
19. Ofsted, Rising to the Challenge: a review of the Teach First initial teacher training programme, 25th January 2008, www.ofsted.gov.uk, Pg. 10.
20. Teach First, www.teachfirst.org.uk/graduates
21. Times Educational supplement, For Richer for Poorer, 11th July 2008, Pg.22-23.
22. Scott, Professor Stephen, Sunday Times, 24th August, 2008, Pg. 7.
23. Litch, Lord, Review of Skills, Prosperity for all in the global economy – world class skills, final report, December 2006, Cabinet Office, Para 6.5
24. Goodman Alissa and Gregg Paul (Editors), Poor children's educational attainment: how important are attitudes and behaviours? Joseph Rowntree Foundation, March 2010, Pg. 34.
25. Institute of Education, University of London, Effective provision of Pre-School, Primary and Secondary Education, July 2008, www.ioe.ac.uk, Executive summary Pg. IV.
26. Ibid, Pg. 104
27. Goodman Alissa and Gregg Paul (Editors), Poor children's educational attainment: how important are attitudes and behaviours? Joseph Rowntree Foundation, March 2010, Pg. 22
28. McKinsey and Company, How the world's best-performing school systems come out on top, September 2007, Pg. 41
29. Goodman Alissa and Gregg Paul (Editors), Poor children's educational attainment: how important are attitudes and behaviours? Joseph Rowntree Foundation, March 2010, Pg. 36
30. Abid, Pg. 5
31. Times Educational supplement, 8th August 2008, Pg. 11.
32. OECD, How does the social attainment gap in England compare with countries internationally, April 2012, Pg. 2 www.oecd.org.
33. Hattie, Professor John, Visible Learning: A synthesis of over 800 meta-analyses relating to achievement, Routledge, 2009, Pg. 66.
34. LSC, 'Getting that dream career is easy, July 2008, www.lsc.gov.uk
35. Steer, Sir Alan, Learning Behaviour, Department for Education and Skills, October 2005, Para.166.

36. Ofsted, Narrowing the Gap: the inspection of Children's services April 2007, www.ofsted.gov.uk
37. Ofsted, Handbook for Inspecting Colleges, September 2008, Para 234
38. Ofsted, Twelve outstanding secondary schools: excelling against the odds, 2009, Para 112.
39. Ofsted, Alder Grange Community and Technology School Inspection Report, November 2006, www.ofsted.gov.uk
40. DFES, Gender and Education: the evidence on pupils in England, 2007, para 6.3
41. Times Educational Supplement, 26th September, 2008, Pg.46.
42. Ofsted, The evaluation schedule for the inspection of maintained schools and academies, April 2012, Pg. 15.
43. Palmer Sue, Toxic Childhood, How the modern world is damaging our children and what we can do about it, Orion, 2006, Pg.316.
44. The Times, 24th April 2008, Pg. 21.
45. Self HarmUK, The truth about self harm, www.selfharmuk.org, 2006.
46. Lifelong Learning, Professional standards for teachers, tutors and trainers in the Lifelong Learning Sector, www.lluk.org/standards, Domain C. BP1.3
47. Ofsted, inspection reports, 2005-09 www.ofsted.gov.uk
48. Ofsted, Identifying good practice: a survey of college provision in Engineering and manufacturing technologies, January 2008, Para 31.
49. Ofsted, Identifying good practice: a survey of college provision in agriculture, horticulture and animal care, January 2008, Pg. 8
50. Hutter Dexter, Sir, Times Educational Supplement, October 2008, Pg.38.
51. Pearson Teaching awards, Secondary Teachers of the Year, Cathy McGowan, 2012, www.teachingawards.com
52. Ofsted, Why Colleges Succeed, November 2004, www.ofsted.gov.uk
53. Ofsted, Twelve outstanding secondary schools: excelling against the odds, 2009, Pg. 22..
54. Atkinson, William Sir, Times Educational Supplement, 30th May 2008, Pg. 24.
55. Steer, Alan Sir, The Independent, 13th October 2005 www.independent.co.uk/news/education/news
56. Ofsted, Why Colleges Succeed, November 2004, www.ofsted.gov.uk
57. Board of Education, Handbook of suggestions for teachers, 1927, Pg. 27
58. Ofsted, Kendal college, inspection report, December 2010, Pg. 10, Para 20. www.ofsted.gov.uk
59. Grylls, Bear, Times Educational Supplement, magazine, 8th August 2008, Pg.6.
60. Press Release, Teachers lack of knowledge of VQ harms learners prospects, 21st June 2012, www.vqday.org.uk
61. City and Guilds, Rich list, www.city-and-guilds.co.uk

Chapter Four

1. Home Office, The Equality Strategy: Building a Fairer Britain, December 2010, www.homeoffice.gov.uk, Pg. 6-7
2. Ofsted, The evaluation schedule for the inspection of maintained schools and academies, April 2012, Pg. 5
3. Ofsted, Handbook for the inspection of Further Education and Skills, 2012, www.ofsted.gov.uk, Pg.37-8
4. Ofsted, The evaluation schedule for the inspection of maintained schools and academies, April 2012, Pg. 4
5. Abid, Pg. 6.
6. Ofsted, Handbook for the inspection of Further Education and Skills, 2012, www.ofsted.gov.uk, Pg.39.
7. Abid, Pg. 48-9.

8. Abid, Pg. 49-52
9. Abid, Pg. 57.
10. Equality and Human Rights Commission, Sex and Power, August 2011, www. Equalityhumanrights.com
11. Financial Times, Poor white pupils lag behind black peers, 26th April 2011, www.ft.com
12. Department for Education, Statistical First Release, 9th February 2012, www.education.gov.uk
13. Guardian, education supplement, 20th January, 2009, Pg. 9
14. www.statistics.gov.uk /cci/nugget.asp?id=458
15. Lammy David, Fatherhood in the 21st Century, 15th March 2010, www.davidlammy.co.uk
16. http://www.dailymail.co.uk/news/article-436527/scandal-absent-fathers
17. Lammy David, Fatherhood in the 21st Century, 15th March 2010, www.davidlammy.co.uk
18. www.nytimes.com http://www.nytimes.com/2008/06/16/us/politics/15cnd-obama.html?scp=1&sq=obama%20sharply%20assails%20absent%20black%20fathers&st=cse)
19. http://www.nytimes.com/2009/07/17/us/politics/17obama.html
20. Swann Lord, Education for All, Report of the committee of Enquiry into the Education of children from Ethnic Minority Groups, HMSO, 1985.
21. www.equalityhumanrights.com , All together Now? A portrait of Race in Britain., Pg. 5.
22. Abid, Pg. 2.
23. Hattie, Professor John, Visible Learning: A synthesis of over 800 meta-analyses relating to achievement, Routledge, 2009, Pg. 128
24. Abbot Diane, www.guardian.co.uk/politics/2002/jan/06/publicservice.race
25. Ofsted, The evaluation schedule for the inspection of maintained schools and academies, April 2012, Pg. 6
26. Abid, Pg. 7

Chapter Five

1. Wiliam, Professor Dylan, Times Educational Supplement, Steadier progress by regular rendezvous, 28th July 2006.
2. Black Paul and Wiliams Dylan, Inside the Black Box, 1998, Pg. 3
3. Black Paul and Wiliams Dylan, Inside the Black Box, 1998, Pg. 13
4. Ofsted, Handbook for the inspection of Further Education and Skills, 2012, www.ofsted.gov.uk, Pg.45
5. Ofsted, The evaluation schedule for the inspection of maintained schools and academies, April 2012, Pg. 12.
6. Ofsted, Why Colleges Fail, November 2004.
7. Black Paul and Wiliams Dylan, Inside the Black Box, 1998, Pg. 6
8. Ofsted, Improving Attendance and Behaviour in Secondary Schools, 2001, Para 69
9. Hattie, Professor John, Influences on Learning, University of Auckland 2nd August 1999, Pg. 12.
10. Assessment Reform Group, Assessment for Learning: Beyond the Black Box, www.qca.org.uk, Pg.4
11. Hattie, Professor John, Visible Learning: A synthesis of over 800 meta-analyses relating to achievement, Routledge, 2009, Pg. 239.
12. DfES, Vision 2020, Report of the Teaching and Learning 2020 Review Group, December 2006, Pg. 17
13. DCSF, Assessment for Learning Strategy, April 2008, Pg.4
14. Ofsted, Handbook for the inspection of Further Education and Skills, 2012, www.ofsted.gov.uk, Pg. 44

15. Abid, Pg. 46
16. Ofsted, The evaluation schedule for the inspection of maintained schools and academies, April 2012, Pg. 11
17. Ofsted, Annual report of the Chief Inspector, November 2011, Pg. 95
18. Ofsted, Assessment for Learning: the impact of national strategy support, 2008, Pg.
19. Hattie, Professor John, Visible Learning: A synthesis of over 800 meta-analyses relating to achievement, Routledge, 2009, Pg. 241
20. Abid. Pg. 239
21. Ofsted, Improving Attendance and Behaviour in Secondary Schools, www.ofsted.gov.uk, 2001, Para 107
22. Ofsted, Handbook for the inspection of further education and skills from September 2009, www.ofsted.gov.uk, Pg. 47.
23. Black Paul and Wiliams Dylan, Assessment for Learning, Putting it into practice, Open University Press, 2007, Pg. 33
24. Abid, Pg. 33
25. Board of Education, Handbook of suggestions for teachers, 1927, Pg. 110
26. Black Paul and Wiliams Dylan, Assessment for Learning, Putting it into practice, Open University Press, 2007, Pg. 67
27. Abid, Pg. 67
28. Hattie, Professor John, Visible Learning: A synthesis of over 800 meta-analyses relating to achievement, Routledge, 2009, Pg. 23.
29. Ofsted, Handbook for the inspection of further education and skills from September 2009, www.ofsted.gov.uk, Pg. 46-7.
30. Ofsted, The evaluation schedule for the inspection of maintained schools and academies, April 2012, Pg. 11
31. Sutton Trust, The Teaching and Learning Toolkit, Pg.12 www.suttontrust.com
32. Black Paul and Wiliams Dylan, Assessment for Learning, Putting it into practice, Open University Press, 2007, Pg. 50
33. Abid, Pg.173
34. Sutton Trust, The Teaching and Learning Toolkit, Pg.20 www.suttontrust.com
35. Black Paul and Wiliams Dylan, Assessment for Learning, Putting it into practice, Open University Press, 2007, Pg. 61
36. Hattie, Professor John, Visible Learning: A synthesis of over 800 meta-analyses relating to achievement, Routledge, 2009, Pg. 187.
37. Brighouse, Tim Professor Sir, Essential Pieces of the Jigsaw, the jigsaw of a successful school, Research Machines 2006, Pg. 9
38. Hattie, Professor John, Visible Learning: A synthesis of over 800 meta-analyses relating to achievement, Routledge, 2009, Pg. 44.
39. Pablo de Sarasate (1844-1908), The complete pocket positives, Five Mile Press, 2010
40. OECD, Pisa: progress in science, 2010, www.oecd.org
41. Hattie, Professor John, Visible Learning: A synthesis of over 800 meta-analyses relating to achievement, Routledge, 2009, Pg. 48.
42. Obama Barack President, Back to School Event, 8th September, 2009, Pg. 1, www.bbc.co.uk/education
43. Hattie, Professor John, Visible Learning: A synthesis of over 800 meta-analyses relating to achievement, Routledge, 2009, Pg. 173
44. Sutton Trust, The Teaching and Learning Toolkit, Pg.17 www.suttontrust.com

Chapter Six

1. Ofsted, Handbook for the inspection of further education and skills from September 2009, www.ofsted.gov.uk, Pg. 49
2. Ofsted, inspection reports, Runshaw College, May 2008, Para 16.
3. Abid, Tameside College, 2004, Para 78.

4. Abid, Oldham Sixth Form College, March 2004, Para 90.
5. Abid, Para 6.
6. Abid, South Downs College, November 2004, Para 57.
7. Abid, Sir John Deane's Sixth Form College, April 2008, Para 12.
8. Abid, South Cheshire College, 2004 Para 115.
9. Abid, Aquinas College, November 2004, Para 10
10. Abid, Sir John Deane's Sixth Form College, April 2004, Para 49.
11. Brighouse, Tim Professor, Essential pieces, the jigsaw of a successful school, Research Machines, 2006, Pg, 17.
12. Board of Education, Handbook of Suggestions for Teachers, H.M. Stationery Office, 1927, Pg. 10.
13. Bilborough College, Learner involvement strategy, October 2008, www.bilborough.ac.uk
14. Ofsted, Handbook for the inspection of further education and skills from September 2009, www.ofsted.gov.uk, Pg.51
15. Northampton College, Learner involvement strategy, 2008, www.northamptoncollege.ac.uk
16. Ofsted, Handbook for the inspection of further education and skills from September 2009, www.ofsted.gov.uk, Pg.23

Chapter Seven

1. Ofsted, Inspection reports, Kendal College, November 2010, Pg.10, Para 20.
2. Abid, South Cheshire College, February 2004, Para 123.
3. Hattie, Professor John, Visible Learning: A synthesis of over 800 meta-analyses relating to achievement, Routledge, 2009, Pg. 128.
4. Abid, Pg. 119
5. Ofsted, Identifying good practice: a survey of business, administration and law in colleges, www.ofsted.gov.uk, January 2008, Para 14.
6. Abid, Para 20.
7. Ofsted, Inspection reports, www.ofsted.gov.uk Runshaw College, May 2008, Para 16.
8. Abid, Nelson and Colne College, April 2008, Para 17.
9. Hattie, Professor John, Visible Learning: A synthesis of over 800 meta-analyses relating to achievement, Routledge, 2009, Pg. 37
10. Ofsted, Inspection reports, www.ofsted.gov.uk Priestley College, May 2007, Para 18.
11. Ofsted, 'A comparison of the effectiveness of level 3 provision in 25 post-16 providers', www.ofsted.gov.uk September 2008,Para 19.
12. Ofsted, Inspection report, www.ofsted.gov.uk Winstanley College, October 2004, Para 89.
13. Abid, Greenhead Sixth Form College, January 2004, Para 40
14. Ofsted, Annual Report of the Chief Inspector, November 2011, Pg. 97.

Chapter Eight

1. Ofsted, Highbury College, inspection report June 2011, Pg.8, Para 17.
2. Parkinson Michael, Parky, My autobiography, Hodder and Stoughton 2008, Pg. 31
3. Times Educational Supplement, 23rd January 2009, Pg. 36.
4. Abid.
5. MIT Survey, http://news.bbc.co.uk/i/hi/sci/tech/1834682.stm
6. Tube Mogul, http://www.tubemogul.com
7. BBC, 'TV reduces children's attention', 14th April 2009, www.bbc.co.uk/1/hi/education/7191707.stm

8. Hattie, Professor John, Visible Learning: A synthesis of over 800 meta-analyses relating to achievement, Routledge, 2009, Pg. 250.
9. Times Educational Supplement, 9th January 2009, Pg.12
10. Ofsted, Annual report of the Chief Inspector, November 2011, Pg. 97, Para 262
11. Board of Education, Handbook for teachers, 1928, Pg. 119.
12. Abid, Pg. 57.
13. Ofsted, A comparison of the effectiveness of Level 3 provision in 25 Post 16 providers, www.ofsted.gov.uk, September 2008.Para. 19.
14. Marzano Robert J et al, Classroom instruction that works, Association for Supervision and Curriculum Development (ASCD), 2001, Pg. 127.
15. Ofsted, Annual report of the Chief Inspector, Learning and Skills, November 2010
16. Ofsted, Annual report of the Chief Inspector Learning and Skills, November 2011, Pg.97
17. Marzano Robert J et al, Classroom instruction that works, Association for Supervision and Curriculum Development (ASCD), 2001, Pg. 113.
18. Abid, Pg.113
19. Hattie, Professor John, Visible Learning: A synthesis of over 800 meta-analyses relating to achievement, Routledge, 2009, Pg. 28.
20. Ofsted, Annual report of the Chief Inspector for Schools, November 2011, Pg. 52, Para 124.
21. Hattie, Professor John, Visible Learning: A synthesis of over 800 meta-analyses relating to achievement, Routledge, 2009, Pg. 239.
22. Ofsted, www.ofsted.gov.uk, 'Identifying good practice: a survey of Post-16 science in colleges and schools, January 2008, Para 12.
23. Marzano Robert J et al, Classroom instruction that works, Association for Supervision and Curriculum Development (ASCD), 2001, Pg. 55.

Chapter Nine

1. Marzano Robert J et al, Classroom instruction that works, Association for Supervision and Curriculum Development (ASCD), 2001, Pg. 87.
2. Ofsted, Handbook for the inspection of Further Education and Skills, 2012, www.ofsted.gov.uk, Pg.40.
3. Abid
4. Ofsted, The evaluation schedule for the inspection of maintained schools and academies, April 2012, Pg. 4
5. Ofsted, inspection reports, www.ofsted.gov.uk Macclesfield College, 2002, Para 45.
6. Abid, Priestley College, 2003, Para 101.
7. Marzano Robert J et al, Classroom instruction that works, Association for Supervision and Curriculum Development (ASCD), 2001, Pg. 16.
8. Abid, Pg.73
9. Ofsted, Inspection reports, www.ofsted.gov.uk, Barrow-in-Furness College, April 2005, Para. 73.
10. Ofsted, Identifying good practice: a survey of business, administration and law in colleges, www.ofsted.gov.uk, January 2008, Para 26.

Chapter Ten

1. Ofsted, Handbook for Inspecting Colleges, www.ofsted.gov.uk September, 2008, Pg. 85.
2. Marzano Robert J et al, Classroom instruction that works, Association for Supervision and Curriculum Development (ASCD), 2001, Pg. 63.

Chapter Eleven

1. Hattie, Professor John, Visible Learning: A synthesis of over 800 meta-analyses relating to achievement, Routledge, 2009, Pg. 37
2. Board of Education, Handbook of suggestions for teachers, 1927, Pg. 57
3. Ofsted, Annual Report of the Chief Inspector 2007-08, November 2008, www.ofsted.gov.uk Para 461.
4. Hattie, Professor John, Visible Learning: A synthesis of over 800 meta-analyses relating to achievement, Routledge, 2009, Pg. 250
5. Ofsted, Handbook for Inspecting Colleges, www.ofsted.gov.uk September, 2008, Para 245
6. Ofsted, Handbook for the inspection of Further Education and Skills, 2012, www.ofsted.gov.uk, Pg.44.
7. Abid, Pg. 45
8. Ofsted, The evaluation schedule for the inspection of maintained schools and academies, April 2012, Pg. 11.
9. Lifelong Learning UK, New Overarching professional standards for teachers, tutors and trainers in the lifelong learning sector, 2007, Criteria BP 2.2 and BP 2.3. www.lsis.org
10. Ofsted, Handbook for Inspecting Colleges, www.ofsted.gov.uk September, 2008, Pg. 93.
11. Ofsted, Inspection reports, www.ofsted.gov.uk,, Sir John Deane's Sixth Form College, April 2008, Para 12.
12. Ofsted, A comparison of the effectiveness of Level 3 provision in 25 Post 16 providers, www.ofsted.gov.uk September 2008.Para. 21.
13. DfES, Vision 2020, Report of the Teaching and Learning 2020 Review Group, December 2006, Pg.6.
14. Teaching and Learning Research Programme, www.tlrp.org/themes/themes/tenprinciples.html 19th February 2008.
15. Ofsted, Why Colleges succeed, www.ofsted.gov.uk, November 2004.
16. The Times, 'Gifted and talented programme extended to one million pupils' , 2nd November 2007, Pg 2.
17. DfES, Vision 2020, Report of the Teaching and Learning 2020 Review Group, December 2006, Pg. 21.
18. Ofsted, Handbook for Inspecting Colleges, September, 2008, Pg.94.
19. Karpinski, Aryn, Facebook low scores, http://researchnews.osu.edu/archive/facebookuser.htm, 12th March 2009.
20. Times Educational Supplement, Stuck in the middle, 18th May 2007.
21. Hattie, Professor John, Visible Learning: A synthesis of over 800 meta-analyses relating to achievement, Routledge, 2009, Pg. 37.
22. Ofsted, Why Colleges Fail, www.ofsted.gov.uk, November 2004.
23. Ofsted, Handbook for Inspecting Colleges, www.ofsted.gov.uk September, 2008, Para 242.
24. Steer, Sir Alan, Learning Behaviour: Lessons learned, DCSF, 15th April 2009, Pg. 42
25. Ofsted, Annual Report of the Chief Inspector 2007-08, www.ofsted.gov.uk November 2008, Para 351.
26 Steer, Sir Alan, Learning Behaviour: Lessons learned, DCSF, 15th April 2009, Pg. 43.
27. DfES, Secondary Teachers journal, July 2005, No. 39, Pg. 12.
28. Marzano Robert J et al, Classroom instruction that works, Association for Supervision and Curriculum Development (ASCD), 2001, Pg. 50.

Chapter Twelve

1. Steer, Sir Alan, Learning Behaviour: Lessons learned, DCSF, 15th April 2009, Pg. 32
2. Ofsted, Twelve outstanding secondary schools: excelling against the odds, www.ofsted.gov.uk 2009, Para. 61.
3. Abid, Para. 60.
4. Ofsted, Why Colleges succeed, www.ofsted.gov.uk, November 2004.

Index

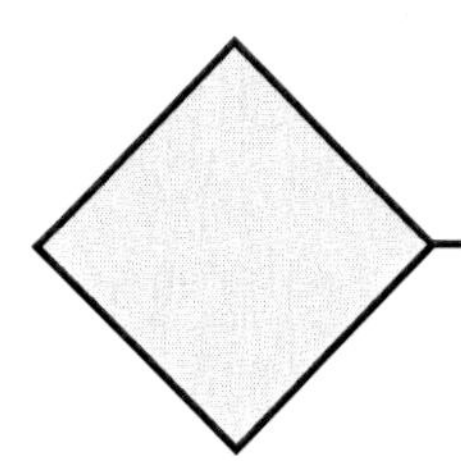